PKI Uncovered

D1453908

Andre Karamanian
Srinivas Tenneti
Francois Dessart

Cisco Press

800 East 96th Street

Indianapolis, IN 46240

PKI Uncovered

Andre Karamanian

Srinivas Tenneti

Francois Dessart

Copyright© 2011 Cisco Systems, Inc.

Published by:
Cisco Press
800 East 96th Street
Indianapolis, IN 46240 USA

Printed in the United States of America

First Printing   February 2011

Library of Congress Cataloging-in-Publication Data:

Karamanian, Andre.

  PKI uncovered / Andre Karamanian, Srinivas Tenneti, Francois Dessart.

    p. cm.

Includes index.

  ISBN-13: 978-1-58705-916-2 (pbk.)

  ISBN-10: 1-58705-916-9 (pbk.)

 1. Public key infrastructure (Computer security) 2. Computers—Access control. 3. Computer networks—Security measures. I. Tenneti, Srinivas. II. Dessart, Francois. III. Title.

  QA76.9.A25K346 2011

  005.8—dc22

                              2011002835

ISBN-13: 978-1-58705-916-2

ISBN-10: 1-58705-916-9

Warning and Disclaimer

Trademark Acknowledgments

All terms mentioned in this book that are known to be trademarks or service marks have been appropriately capitalized. Cisco Press or Cisco Systems, Inc., cannot attest to the accuracy of this information. Use of a term in this book should not be regarded as affecting the validity of any trademark or service mark.

Corporate and Government Sales

The publisher offers excellent discounts on this book when ordered in quantity for bulk purchases or special sales, which may include electronic versions and/or custom covers and content particular to your business, training goals, marketing focus, and branding interests. For more information, please contact: **U.S. Corporate and Government Sales**   1-800-382-3419   corpsales@pearsontechgroup.com

For sales outside the United States, please contact: **International Sales**   international@pearsoned.com

Feedback Information

At Cisco Press, our goal is to create in-depth technical books of the highest quality and value. Each book is crafted with care and precision, undergoing rigorous development that involves the unique expertise of members from the professional technical community.

Readers' feedback is a natural continuation of this process. If you have any comments regarding how we could improve the quality of this book, or otherwise alter it to better suit your needs, you can contact us through email at feedback@ciscopress.com. Please make sure to include the book title and ISBN in your message.

We greatly appreciate your assistance.

Publisher: Paul Boger

Associate Publisher: Dave Dusthimer

Executive Editor: Brett Bartow

Managing Editor: Sandra Schroeder

Project Editor: Seth Kerney

Editorial Assistant: Vanessa Evans

Book Designer: Louisa Adair

Indexer: Tim Wright

Business Operation Manager, Cisco Press: Anand Sundaram

Manager Global Certification: Erik Ullanderson

Development Editor: Kimberley Debus

Copy Editor: Apostrophe Editing Services

Technical Editor: Alex Teichmann

Proofreader: Sheri Cain

Composition: Mark Shirar

Cisco Systems, Inc.
San Jose, CA

Asia Pacific Headquarters
Cisco Systems (USA) Pte. Ltd.
Singapore

Europe Headquarters
Cisco Systems International BV
Amsterdam, The Netherlands

Cisco has more than 200 offices worldwide. Addresses, phone numbers, and fax numbers are listed on the Cisco Website at www.cisco.com/go/offices.

CCDE, CCENT, Cisco Eos, Cisco HealthPresence, the Cisco logo, Cisco Lumin, Cisco Nexus, Cisco StadiumVision, Cisco TelePresence, Cisco WebEx, DCE, and Welcome to the Human Network are trademarks; Changing the Way We Work, Live, Play, and Learn and Cisco Store are service marks; and Access Registrar, Aironet, AsyncOS, Bringing the Meeting To You, Catalyst, CCDA, CCDP, CCIE, CCIP, CCNA, CCNP, CCSP, CCVP, Cisco, the Cisco Certified Internetwork Expert logo, Cisco IOS, Cisco Press, Cisco Systems, Cisco Systems Capital, the Cisco Systems logo, Cisco Unity, Collaboration Without Limitation, EtherFast, EtherSwitch, Event Center, Fast Step, Follow Me Browsing, FormShare, GigaDrive, HomeLink, Internet Quotient, IOS, iPhone, iQuick Study, IronPort, the IronPort logo, LightStream, Linksys, MediaTone, MeetingPlace, MeetingPlace Chime Sound, MGX, Networkers, Networking Academy, Network Registrar, PCNow, PIX, PowerPanels, ProConnect, ScriptShare, SenderBase, SMARTnet, Spectrum Expert, StackWise, The Fastest Way to Increase Your Internet Quotient, TransPath, WebEx, and the WebEx logo are registered trademarks of Cisco Systems, Inc. and/or its affiliates in the United States and certain other countries.

All other trademarks mentioned in this document or website are the property of their respective owners. The use of the word partner does not imply a partnership relationship between Cisco and any other company. (0812R)

About the Authors

Andre Karamanian, CCIE R/S No. 10228, attended Capitol College where he received his master's degree in network security and where he is currently a doctoral student in information assurance. He is currently a security consultant at Cisco. He has worked in the field of security for approximately 11 years. Before he came to Cisco, Andre worked as a security leader at a large service provider for its large custom clients. He is highly credentialed with many industry certifications and has been a presenter at Networkers at Cisco Live for two years.

Srinivas Tenneti, CCIE R/S, Security, No. 10483, is currently working as an Enterprise systems engineer at Cisco. He has published design guides, white papers, and presentations on end-to-end solutions for enterprise and commercial customers. He also worked with several service providers to validate their network designs and architectures. Before he came to Cisco, he worked as a network specialist for a large service provider where he designed WANs for enterprise customers.

Francois Dessart, CCIE Security No. 15962, is currently a security consultant at Cisco. Before joining the European Advanced Services organization, he spent 4 years in the Security TAC in Brussels, solving complex PKI and VPN issues for Cisco customers. Francois has a master's degree in electrical engineering from Université Catholique de Louvain and recently received his master's degree in management from the Louvain School of Management.

About the Technical Reviewers

Alex Teichmann is a consultant for Cisco. He has helped developed leading practices for PKI and has personally worked on several IPsec and PKI deployments with great success and accolades. Alex Teichmann has an unmatched knowledge of PKI and is a leader in the field.

Piotr Jarzynka, CCIE R/S, Security, No.4737, is a Solutions Architect at Cisco. He is currently focusing on the security of Unified Communications (UC) for which he has developed a complete services portfolio, helping organizations to secure their UC environment. He has also created leading practices for the application of PKI within UC and has worked on several large customer implementations.

Dedications

Andre Karamanian: To my wife and family.

Srinivas Tenneti: To my wife, children, and my parents.

Francois Dessart: To my wife Anne-Sophie and my son Grégoire.

Acknowledgments

We'd like to give special recognition to Alex Teichmann for providing his expert technical knowledge in editing this book. He's also been as good a colleague as anyone could hope to have.

Contents at a Glance

Contents

Icons Used in This Book

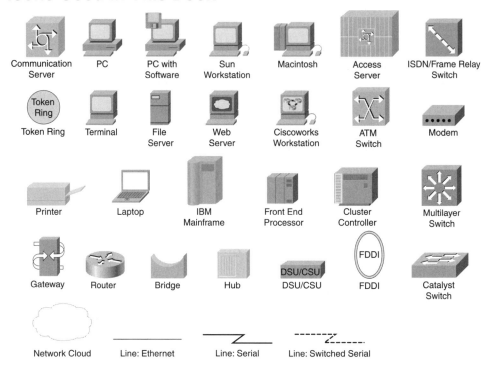

Command Syntax Conventions

The conventions used to present command syntax in this book are the same conventions used in the IOS Command Reference. The Command Reference describes these conventions as follows:

- **Boldface** indicates commands and keywords entered literally as shown. In actual configuration examples and output (not general command syntax), boldface indicates commands manually input by the user (such as a show command).

- *Italic* indicates arguments for which you supply actual values.

- Vertical bars (|) separate alternative, mutually exclusive elements.

- Square brackets ([ ]) indicate an optional element.

- Braces ({ }) indicate a required choice.

- Braces within brackets ([{ }]) indicate a required choice within an optional element.

Introduction

With the increasing focus on IT Security comes a higher demand for identity management in the modern business. This requires a flexible, scalable, and secure authentication method. Identity control is made mandatory by many public standards, such as PCI, and PKI is an essential component to set up authentication in many technologies, such as VPN. Public Key Infrastructure (PKI) plays a key role in achieving the required degree of security and scalability. Other approaches have been either scalable but not secure, or secure but not scalable. Not only does PKI provide the framework for security and scalability, it also is a standard adaptable for the coming years. This book's unique approach illustrates the techniques to practically apply PKI into solutions while developing the foundational concepts of the technology. Consequently, this book makes deploying this complex and essential technology simple.

Goals and Methods

This book is tailored to enable you to deploy PKI-based solutions in a simple, efficient, and manageable way. The book achieves this goal by taking a layered approach. First, it presents the foundations of PKI to ensure that you have the required theoretical background to properly understand the mechanisms. Then the book modularly takes those foundations into generic design considerations: The goal is to help you to perform the choices most suitable for the targeted environment; guidance is provided through sharing best practices and experiences acquired in production customer deployments. Those design modules are pieced together into hierarchical models, which are then applied to comprehensive solutions. Through the book, troubleshooting sections are included to ensure smooth implementations and enable you to gain a deep understanding of the internals.

Who Should Read This Book?

This book has been written primarily for enterprise network security designers, planners, architects, operators, and support personnel. These are the people responsible for the design, deployment, and support; and they can find the topic, scope, and level of detail beneficial. The book's structure is layered, starting from foundational topics, moving toward high-level architectures, and finally into detailed designs. This layered and modular approach can benefit both the intermediate reader and the advanced reader or individuals seeking a practical view of PKI. They can read the modules of interest or start from the beginning and learn the solutions throughout.

This book is also of interest to the user and purchaser of enterprise networks, including IT directors and CIOs or CTOs in small, medium-sized, and large enterprises and network engineers and support staff. Technical sales personnel both at network vendors and their integration partners can also greatly benefit from this book.

How This Book Is Organized

Although this book could be read cover-to-cover, it is designed to be flexible and enable you to easily move between chapters and sections of chapters to cover just the material that you need more work with. Chapter 1, "Crypto Refresh," provides an overview of the encryption-related technologies to provide a foundation and review of core concepts. Chapters 2 through 11 can be covered out of order; however, they are designed to build on each other. If you intend to read them all, the order; in the book is an excellent sequence to use.

The book is broken out into three major sections. The first section provides theoretical knowledge and background. The second section covers design principals and solutions. The third section discusses case studies for PKI and specific use cases. Chapters 2 through 11 cover the following topics:

- Chapter 2, **"Understanding PKI Building Blocks"**—Discusses analyzing criteria for placing the foundational pieces used to build a PKI and certificates and certificate authorities.

- Chapter 3, **"PKI Processes and Procedures"**—Discusses the basic processes required for a PKI to function, including enrollment, expiration, renewal, verification, and enforcement.

- Chapter 4, **"Troubleshooting"**—Covers how to troubleshoot basic PKI deployments, specifically key generation problems, enrollment problems and certificate verification problems.

Part II: Design and Solutions

- Chapter 5, **"Generic PKI Designs"**—Starts by covering a basic, small-style PKI design. It then covers a more involved hierarchical design, which is common among complex and larger deployments.

- Chapter 6, **"Integration in Large-Scale Site-to-Site VPN Solutions"**—Covers the two most popular large scale VPN deployments using certificates and examines how to deploy GET-VPN and DMVPN using PKI.

- Chapter 7, **"Integration in Remote Access VPN Solutions"**—Covers remote access VPN solutions. It covers ASA-based IPsec VPN remote access connections, ASA SSL VPN, and the Cisco VPN client.

- Chapter 8, **"Using 802.1x Certificates in Identity-Based Networking"**—Covers the basics of how to deploy certificates to control access at the switchport level.

- Chapter 9, **"PKI in Unified Communications"**—Covers the use of certificates in IPT-based systems to drive identity. This chapter covers Call Manager and IP phones' implementation of certificates.

Part III: Case Studies

■ **Chapter 10, "Understanding Cisco Virtual Office Overview"**—Builds upon previous chapters' topics and weaves together a variety of certificate-based solutions. This topic uses 802.1x, DMVPN, and PKI architecture to build a cohesive virtual office solution.

■ **Chapter 11, "Deploying VPNs with PKI Using Cisco Security Manager"**—Covers the use of Cisco Security Manager for PKI-based systems. It also covers how to migrate from preshared keys for IKE authentication to PKI.

Chapter 1

Crypto Refresh

This chapter covers the following topics:

- Confidentiality, Integrity, Authenticity, Nonrepudiation

- Symmetric Encryption

- Asymmetric Encryption

- Other Crypto Functions

- Internet Key Exchange (IKE)

- Device Configuration: Certificates

Cryptography has been used throughout history to hide messages and keep secrets. There have been various techniques used that have been concurrent with the technology available for that time. In today's world, ever increasing high-powered computing systems networked together have created a new paradigm. This complexity to provide data and identity security requires a new paradigm of information security.

This book assumes you are a network engineer who has been exposed to the basics of encryption technology. One of the goals of this chapter is to provide a refresher, but it also dives deeper into the theory of the core concepts than most engineers might have seen in the past. This is necessary because these foundations are at the heart of the concepts covered in this book.

This chapter covers the basics of encryption, which essentially is the mathematical concatenation of data with a key. This chapter sets the foundation of the topics to follow.

The basic concept of encryption is simple. Cryptography attempts to take unencrypted (clear text) data and mathematically manipulate it to create encrypted ciphertext. Following best practices for encryption provides the best possible chances for confidentiality, integrity, authenticity, and nonrepudiation.

Confidentiality, Integrity, Authenticity, Nonrepudiation

The core concepts of confidentiality, integrity, authenticity, and nonrepudiation are integral to all schemes of encryption. Secure delivery of data depends on all elements. Varying techniques provide different levels of strengths in these areas. PKI's objective in IPsec is to provide the best methods for authenticity and nonrepudiation. PKI's goal is not necessarily to provide a method for confidentiality.

Confidentiality

Corporations, the military, financial institutions, and even an end user sitting at a computer have sensitive data that should remain confidential. Ensuring confidentiality for this data keeps a corporation from losing a corporate secret, the military from losing a battle or lives, and financial institutions from losing personal credit information.

If you look closely, confidentiality is a part of your everyday lives. Every time you use an ATM to draw money, you probably look over your shoulder to make sure no one is looking while you enter the PIN. Even in nontechnical areas of life, there are personal and private things that we don't want to make public.

We might want to share these private details about life only with someone like a close friend or family member. That takes us to the core of confidentiality. Confidentiality's goal is to provide information only to those people with whom you want to share it and make information unviewable by others.

Figure 1-1 simply illustrates this concept. If Bob is at a ball game and wants to tell Alice he has poison ivy, he will not go up to the speaker system and tell Alice over the loudspeaker in plain English, "Hey Alice, I have poison ivy." Assuming Alice and Bob are the only two people in the stadium that speak French, he might choose to announce it in French. If other people try to listen, they will likely be unable to understand what was said. Confidentiality of the conversation is maintained.

Confidentiality has legal, physical, and financial consequences. Should a financial institution not perform due diligence as defined in the PCI standard (Visa's personal credit information standard) to protect personal credit information, that institution could face legal and financial consequences.

Integrity

The goal of integrity in cryptography is simple: to maintain the original message. While a message is in transit, it might be modified, and the original message might get changed by some intermediate vector.

Integrity verification detects an attempted change. You can use various techniques to verify integrity. One technique often used is hashing the original message and then encrypting the hash along with the message. If the message were altered in any way, the decrypted hash would not match the new hash. Consequently, the disruption of the message would be detected.

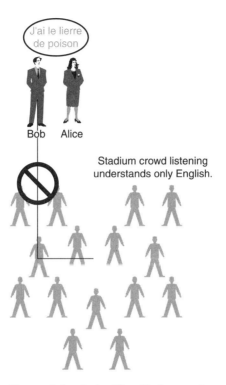

Figure 1-1 *Only Alice Understands What Bob Is Saying*

Authenticity and Nonrepudiation

Authenticity and nonrepudiation both involve identification as a way to protect data. Authenticity is the process to identify a sender. This is a necessary condition for nonrepudiation but not a sufficient one. For nonrepudiation to occur, the sender's message must be proven beyond a doubt to have been sent by the sender. In PKI, this is achieved by using certificates.

Authenticity and nonrepudiation are one of the key objectives of most certificate systems. Typically, a digital signature is created using asymmetric key pairs (discussed later in the "Asymmetric Encryption" section and contrasted to symmetric encryption). The sender "signs" a message. A certificate is granted by a trusted third party who vouches for someone's signature, consequently "certifying" the sender's signature.

Symmetric Encryption

Symmetric encryption is a form of changing plain text to cipher text while using a shared secret. The shared secret is only known to the sender and receiver. Both parties use the same key to encrypt and decrypt.

This form of encryption has the most history and wide-spread use. Documented uses go far back into pretechnical eras. You can use a number of encryption ciphers, including straight substitutions and transformations.

All approaches have one element in common: the use of the shared secret, which is also a place of vulnerability. The goal to break this form of encryption is to obtain the common key or shared secret. Consequently, secure mechanisms must be used to exchange the shared secret. Diffie-Hellman is an example of an approach to exchanging a shared secret.

Advantages

The advantage of using symmetric encryption is in its fundamental simplicity. Performance becomes an advantage in this case. Also the strength of encryption is dependent on the key length for any given algorithm. The longer the shared secret, the longer it can take a hacker to decode it, and consequently, the stronger the confidentiality provided.

Challenges

A major disadvantage of symmetric encryption is in distribution of the shared secret. For this form of encryption to work, all parties must know the common key.

This creates two principal issues that have a common theme in security: availability versus security. First, a secure method to deliver the shared secret is required, which centers around availability. Without the shared secret being delivered to all parties, encryption or decryption can not be performed. The second issue is with security, which hinges on knowledge of the shared secret. If the shared secret is compromised by brute force, crypto analysis, or erroneous exposure, all transmissions will be compromised.

This introduces another related and significant challenge, arriving at a sufficiently strong shared secret. The shared secret, if compromised, would result in all conversations becoming readable. One approach to solve this problem is to use Diffie-Hellman.

Example Algorithm: DES and 3DES

DES is a symmetric encryption algorithm. The key used for encryption and decryption is the same. Portions of the cleartext are logically operated on by the "exclusive or" on portions of the key. Then this goes through other manipulations such as substitution by S-boxes (developed as part of collaboration between the NSA and IBM). Decryption uses the same key, although in the reverse order. The algorithm is considered symmetric because the same key decrypts the cipher text.

Asymmetric Encryption

Unlike symmetric encryption that uses a shared secret, asymmetric encryption uses multiple keys. Each sender has two keys: a public key and a private key. The public key is available to anyone and is freely distributed. The private key is kept hidden and known only to the sender. The private key being known only to the sender is a critical assumption to asymmetric encryption.

Converting plain text into cipher text uses a different paradigm in asymmetric encryption. Depending on the purpose of the transmission, either the private or the public key can encrypt data. The receiver uses the opposite key to decrypt data. To illustrate this further, now examine the two major applications in which asymmetric encryption are used.

Asymmetric Encryption Application: Authentication

Authentication is the principal application of most PKI solutions. The goal of authentication is not to provide confidentiality of information, but to verify the sender's identity. Authentication in asymmetric encryption uses the sender's private and public key. If any message is encrypted using the sender's private key, the receiver can use the senders public key to decrypt it. Because the assumption is that the only user with the private key is the sender, and the message is successfully decrypted by the receiver with the public key, the message must have been sent by the sender. QED authentication is successful. Digital signatures use a specific schema of this form of authentication. A discussion on digital signatures is found later in this chapter in the "Digital Signatures" section.

In Figure 1-2, Bob encrypts the message "Hello" with his private key. Because Alice can decrypt the message with Bob's public key, Bob must have sent the message (only Bob has the public key), and thus the message is authenticated.

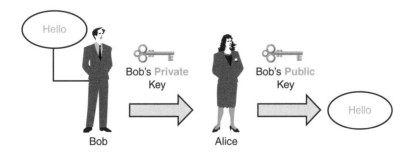

Figure 1-2   *Alice Verifies Bob Is the Sender of the Message*

Asymmetric Encryption Application: Encryption

Encryption using an asymmetric schema uses the receiver's public and private key. The sender obtains the receiver's public key. Then the sender encrypts the message with the sender's public key. It is assumed that the private key of a party is known only by that party; that is, the receiver is the only one with the private key. Consequently, when the receiver obtains a copy of the encrypted message, the receiver and only the receiver can decrypt it using the private key.

In Figure 1-3, Bob sends the message "Hello" to Alice. He uses Alice's public key to encrypt the message. Because only Alice has her private key, she is the only one who can decrypt the message. Confidentiality of the message is maintained between Alice and Bob.

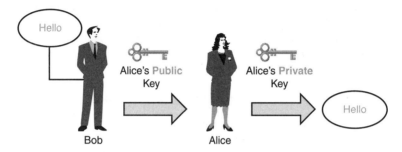

Figure 1-3 *Alice Decrypts Bob's Secret Message*

Advantages

The principal advantage of using the asymmetric schema is availability. A shared secret does not need to be distributed to all communicating members; the public key is freely distributed.

Challenges

The major challenge in the asymmetric schema is the complexity of the algorithms. Typically, they require more processing power and take longer to perform encryption.

Example: RSA

The RSA algorithm has two keys: a public and a private key. The public key can decrypt ciphertext created with the private key and vice versa.

RSA finds its strength in a number of assumptions. One assumption is that it is easy to multiply two prime numbers together, and conversely, it is difficult to determine the prime factors used, assuming that the resultant is large. The public and private keys are inverse functions of one another, the function of which is related to the multiplicative product of both primes. To determine the inverse, the prime factors of the resultants must be determined, which is computationally expensive.

Other Crypto Functions

The two critical supporting functions for cryptography are hashes and digital signatures.

Hashes

The capability to take a multilength string and convert it to a fixed length unique string is a useful mechanism in cryptography. Creating the fixed-length unique string is computationally low cost. The reverse is computationally high cost, relatively speaking.

In Figure 1-4, hashes take mixed length generic inputs and produce fixed length, pseudo random outputs.

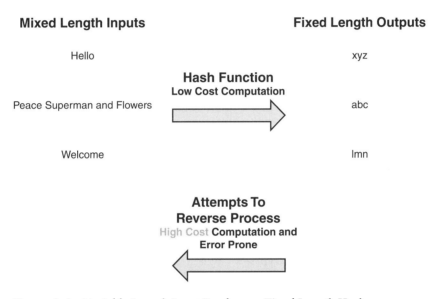

Figure 1-4   *Variable Length Input Produces a Fixed Length Hash*

Because of the irreversibility of hash functions, hashes are often used as methods to validate the integrity of a communication.

Digital Signatures

A sender uses digital signatures to authenticate a message. Digital signatures use asymmetric cryptography; specifically, digital signatures are based on the method of authentication in asymmetric cryptography.

Digital signatures operate in two distinct functions: signature construction and signature verification. Following are the steps in signature construction:

1.   A message is created by the sender.

2.   A hash is taken of that message.

3.   That hash is encrypted with the sender's private key.

4.   The encrypted hash, the digital signature, is sent with the original message.

In Figure 1-5, a digital signature takes a copy of a message, hashes it, and then encrypts it with the sender's private key. It is not used for confidentiality, but rather for authentication.

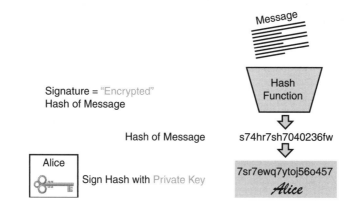

Figure 1-5   *Creating a Digital Signature*

Following are the steps in signature verification:

1. The encrypted hash is separated from the original message.

2. A hash is taken of the original message.

3. The encrypted hash is decrypted with the sender's private key.

4. The decrypted hash is compared with the hash of the original message.

5. If both hashes are the same, the signature, and consequently the sender's identity, is verified.

In Figure 1-6, a signature is verified by taking a hash of the message and comparing that hash to the decrypted copy of the signature, which is decrypted by using the sender's public key. If both match, the signature of the message is verified.

In summary, a digital signature is the hash of a message, which is encrypted with the sender's private key. The signature must be verified to verify the sender's identity. This is done by the receiver, who decrypts the signature with the sender's public key, makes a hash of the original message, and compares both hashes. If both are the same, the sender's identity is verified.

Internet Key Exchange (IKE)

IKE is a method of exchange keys with the intent of establishing a peer relationship. This peer relationship enables a secure and authenticated exchange of cryptographic material. This exchange is followed by the encryption of data between peers. IKE is the control plane for an IPsec tunnel, which encrypts user data.

Separate the message from the signature.

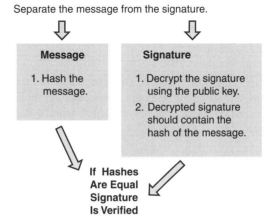

Figure 1-6   *Verifying a Digital Signature*

IKE can be broken into two distinct phases. Phase 1 establishes a secure, authenticated channel. By default, Cisco routers execute this phase in *main mode*. A less secure, but quicker approach, called *aggressive mode* for IKE authentication, can be configured.

Phase 2 negotiates the data plane security associations. In this discussion this is the IPsec parameters. This approach is referred to as *quick mode*. In this paradigm, certificates are used for authentication. Authentication occurs in Phase 1 of IKE; consequently, we focus on Phase 1.

For the authentication discussion for IKE assume that in a successful transaction, both sender and receiver have received a certificate from the same certification authority (CA). Consequently, both the sender and receiver have a copy of the CA's public key.

At a high level, certificate authentication can involve verifying digital signatures. The digital signature of the IKE peer is verified. Also, the digital signature of the CA is verified to ensure the certificate provided by the authenticator has truly been issued by the CA. For the peer to receive a certificate from the CA, the peer must first have a public private key pair (typically RSA). This key pair is signed by the CA and used as part of the digital signature offered by the peer described later in this chapter.

IKE Phase 1

Main mode Phase 1 can be broken up into three main packet exchanges of two packets each. The first set of packets exchange negotiates the method, the SA (security association), used for IKE. These first two packets define the algorithms and hashes used to secure the IKE communications and are agreed upon in matching IKE SAs in each peer. In other words, the first exchange defines which IKE security association will be used. The second exchange sets up the secure channel and sets the stage for authentication. This exchange uses a Diffie-Hellman exchange, which is a process that generates a shared secret. This is done by using a method of exchanging nonces, which are random numbers sent to the other party. These nonces are digitally signed and returned as part of authen-ticating the communication channel. The third packet exchange proves the identity of the both peers to one another. This is where the authentication is completed. After all three packet exchanges are completed, a secure, authenticated control channel is created.

In Phase 1, six packets are exchanged. The contents of the packets vary if certificates or preshared keys are used for authentication. In each case, the general theme of each set of exchanges is the same. The first two packets negotiate the IKE SAs; the next two set up the secure channel; and the last two authenticate the other side.

In Figure 1-7, IKE main mode is handled in three distinct sets of packet exchanges: SA negotiation, secure channel creation, and authentication.

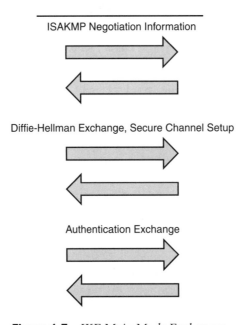

Figure 1-7   *IKE Main Mode Exchanges*

In Figure 1-8, preshared keys are authenticated in the last two packets exchanged in main mode.

When using certificates, the first packet exchange has the same purpose, to negotiate the Phase 1 SAs. In the second exchange, Diffie-Hellman creates a secure channel. In the third exchange each sender sends their respective certificates. This message is signed with the sender's private key and verified with the sender's public key. The sender's certificate is verified using the CA's public key.

Figure 1-9 shows certificates in IKE main mode that are requested in the second exchange and delivered in the third exchange.

IKE Phase 1 Negotiation

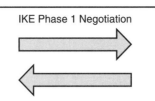

DH Key Exchange, Shared Secret Derived
via Nonce Exchange

Verifies the other side's identity. The
identity value is the IPsec peer's IP
address and preshared key in encrypted form.

Figure 1-8 *Phase 1 Using Preshared Keys*

IKE Phase 1 Negotiation

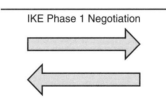

DH Exchange, Certificate Request

Cert, {Hash} private key encrypted,
verifies the other side's identity.

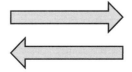

Figure 1-9 *Phase I Using Certificates*

IKE Phase 2

IKE Phase 2 negotiates SAs for the data plane protocol in most cases, IPSEC SAs. This negotiation process is protected by the control channel established in Phase 1. Phase 2, also called *quick mode*, refreshes SAs periodically for increased security.

The Phase 2 exchange consists of three packets. These packets negotiate the IP addresses of the peers, the protected traffic, and the transforms that will be protecting that traffic. In the first two packets, each peer sends over its SA information. The third packet is a confirmation and keepalive message. Every packet is protected by the IKE secure channel (header) as indicated by HDR in Figure 1-10 and is also protected by a hash to ensure integrity of the transmission.

Figure 1-10 shows that in IKE quick mode, the dataplane (common IKE) encryption SAs are negotiated.

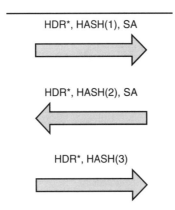

HDR*, HASH(1), SA

HDR*, HASH(2), SA

HDR*, HASH(3)

Figure 1-10   *IKE Quick Mode Negotiation*

Device Configuration: Certificates

The default configuration for the Isakmp policy is to use certificates. For this to be done, RSA keys need to be generated, and the router must be enrolled with a CA. (This process is covered in detail in Chapter 3.) The command **crypto key generate rsa** creates RSA keys locally in the router and must be done first.

Example 1-1   *Configuration of the Router Using Certificates. Default Authentication Uses Certificates.*

```
Router(config)# crypto key generate rsa usage-keys label localkeys  modulus 1024
Router#
*Mar  1 00:05:47.627: %SYS-5-CONFIG_I: Configured from console by consoleconf t
Enter configuration commands, one per line.  End with CNTL/Z.
Router(config)# $generate rsa usage-keys label localkeys modulus 1024
The name for the keys will be: localkeys
```

```
% The key modulus size is 1024 bits
% Generating 1024 bit RSA keys ...[OK]
% Generating 1024 bit RSA keys ...[OK]

end

sh run
......
crypto isakmp policy 1
encr 3des
hash sha
....
crypto pki trustpoint root-ca
 enrollment url http://10.254.0.10:80
 revocation-check crl none
 rsakeypair localkeys
```

Summary

The basics covered in this chapter set a baseline understanding of encryption. Some key points to remember are that symmetric encryption uses the same key to encrypt and decrypt, where asymmetric encryption uses a private/public key pair. In asymmetric encryption, the private and public keys perform opposite functions. If data is encrypted with the public key, the private key decrypts it and vice versa.

One place certificates come into play is as part of IKE. During IKE certificates are used as a method of authentication. Certificates heavily depend on asymmetric encryption. The framework of how to generate and deliver certificates in a secure, scalable, and reliable fashion is the foundation of this text.

Chapter 2

Understanding PKI Building Blocks

This chapter covers the following topics:

- Certificates

- Certification Authorities (CA)

- Subordinate Certification Authorities (Sub-CA)

- Registration Authorities (RA)

- Endpoint Entities: Users and Devices

- Key and Certificate Storage

The principles and functions of cryptography are the building blocks for Public Key Infrastructure (PKI). This chapter describes digital certificates, the surrounding environment, and the various forms of Certification Authorities (CA).

Certificates

In the digital world, certificates establish the link between an identity (associated with either an individual or a device of any type) and the corresponding electronic material. In this case, the material is cryptographic information, commonly known as encryption keys. A digital certificate is therefore a set of initially independent digital information combined and signed by an authority. An authority is an administrative entity that has some level of trust by the users; examples are government organizations or some companies.

Structure and Content

The main information contained in a certificate follows:

- An **identity** (that is, a name or a reference to an object, human, or material).

- Some **attributes**, attached to either the identity itself or the authorized uses of the certificate. Attribute types can vary to a wide extent; the most common ones will be explained later in this chapter.

- A **public key** performs a given set of cryptographic operations. It is included in the certificate so that it is published at the same time and therefore becomes available to third parties (all entities different from the owner). Absolutely nothing is secret or confidential in the public key, so no security is required.

- A **signature** from a Certification Authority (CA), covering all preceding information fields. The signature authenticates the binding between all the information contained in the *package*.

Along with those four items, additional information can also be included, either to add more security or to automate operations inside the PKI.

The typical certificate is structured as follows:

- Certificate

  - Version

  - Serial Number

  - Algorithm ID

  - Issuer

  - Validity period

    — Not Before

    — Not After

  - Subject Name

  - Subject Public Key Info

    — Public Key Algorithm

    — Subject Public Key

  - Issuer Unique Identifier (Optional, Version 2 and above)

  - Subject Unique Identifier (Optional, Version 2 and above)

  - Extensions (Optional, Version 3 and above)

    — ...

- Certificate Signature Algorithm

- Certificate Signature

OpenSSL libraries offer convenient tools to work with and view certificates. Example 2-1 shows the certificate content.

Example 2-1 *OpenSSL Output of Certificate Content*

```
Certificate:
    Data:
        Version: 3 (0x2)
        Serial Number: 61 (0x3d)
        Signature Algorithm: md5WithRSAEncryption
        Issuer: O=Cisco, OU=VPN Lab, CN=LAB-CA
        Validity
            Not Before: Dec  8 17:28:17 2006 GMT
            Not After : Nov  2 18:01:34 2011 GMT
        Subject: O=Cisco, OU=VPN Lab, CN=vpn-A.cisco.com
        Subject Public Key Info:
            Public Key Algorithm: rsaEncryption
            RSA Public Key: (1024 bit)
                Modulus (1024 bit):
                    00:b8:00:3a:53:b0:12:fb:80:4a:76:c1:6f:82:0f:
                    f9:cf:5a:5a:f1:7b:4f:1c:ba:ee:ce:6c:2d:44:71:
                    ce:16:28:33:5b:af:56:c2:1f:53:80:95:8d:86:96:
                    68:a3:cc:03:ed:a4:2b:30:a9:77:5f:7f:0d:3e:52:
                    1f:72:12:11:12:59:e6:9a:09:4e:c3:3d:03:37:d5:
                    a4:e9:7a:10:17:a8:2a:44:a6:f0:b6:e0:f3:7a:27:
                    aa:f5:e5:bb:8d:ca:c6:6f:3b:1c:c3:90:79:f8:a4:
                    68:dc:ac:59:bc:f9:99:07:5b:ee:28:e8:52:2a:af:
                    10:db:73:95:d4:01:ac:2d:ad
                Exponent: 65537 (0x10001)
        X509v3 extensions:
            X509v3 Key Usage: critical
                Digital Signature, Key Encipherment
            X509v3 Authority Key Identifier:
                keyid:03:50:7F:E1:AD:84:A8:13:8D:CC:9A:37:C8:0C:38:3B:02:EC:91:98

            X509v3 Subject Key Identifier:
                05:A6:1F:52:5B:3E:71:0B:F3:4E:79:74:2F:38:AA:A6:FF:44:61:19
    Signature Algorithm: md5WithRSAEncryption
        3d:26:d5:b0:63:df:dc:3e:cb:26:87:68:5d:f8:95:ce:a1:df:
        53:ec:59:6d:1e:20:e1:cb:d8:be:36:c3:6f:e3:f6:3c:d3:81:
        5d:93:fc:76:41:47:5d:4a:3a:c1:65:3d:75:2f:f9:03:47:b0:
        67:99:c1:d5:c6:2b:86:e8:b6:5e:09:ef:45:71:b1:c1:34:78:
        4a:aa:f3:0f:91:07:c6:3c:89:40:ca:43:4b:29:59:c9:2a:76:
        51:02:27:6d:2e:69:56:8c:09:42:3e:30:cd:3b:9d:97:37:fa:
        6b:96:88:48:a7:1b:49:17:ab:24:a9:31:ab:8a:0b:0e:73:90:
        2c:60:31:01:27:c0:8e:dd:ac:e9:5a:96:d0:82:65:62:94:0d:
        f4:da:17:40:99:50:5a:f6:16:d5:3f:2a:31:47:7d:1c:13:dc:
        91:0c:e7:aa:eb:22:e9:67:6e:d4:2e:e0:a8:e9:e9:d0:66:f8:
```

```
a3:a7:c1:aa:53:d1:5f:07:81:fb:54:91:d9:ea:b8:6c:0c:59:
72:0b:7b:cc:83:ad:2b:35:aa:85:f4:2b:52:d8:d9:7d:c5:48:
03:5d:b3:ee:3f:d0:a2:5e:06:5c:62:e7:d6:60:4b:06:67:5e:
21:f6:fd:61:cb:8e:a2:1d:f0:7d:a7:47:c6:41:36:c5:bb:b7:
22:a8:e2:da
```

Following is a description of each field based on RFC-5280:

■ **Version:** To date, three versions of the X.509 standard have been defined. Since 1996, the latest and most commonly used version for Internet purposes is v3. The differences between versions are that additional fields have proven to be necessary over time, triggering updates in the defined standards.

■ **Serial number:** Uniquely identifies a certificate among all the certificates issued by a given CA.

■ **Algorithm ID:** Identifier for the algorithm used by the CA to sign the certificate.

■ **Issuer:** Information about the particular CA that has issued and signed the certificate.

■ **Validity period:** Defines the time interval during which the CA warrants that it will maintain information about the status (valid or revoked) of the certificate. After the expiration date, the certificate is invalid. This field contains two dates: "not before" and "not after" (therefore defining a time interval), expressed in universal time (UTC/GMT).

■ **Subject Name:** Identifies the entity to which the public key belongs. The subject name takes the form of an X.500 distinguished name (DN). Typical Distinguished Name structures include Country, Organization, Organizational Unit, and Common Name and can be organized in a hierarchical way.

■ **Public Key Algorithm:** Algorithm with which the subject public key can be used (that is, RSA or DSA).

■ **Subject Public Key:** The public key associated with the entity identified in the Subject Name field. This is one of the keys used for cryptographic operations.

■ **Subject Unique Identifier:** A unique identifier bound to the subject entity. This optional field can be used in case multiple entities (users or devices) have similar subject names.

■ **Issuer Unique Identifier:** A reference to the subject unique identifier used in the CA certificate, in case multiple CAs have similar subject names.

■ **Certificate Signature Algorithm:** An identifier for the algorithm used by the CA to sign the certificate. An example of such algorithm is MD5 with RSA encryption. This field must contain the same algorithm identifier as in the Algorithm ID field.

■ **Certificate Signature:** The digital signature computed on the certificate fields, added by the CA when creating the certificate. By generating this signature, a CA certifies the validity and authenticity of the information in the fields. In particular, the CA certifies the binding between the public key material and the subject of the certificate. When receiving a certificate from a peer, one of the first steps is to verify the signature to ensure that the certificate has not been tampered with.

■   **Extensions:** Provide a way to associate various attributes to user or public keys. Private extensions can be defined as required by the implementation.

   Each extension is marked as either *critical* or *noncritical*. If a system cannot understand or process a critical extension, it must reject the certificate. Meanwhile, noncritical extensions might be ignored in similar situations. Therefore, caution must be taken before flagging an extension as critical in a PKI deployment.

Following is a review of the most common standard extensions seen in PKI implementations:

■   **Authority Key Identifier:** Provides a way to uniquely identify the key pair used to sign a certificate. This is useful if the CA has multiple certificates.

■   **Subject Key Identifier:** Provides a way to uniquely identify certificates that contain a particular public key. This extension is mandatory for CA certificates and optional for others.

■   **Key Usage:** Defines the usage that can be done with the key contained in the certificate. Typical usages are encipherment, digital signatures, CRL signing, and certificate signing.

■   **Subject Alternative Name:** Binds identities to the subject of the certificate. Those identities can be an email address, a DNS name, or an IP address.

■   **Basic Constraints:** Identifies whether the subject of the certificate is a Certification Authority (allowed to issue child certificates) and the maximum depth of valid certification chain (including this certificate).

■   **Extended Key Usage:** Indicates purposes for which the certified public key can be used, in addition to or in place of the basic purposes indicated in the key usage extension. Examples key usages include TLS Web server authentication, TLS Web client authentication, signing of downloadable executable code, email protection, or signing OCSP responses.

■   **CRL Distribution Points:** Defines how CRL information should be retrieved. That field contains most commonly an HTTP or LDAP URI.

Standards

X.509v3 is *the* standard for Internet PKI. It is based on a hierarchical model and is described in RFC-5280, published by IETF.

Although there is little discussion about the format (X.509 is the standard), the encoding used often causes headaches or nightmares for the individual trying to understand and deploy a PKI. The objective of this section, therefore, is to shed some light in that area so that you can become efficient in working with PKI.

The Privacy Enhanced Mail **(PEM)** encoding is common for representing certificates in text format. It can be easily identified through the use of headers and trailers indicating the content (certificate, private key, and so on). Example 2-2 shows a certificate in PEM format.

Example 2-2   *Certificate in PEM Format*

```
-----BEGIN CERTIFICATE-----
MIICuDCCAaCgAwIBAgIBPTANBgkqhkiG9w0BAQQFADBEMQ4wDAYDVQQKEwVDaXNj
bzEUMBIGA1UECxMLU3R1YWx0aCBWUE4xHDAaBgNVBAMTE2Ftcy1jbGwLXN0ZWFs
...
o6fBqlPRXweB+1SR2eq4bAxZcgt7zIOtKzWqhfQrUtjZfcVIA12z7j/Qol4GXGLn
1mBLBmdeIfb9YcuOoh3wfadHxkE2xbu3Iqji2g==
-----END CERTIFICATE-----
```

In between those headers, the certificate itself is actually represented using Distinguished Encoding Rules (DER) encoding.

DER provides the advantage to have a unique way of encoding each ASN.1 value. Now you might wonder what an ASN.1 value is. ASN.1 provides a set of rules for representing, encoding, transmitting, and decoding data structures. Example 2-3 shows ASN.1 parsing with OpenSSL.

Example 2-3   *Parsing ASN.1 with OpenSSL*

```
openssl asn1parse -in cert1.pem
    0:d=0  hl=4 l= 696 cons: SEQUENCE
    4:d=1  hl=4 l= 416 cons: SEQUENCE
    8:d=2  hl=2 l=   3 cons: cont [ 0 ]
   10:d=3  hl=2 l=   1 prim: INTEGER           :02
   13:d=2  hl=2 l=   1 prim: INTEGER           :3D
   16:d=2  hl=2 l=  13 cons: SEQUENCE
   18:d=3  hl=2 l=   9 prim: OBJECT            :md5WithRSAEncryption
   29:d=3  hl=2 l=   0 prim: NULL
   31:d=2  hl=2 l=  68 cons: SEQUENCE
   33:d=3  hl=2 l=  14 cons: SET
   35:d=4  hl=2 l=  12 cons: SEQUENCE
   37:d=5  hl=2 l=   3 prim: OBJECT            :organizationName
   42:d=5  hl=2 l=   5 prim: PRINTABLESTRING   :Cisco
   49:d=3  hl=2 l=  20 cons: SET
   51:d=4  hl=2 l=  18 cons: SEQUENCE
   53:d=5  hl=2 l=   3 prim: OBJECT            :organizationalUnitName
   58:d=5  hl=2 l=   7 prim: PRINTABLESTRING   :LAB VPN
```

```
 71:d=3  hl=2 l=   28 cons: SET
 73:d=4  hl=2 l=   26 cons: SEQUENCE
 75:d=5  hl=2 l=    3 prim: OBJECT            :commonName
 80:d=5  hl=2 l=    6 prim: PRINTABLESTRING   :LAB-CA
101:d=2  hl=2 l=   30 cons: SEQUENCE
103:d=3  hl=2 l=   13 prim: UTCTIME           :061208172817Z
118:d=3  hl=2 l=   13 prim: UTCTIME           :111102180134Z
133:d=2  hl=2 l=   43 cons: SEQUENCE
135:d=3  hl=2 l=   41 cons: SET
137:d=4  hl=2 l=   39 cons: SEQUENCE
139:d=5  hl=2 l=    9 prim: OBJECT            :unstructuredName
150:d=5  hl=2 l=   20 prim: IA5STRING         :vpn-router.cisco.com
178:d=2  hl=3 l=  159 cons: SEQUENCE
181:d=3  hl=2 l=   13 cons: SEQUENCE
183:d=4  hl=2 l=    9 prim: OBJECT            :rsaEncryption
194:d=4  hl=2 l=    0 prim: NULL
196:d=3  hl=3 l=  141 prim: BIT STRING
340:d=2  hl=2 l=   82 cons: cont [ 3 ]
342:d=3  hl=2 l=   80 cons: SEQUENCE
344:d=4  hl=2 l=   14 cons: SEQUENCE
346:d=5  hl=2 l=    3 prim: OBJECT            :X509v3 Key Usage
351:d=5  hl=2 l=    1 prim: BOOLEAN           :255
354:d=5  hl=2 l=    4 prim: OCTET STRING      [HEX DUMP]:030205A0
360:d=4  hl=2 l=   31 cons: SEQUENCE
362:d=5  hl=2 l=    3 prim: OBJECT            :X509v3 Authority Key Identifier
367:d=5  hl=2 l=   24 prim: OCTET STRING
   [HEX DUMP]:3016801403507FE0AD84A9138DCC9F37C80C383B02EC9198
393:d=4  hl=2 l=   29 cons: SEQUENCE
395:d=5  hl=2 l=    3 prim: OBJECT            :X509v3 Subject Key Identifier
400:d=5  hl=2 l=   22 prim: OCTET STRING
   [HEX DUMP]:041405A61F525B3E710BF34E79742F38AAA6FF446119
424:d=1  hl=2 l=   13 cons: SEQUENCE
426:d=2  hl=2 l=    9 prim: OBJECT            :md5WithRSAEncryption
437:d=2  hl=2 l=    0 prim: NULL
439:d=1  hl=4 l=  257 prim: BIT STRING
```

PKCS#7: .p7b .p7c file extensions

This is a standard for enveloping data. It is defined in RFC-2315. In a PKCS#7 envelope, you can, for example, place a user certificate and the issuing CA root certificate so that the receiver has all the material required to start using the certificate.

PKCS#12: .p12 .pfx file extensions

This is used to exchange public and private objects in a single file. It can therefore contain a certificate and the associated private key. It provides an encryption mechanism so

that private keys can be protected. This is the Cisco preferred format for carrying PKI
material.

Note PEM files can also contain private keys, with the corresponding headers. Example
2-4 shows a PEM key pair, resulting from the export function on a Cisco IOS router. The
key must have been generated with the *exportable* option to be allowed to export it.

Example 2-4 *Exporting a Key Pair from a Cisco IOS Router*

```
vpn-router(config)# crypto key export rsa testkey pem terminal 3des cisco123
% Key name: testkey
   Usage: General Purpose Key
   Key data:
-----BEGIN PUBLIC KEY-----
MIGfMA0GCSqGSIb3DQEBAQUAA4GNADCBiQKBgQC6APS9LkyB21J9e7wlFFnvM+cG
lj6duEBoFMp4yOYmgz+HAgLdu8XClWqR0lAlJkUkBdsaLJ4ogzqDzhEljV5AS8MQ
0TpE4Yx6T7Mm+WSgWB9RB5qsf78Uowh9YGeNoKJPiXiqC2MOlpJ1YfbX1X4Hr81x
NckdQ3uKR19Sd1Lr9QIDAQAB
-----END PUBLIC KEY-----
-----BEGIN RSA PRIVATE KEY-----
Proc-Type: 4,ENCRYPTED
DEK-Info: DES-EDE3-CBC,75FA73FE3E475900

13dfwWoNBjZk7oFz1Dy3xMmmCADTgArR0obzAdftWz76LOlNJ/TnGym1Is6ooZv6
APzJbqQPKFLel+bsZ9RG5k6tUCy5S/iQQw0+lQUI0OTrcvBEE/FMTSoe+pZq4csK
wdYxKjoSflPBpKCbZSAQz5QkIjojNCjLoUAtQcGa0ByiY04TVNJGYITFx2pw7Z5f
8H37QXf4nvrFx7QkFlVdpFrTissihzYCZPx4z1orBTYKjwcmA43l/IicHS9kTjOf
MhaukRwpWG8wlIS+Ez09dkXDklk8MMu2bnhR9uoo3vRTbnPjOBF0QiblsTTdlQzt
2uLflSnS+/uGZ2l4embm4jqjFpEJvE8l1KQFQcTAxmriQgI4MK0Brrxq1fQk7Em7
bQrlet25iZ860nZbFE+dGpMiDdbS+ghURyYSM+BGBfGqLqXh9IXSvGCtJcDXYjSj
ngEL5F7hzyNm0cQGTTl83rqHqWVnlYI2VCcvPs5GSUaV0He6MBETKEpvW/UvbDHo
Wz+NRlFFVAuU5/WszL7JQAxIEh92etpIu6lzqV6XZDPDQK0Cxy4PWosxrpP3OIOm
ccM+uHQf7dM8jpSDTeObEM8ulSPob6IS/Gotds9jTUhqdwpOeMqyd9SIs9akuZ0l
kJV+7eYf3EPMEoREVxR1BpVFqtP9ZQWfxIQ+TaVdjgBNVov9RfW5qvGmCRezTfMH
a+ocMXAQsH75PHDzXDMpU1a9L+GluDFtK3TEmiGJGHHDU4DXu+sykBIrGuOMyEMb
o21YPQlNmfhCfM4yjPpWaao/w34Qi6r2ngtsPEnD4EKadyyWiPC12Q==
-----END RSA PRIVATE KEY-----
```

Certification Authority (CA)

You now know what a certificate is and what it contains. Now we look at the CA responsible for creating and distributing them.

Role and Functions

A certificate creates a relationship between an identity and a key pair. Now, an external entity is called into the game to formally state and guarantee the existence of that link. The idea is to build a trusted relationship with the authority. This authority is then responsible to validate the authenticity of certificate requests: to guarantee that the identity requested to be included in the certificate is the actual identity of the requester or the entity that will own and use the certificate.

For example, if someone is requesting a certificate with the name "Alice" in it, the certification authority is responsible for validating that it is actually Alice asking for it (and owning the corresponding keys) and not Bob. To document the involvement of the certification authority, the CA digital signature (generated with a private key) is added to the certificate as a proof. As the certification authority is also trusted by the other members of the PKI, verifying the CA signature on a certificate guarantees its authenticity and therefore the identity of its owner.

The CA is the most important link in a PKI system. If the CA is ever compromised, the entire PKI implementation can no longer be trusted. Further sections show how the CA can be efficiently protected to minimize the risk.

Private Versus Public CAs

As you have seen, one of the main roles of the CA is to guarantee a trusted relationship. For that to happen, the CA must be "known" (and also trusted) by all parties involved in the PKI. Depending on the targeted scope and scale of the PKI deployment, you can differentiate two types of CAs: private and public.

Private CAs are entirely created, operated, and maintained by a limited private organization, usually a company or even a single department within a company. The private CA provides its services only for functions that are internal to the company (or department). An external component will typically not know or trust a private CA. Everyone can choose to deploy his own private CA; however, it will then be limited in terms of trusted relationships. The main advantage of a private CA is that it offers you complete freedom in terms of structure (multiple levels of sub-CAs, for example) and content of certificates. (Names and attributes can be chosen to accommodate the requirements.) A private CA is free in the sense that there is no subscription fee to create it or obtain certificate from it. The main limitation has already been mentioned, and the trust relationships are limited; although, it is always possible to cross-link multiple private PKI.

Public CAs, on the other hand, are well known, reachable, and trusted on a more global basis (at the Internet level). They are usually operated and maintained by dedicated companies for which running a CA is a core business. Some of the most popular ones include Verisign, Entrust, GlobalSign, and Thawte. They are so widely used that the corresponding root certificates are installed by default in popular Internet web browsers. To make use of their services (that is, get a certificate issued from them), a fee must usually be paid. The content of the certificate (name format and attributes) is usually more constrained. More and more government authorities are also creating their own CAs so that public services and institutions can make use of them. In some countries (Belgium, for example), each citizen now receives a personal certificate, usually stored on a personal identity card in the form of a smartcard.

Subordinate Certification Authorities (Sub-CA)

When the number of enrolled entities is increasing, to scale while keeping manageability, it is necessary to introduce hierarchical levels for the certification authority functions. The role and functions of the CA become distributed to multiple sub-CAs.

Role and Functions

The roles and functions of a sub-CA are exactly the same as the ones of a CA:

- Act as trusted authority
- Verify identities of requesters
- Issue certificates

The only difference is that although a CA can be seen as an autonomous, or top of structure, PKI component, a sub-CA is always a child of a CA.

Hierarchies

Hierarchical PKIs are created to answer scalability and management challenges. They use a tree model with the root CA at the top and sub-CAs at intermediate levels. The top CA (also called the root CA) stays the central point of aggregation; however, it can now delegate some of its responsibilities to the subordinate CAs so that scalability is restored.

Figure 2-1 shows a typical enterprise hierarchical PKI. The central security department owns and operates the root CA. It then creates a subordinate CA for each department in the company that will be operated by the department itself. Now each department can use it according to its needs: The network department uses it to enroll network devices, and the computer department generates certificates for servers and user laptops.

It was mentioned previously that one of the roles of the CA is to establish the trust relationship between two enrolled entities. What's happening now within a hierarchical PKI? Now look deeper at the example.

Imagine that you would like to connect a user laptop through a VPN service using certificates for authentication. Focus on the trust relationships, not on the technical details of the VPN.

The following components are part of the infrastructure:

- **Root CA:** CA at the top of the hierarchy.
- **SubCA-network:** Sub-CA administered by the networking department

- **SubCA-computers:** Sub-CA administered by the computer department

- **Laptop:** Certificate installed (with the corresponding key pair) on the laptop

- **Router:** Certificate installed (with the corresponding key pair) on the VPN router

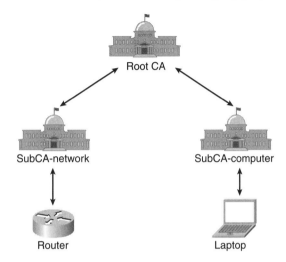

Figure 2-1   *PKI Hierarchy Example*

The laptop certificate has been issued by *SubCA-computers*; therefore, the laptop trusts the *SubCA-computers* sub-CA. But *SubCA-computers* has been issued by the *Root CA*, so the laptop also trusts the *Root CA*.

The router certificate has been issued by *SubCA-network*; therefore the router trusts the *SubCA-network* sub-CA. But the *SubCA-network* has been issued by the *Root CA*, so the router also trusts the *Root CA*.

The common point between the two trust branches is the *Root CA*, which is trusted by both the laptop and the router. As a result, all other children of *Root CA* will be trusted by the router and laptop. Therefore, using the entire chain back to the common point (*Root CA* in this case), the laptop can verify and potentially trust the certificate installed on the router, using the intermediate step of verifying the *SubCA-network* certificate before trusting it. The same is valid in the reverse direction. (The router can trust the certificate installed on the laptop.)

You are not limited to a single level of subordination: It is quite common to have several layers of sub-CAs, as shown in Figure 2-2.

In addition, the different branches do not have to be symmetric in any way: Both the number of horizontal and vertical levels can be different in each branch. Another good reason to build your PKI using hierarchical sub-CAs is that it enables you to put the root CA offline, hence increasing its security. If a sub-CA is compromised, only the underlying subtree would be impacted. A good approach is therefore to align your PKI topology to the administrative responsibility of your organization.

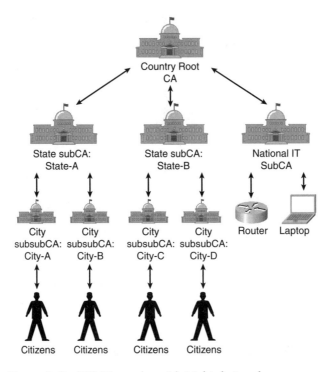

Figure 2-2   *PKI Hierarchy with Multiple Levels*

Registration Authority (RA)

A Registration Authority (RA) is also a child in the hierarchy of a CA (or sub-CA); how-ever, its roles and functions are more limited.

Role and Functions

Although a sub-CA has the same roles, responsibilities, and functions as a root CA, an RA receives delegation only for the administrative tasks:

■ Receive certificate requests

■ Verify requester identity

After those have been performed, the RA contacts its parent CA (or sub-CA) to have the certificate created and issued. The new certificate will then be returned to the RA first, that then handles the final distribution to the requester. Figure 2-3 shows the enrollment process involving an RA.

An RA is only a frontend to the actual CA. Except to authenticate the transaction with the RA, the requester does not need to establish a trust relationship with the RA because the registration authority does not actually sign any certificate. That means that several RAs can work for the same CA, or that the RA can be replaced easily by another one. The main purpose of the RA is to reduce the load on the CA by delegating some of the admin-istrative tasks: You can see the RA as the front-facing agent, working for the CA.

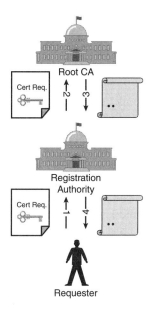

Figure 2-3   *Enrollment Using an RA*

A trust relationship does exist between the RA and the CA because the CA must rely on the requester identity verification performed by the RA on its behalf.

Endpoint Entities: Users and Devices

This section dedicated to users and devices covers the actual recipients of digital certificates.

Role and Functions

The user or device is a leaf of the PKI tree: It is an endpoint. That means that it cannot issue child certificates further down the chain, so the only thing that can be done with such a certificate is to use it for cryptographic operations involving the endpoint directly. Some more popular uses are authentication toward an IT system (VPN, web server, and so on), digital signature of emails, and content encryption.

Security Considerations

The digital certificate is the digital identity of the endpoint; therefore, it is critical to ensure that it is protected to avoid identity theft. The certificate itself is public information; however, the associated key pair (more specifically the private key) is secret information because it is the one used to generate cryptographic content linked to the certificate.

Although the private key must stay accessible so that it can actually be used, it must be protected against copy or theft. Later this chapter covers several storage means available that can potentially (or partially) address the security challenges. However, for the most basic PKI system, the key pair can be simply stored somewhere on a laptop hard disk with simple password protection.

In summary, using a certificate-based solution does not mean the overall solution is secure; the certificates and keys must be protected as well.

Users Versus Devices

Although digital certificates for devices or human users are technically identical, their storage and usages can differ. A device "acts as configured" when performing certification validation steps. However for users, the human factor plays a non-negligible part. Few people actually read all certificate warnings displayed by web browsers when navigating through the web. This unfortunately typical behavior means users click *Accept* independently of the message presented, defeating the security mechanisms of PKI. An expired, unknown, or changed certificate should catch your attention that something is not "as expected." With your PKI knowledge and understanding, a more detailed look at the error or the certificate can clarify what's actually happening, and the system administrator should be, at a minimum, notified.

Key and Certificate Storage

Secure storage of certificates and associated keys is of utmost importance. Storage is implemented differently, depending on the operating system or media used.

Generalities

As previously mentioned, the certificate is public information; therefore, it does not require any special protection besides ensuring that a copy is available for use. However the associated keys, more specifically the private key, must be secured so that only the actual owner can use it. For certificates bound to a computer or embedded system (a router for example), this is usually achieved through a file system on which the keys are saved using password-based encryption. Although such a mechanism provides an acceptable solution, it also has limitations: The keys can still be copied or stolen, for example, by reading the computer memory after the keys have been unlocked by the legitimate user and loaded in RAM.

Using such storage, the keys are installed only on a given system; therefore, for more agility or when certificates are issued to human users instead of systems, smartcards are usually preferred because they offer additional advantages that will be reviewed.

Microsoft Windows Certificate Stores

In Microsoft Windows operating systems, certificates are located in dedicated certificate stores that you can manipulate through the Certificates snap-in (reachable through the mmc.exe utility). Multiple stores exist by default, each with a dedicated usage: user, computer, and services stores that contain certificates for use by the respective entity. Within each of those, separate folders host trusted root CAs certificates, personal certificates, and others.

In addition to the operating systems stores, third-party applications can have their own repository. The Cisco IPsec VPN Client is an example. Firefox also uses its own certificate manager.

When accessing the appropriate store, you can perform view, delete, import, or export operations on the certificates.

Linux

In Linux, each application has its own certificates and keys repositories. It is usually implemented through a database file stored in the user home directory. If you look at the example of Firefox, it uses the Mozilla shared crypto library consisting of (among others) the cert8.db and key3.db files. Those files can be manipulated to view, add, delete, and export certificates using the **certutil** utility.

MAC

On MAC, the Apple Keychain is the central security repository for passwords, certificates, and keys. It can be manipulated using the Keychain Access application.

Cisco IOS

In Cisco IOS, keys and certificates are stored through files in NVRAM, as shown in Example 2-5.

Example 2-5 *Certificates Stored on NVRAM*

```
vpn-871# dir nvram:
Directory of nvram:/

  109  -rw-         16122               <no date>  startup-config
  110  ----          1896               <no date>  private-config
  111  -rw-         16122               <no date>  underlying-config
    1  ----            50               <no date>  persistent-data
    2  -rw-             0               <no date>  ifIndex-table
    3  -rw-           595               <no date>  IOS-Self-Sig#3601.cer
    4  -rw-           700               <no date>  CAServerA#3D.cer
    5  -rw-           874               <no date>  CAServerA#1CA.cer

131072 bytes total (105834 bytes free)
```

Materials can be added through the CLI configuration mode, and part of the information can be displayed through **show** commands, as shown in Example 2-6.

Example 2-6 *Displaying Information About Keys and Certificates on Cisco IOS Router*

```
vpn-871# show crypto key mypubkey rsa
% Key pair was generated at: 18:27:13 CET Dec 8 2006
Key name: vpn-key
 Storage Device: private-config
 Usage: General Purpose Key
 Key is not exportable.
 Key Data:
  30819F30 0D06092A 864886F7 0D010101 05000381 8D003081 89028181 00B8003A
  53B012FB 804A76C1 6F820FF9 CF5A5AF1 7B4F1CBA EECE6C2D 4471CE16 28335BAF
  56C21F53 80958D86 9668A3CC 03EDA42B 30A9775F 7F0D3E52 1F721211 1259E69A
  094EC33D 0337D5A4 E97A1017 A82A44A6 F0B6E0F3 7A27AAF5 E5BB8DCA C66F3B1C
  C39079F8 A468DCAC 59BCF999 075BEE28 E8522AAF 10DB7395 D401AC2D AD020301 0001
% Key pair was generated at: 16:36:01 CEST Sep 17 2009
Key name: vpn-key.server
Temporary key
 Usage: Encryption Key
 Key is not exportable.
 Key Data:
  307C300D 06092A86 4886F70D 01010105 00036B00 30680261 0091140D D31903A1
  BA5A35CC E71206DC BE9A7296 6906AB1C 9026C9D6 6368CCC2 8460141E FCC06469
  52D609AB 3D91559F 9DB631E4 04A433F8 F19AE237 AA981C8D 742B8CE2 EE62F0A8
  63CD03CF 64B08B15 178E8172 1387F37F BBA00056 69E522CB 09020301 0001


vpn-871# show crypto pki certificates verbose
Certificate
  Status: Available
  Version: 3
  Certificate Serial Number: 0x3D
  Certificate Usage: General Purpose
  Issuer:
    cn=CAServerA
    ou=MyVPN
    o=Cisco
  Subject:
    Name: vpn-871.cisco.com
    hostname=vpn-871.cisco.com
  Validity Date:
    start date: 18:28:17 CET Dec 8 2006
    end   date: 19:01:34 CET Nov 2 2011
    renew date: 19:58:14 CEST May 7 2011
  Subject Key Info:
    Public Key Algorithm: rsaEncryption
    RSA Public Key: (1024 bit)
```

```
  Signature Algorithm: MD5 with RSA Encryption
  Fingerprint MD5: B2FAA8B9 DC3D6A1C 877E80BD 2FFE2ED5
  Fingerprint SHA1: A3DC553F 305729C3 1D0E9BA8 7D975188 95BE994B
  X509v3 extensions:
    X509v3 Key Usage: A0000000
      Digital Signature
      Key Encipherment
    X509v3 Subject Key ID: 05A61F52 5B3E710B F34E7974 2F38AAA6 FF446119
    X509v3 Authority Key ID: 03507FE0 AD84A913 8DCC9F37 C80C383B 02EC9198
    Authority Info Access:
  Associated Trustpoints: CAServerA
  Storage: nvram:CAServerA#3D.cer
  Key Label: vpn-key
  Key storage device: private config

CA Certificate
  Status: Available
  Version: 3
  Certificate Serial Number: 0x1
```

Certificate Usage: Signature

```
  Issuer:
    cn=CAServerA
    ou=MyVPN
    o=Cisco
  Subject:
    cn=CAserverA
    ou=MyVPN
    o=Cisco
  Validity Date:
    start date: 19:01:59 CET Nov 3 2006
    end   date: 19:01:59 CET Nov 2 2011
  Subject Key Info:
    Public Key Algorithm: rsaEncryption
    RSA Public Key: (2048 bit)
  Signature Algorithm: MD5 with RSA Encryption
  Fingerprint MD5: 65B9F277 7F5D7EF8 5771A7C9 E5EF5931
  Fingerprint SHA1: 93205E75 6C9AB91F 9C7D8F51 F84ABB53 2638872F
  X509v3 extensions:
    X509v3 Key Usage: 86000000
      Digital Signature
      Key Cert Sign
      CRL Signature
    X509v3 Subject Key ID: 03507FE0 AD84A913 8DCC9F37 C80C383B 02EC9198
```

```
    X509v3 Basic Constraints:
        CA: TRUE
    X509v3 Authority Key ID: 03507FE0 AD84A913 8DCC9F37 C80C383B 02EC9198
    Authority Info Access:
  Associated Trustpoints: CAServerA
  Storage: nvram:CAServerA#1CA.cer
```

Using the **show running-config** command, certificates are displayed using a hexadecimal representation of the DER encoding. Using some PERL scripts for example, you can convert the output to a human readable format.

In Cisco IOS, note that keys cannot be exported unless they have been explicitly marked as *exportable* at the time of generation.

Cisco ASA

In Cisco ASA (version 8.2 and above), keys and certificates are stored in hidden files on the flash file system. Therefore, the only way to view and manage crypto material is through the command-line interface (CLI), as shown in Example 2-7.

Example 2-7   *Displaying Information About Keys and Certificates on Cisco ASA*

```
ciscoasa# show crypto key mypubkey rsa
Key pair was generated at: 02:35:41 UTC May 21 2008
Key name: <Default-RSA-Key>
 Usage: General Purpose Key
 Modulus Size (bits): 1024
 Key Data:

  30819f30 0d06092a 864886f7 0d010101 05000381 8d003081 89028181 009d3fe8
  135a4389 4c8be082 8c53a971 f03dff25 2a7e3928 5df73cce 549be49b 5e7ffa7c
  e1d7b15d 9b472ba4 4bc9dbb6 08df9f89 b6f0e633 692a7fa8 7919046f 8e8d54d8
  dd933c40 bee9699a 2aadba5c a1183122 a9b0d87f fb031564 73cf74d7 661c3148
  23a87f6b f869c582 824c5c07 f0f13479 f5d703eb c71cd2ef ae7cf3aa 09020301 0001
Key pair was generated at: 21:18:41 UTC Jul 17 2009
Key name: <Default-RSA-Key>.server
 Usage: Encryption Key
 Modulus Size (bits): 768
 Key Data:

  307c300d 06092a86 4886f70d 01010105 00036b00 30680261 0091bfe0 2485547f
  b8f428d7 4c229fec fb4b69a8 d0110901 2dd3db31 cb396773 021f97c0 dffae914
  03a6eece 05c5c653 d9c89399 db9d221c 7c451dde 58da139f 3fc4eae5 7fef4162
  5ca8bb66 945fd2f5 0282203e 5c2970a2 2c4648cb 1e5aa4a8 0f020301 0001
ciscoasa#
```

```
ciscoasa# show crypto ca certificates
CA Certificate
  Status: Available
  Certificate Serial Number: 01
  Certificate Usage: Signature
  Public Key Type: RSA (2048 bits)
  Issuer Name:
    cn=LABPKI
    ou=VPNLAB
    o=Cisco
  Subject Name:
    cn=LABPKI
    ou=VPNLAB
    o=Cisco
  Validity Date:
    start date: 18:01:59 UTC Nov 3 2006
    end   date: 18:01:59 UTC Nov 2 2011
  Associated Trustpoints: GLOBALPKI

CA Certificate
  Status: Available
  Certificate Serial Number: 01
  Certificate Usage: Signature
  Public Key Type: RSA (1024 bits)
  Issuer Name:
    cn=ASA-PKI
    ou=LAB
    o=Cisco
  Subject Name:
    cn=ASA-PKI
    ou=LAB
    o=Cisco
  Validity Date:
    start date: 14:22:31 UTC Sep 28 2009
    end   date: 14:22:31 UTC Sep 27 2012
  Associated Trustpoints: LOCAL-CA-SERVER
```

Similar to Cisco IOS-based devices, certificates are displayed via the **show running-config** command using a hexadecimal representation of the DER encoding.

On Cisco ASA, you can export certificates and keys using **crypto ca export** commands.

Smartcards

The computer system-based storages explained previously have one main drawback: The certificates and keys are bound to the system on which they are installed, and they cannot easily be moved between different systems. Smartcards try to address this limitation by providing mobility capabilities, while increasing the level of security at the same time.

Although the most basic smartcards just act as storage devices, the more advanced ones also offer some embedded computing capabilities, making them more secure.

The most common physical formats of smartcards are credit card-like systems with an embedded chip and USB token devices.

Smartcards offer two main functions for PKI implementations:

■ **Secure storage:** Smartcards offer ways to store keys so that they cannot be exported (or copied) afterward. It is therefore (theoretically) impossible to make a copy of the keys or the card. Of course, it must be mentioned that there is a lot of research (and hacking) done into that area to identify vulnerabilities and bypass the security in place. This results in smartcards becoming increasingly more secure.

■ **Cryptographic functions:** Making the private keys unreadable is a good thing from a security point of view; however, how can those keys perform cryptographic operations (signature, encryption, and so on) if you cannot get access to them?

The solution is provided by the embedded computer chip on which cryptographic functions have been implemented. The chip is the only component that has authorized access to the keys. It can perform the crypto operations requested by the system to which the smartcard is connected. For example, if a signature must be generated, the computer sends the data to the smartcard (through the appropriate smartcard reader or USB port), which then returns the signature as a result.

Smartcards are therefore providing a secure solution for certificate storage and use:

■ Keys are safeguarded.

■ Crypto functions are performed by embedded implementations of the cryptographic algorithm, which can, if certified appropriately, protect against weaknesses as well.

Note Although cryptographic algorithms are usually quite strong, it is their implementations that often introduce weaknesses and vulnerabilities. An example of weakness is a crypto module (hardware or software) on which it is possible to tap the embedded keys during processing. Although exploiting them might require considerable technical knowledge and material, the "reward" is sometimes worth the effort.

When using smartcards (in their various formats), the crypto system becomes isolated from the user system, preventing tampering problems. Indeed, the use of smartcards increases your control over cryptographic components because they become part of the

PKI system you manage. That removes the risk associated with giving the user the possibility to manipulate certificates and keys.

Smartcards also offer some additional advantages for key distribution. The administrators of the PKI can package everything onto the smartcard and ship it to the end user who can then immediately start using it by inserting the smartcard into a reader. Using secure Web access or emails becomes much more user-friendly.

Smartcards also protect the keying material through the use of a PIN, which must be entered by the user before the keys are unlocked and ready for operations. The PIN must be secretly kept by the user and entered into the system through either a keypad on the reader (the most secure solution) or through a graphical user interface on the computer system. This results in a multifactor authentication:

■   Something *you have*: your smartcard

■   Something *you know*: your PIN

Smartcards are becoming quite popular: Most bank and credit cards have been equipped for several years now, and other systems have started using them as well. In Belgium, traditional identity cards (the national version of the passport) have been replaced with smartcards: All citizens now have an official digital certificate issued by the country authorities that they can use to access websites for administration operations, requesting documents, or log in to their bank accounts.

On the device side, all recent Cisco devices are equipped with USB ports to connect cryptographic USB tokens. On ISR routers, Cisco IOS Software already offers a wide set of capabilities to access and use those tokens for all crypto operations and make easier the deployment of PKI-based solutions.

Standards of Interests (ITU-T, PKCS, and ISO)

You can find more information on the protocols and technology referenced in this chapter in the following standards. Although some of these documents are free, others require purchasing from the respective authoring organization:

■   **ITU-T X.509:** "Information technology - Open Systems Interconnection - The Directory: Public-key and attribute certificate frameworks"

■   **ITU-T X.500:** "Information technology - Open Systems Interconnection - The Directory: Overview of concepts, models, and services"

■   **ITU-T X.680:** "Information technology - Abstract Syntax Notation One (ASN.1): Specification of basic notation"

■   **RFC-2315:** "PKCS #7: Cryptographic Message Syntax Version 1.5"

■   **RFC-2898:** "PKCS #5: Password-Based Cryptography Specification Version 2.0"

■   **RFC-2986:** "PKCS #10: Certification Request Syntax Specification Version 1.7"

- **RFC-3447:** "Public-Key Cryptography Standards (PKCS) #1: RSA Cryptography Specifications Version 2.1"

- **RSA PKCS #8:** "Private-Key Information Syntax Standard"

- **RSA PKCS #12:** "Personal Information Exchange Syntax Standard"

- **ISO/IEC 7816:** "Identification cards–Integrated circuit cards"

- **ISO/IEC 14443:** "Identification cards–Contactless integrated circuit cards–Proximity cards"

Summary

This chapter reviewed the different components that constitute a PKI. First, you looked at what a digital certificate is and then compared the various types of certificate authorities and their interactions in a hierarchical PKI. You analyzed the available techniques to store cryptographic materials so that it is available for use by the end user and devices. Finally, the strengths and advantages of smartcards were detailed as they become more widely deployed in your daily lives.

Chapter 3

PKI Processes and Procedures

Several processes need to occur in a PKI network for a deployment to function smoothly. To address these processes, this chapter covers the following topics:

- Enrollment

- Certificate Expiration and Renewal

- Certificate Verification and Enforcement

- PKI Resiliency

Understanding the basics of cryptography and the building blocks of public key infrastructures provides a foundation for exploring the core processes and practical application of PKI. These processes govern how to get a certificate, how to keep a certificate that is current, how to revoke a certificate, and how to keep a PKI up and running if an outage occurs.

Enrollment

Enrollment is the process to obtain a certificate. The two process of enrollment are manual enrollment and a network SCEP-based enrollment. Network-based SCEP is discussed later in this chapter. Simple Certificate Enrollment Protocol (SCEP) is an IETF draft, draft-nourse-scep-20. Whereas both processes follow the same principles, the procedure for implementation varies. The common events for both scenarios are as follows:

- An end host generates an RSA (Rivest, Shamir and Adleman) key pair.

- A certificate request containing the end host's public key is delivered to a certificate authority (CA).

- The CA signs the request with the CA's private key and generates the end host's certificate.

- The certificate is delivered back to the end host.

Manual Enrollment

Sometimes a network connection may not be possible or secure between an endpoint and a certificate server. In this situation a non-network-based approach might be preferred. This approach requires an administrator to manually copy and paste a certificate into the local router.

Manual copy-and-paste enrollment has several steps. The high-level steps are presented here, followed by a detailed example. Example 3-1 through Example 3-6, which illustrates the execution of the following steps:

1. The spoke is configured to use terminal enrollment.

2. The certificate authority exports its certificate to the screen.

3. The spoke authenticates the certificate authority certificate and verifies the fingerprint.

4. The spoke makes an enrollment request.

5. The certificate authority grants the request.

6. The spoke certificate is pasted into the terminal.

Note   In the following example, the name of the sub-ca is ra, which refers to Raleigh, not RA (registration authority).

Step 1.   Configure the spoke to use terminal enrollment, as illustrated in Example 3-1.

Example 3-1   *Configure Spoke to Use Terminal Enrollment*

```
r35-4-1023(config)# crypto pki trustpoint ra
r35-4-1023(ca-trustpoint)# enrollment terminal
```

Step 2.   The certificate authority exports its certificate to the screen, as shown in Example 3-2.

Example 3-2   *CA Exports Certificate*

```
Device: SUB-CA

S-3845-ra-subca(config)# crypto pki export ra-subca pem terminal
% CA certificate:
-----BEGIN CERTIFICATE-----
MIICMDCCAZmgAwIBAgIBCDANBgkqhkiG9w0BAQQFADASMRAwDgYDVQQDEwdyb290
LWNhMB4XDTA5MDEyODE2MjExOVoXDTExMDEyODE2MjExOVowEzERMA8GA1UEAxMI
cmEtc3ViY2EwgZ8wDQYJKoZIhvcNAQEBBQADgY0AMIGJAoGBAPoXSGDFGRqPiVQt
cRscN6uGG+nY1exDTzY18AUaP83laS6ylbHek1P9nzwKNZysO9Ya8+0bhG9SEHCh
XUJd4Y2DovwWnxzFEhqvWI7hVP8vkWmRFZx7EooiWlW/lTxgqrnjdg4/N9OTej0E
```

```
pmExbQfL3TN+ZAckHrVbWl8w7OH7AgMBAAGjgZQwgZEwMQYDVR0fBCowKDAmoCSg
IoYgaHR0cDovLzE3Mi4yNi4xODUuOTkvcm9vdC1jYS5jbcwwDwYDVR0TAQH/BAUw
AwEB/zALBgNVHQ8EBAMCB4AwHwYDVR0jBBgwFoAUDkMCSiWkFtEXEC4a0UrEnEV/
QdAwHQYDVR0OBBYEFOOEC8szKHCxiv4yrUtP+fgFjhTtMA0GCSqGSIb3DQEBBAUA
A4GBAF1IN0RnKRKmj2SwrygZcYdgmMPkzaXFW+9c7xEq8UWO25bG3MqKLEwEURgU
DcZ1jMgJeciGiQMO6N0kpWwYwVI1w0dJZ5Ab2Nby9ew892viw/vFWjeTdJvTkrd7
KjLtRgnnslm26gsFhA1X9uvKpXfFsDp4kLnMxZxRIPQUc8m7
-----END CERTIFICATE-----
```

Step 3.   The spoke authenticates the CA certificate and verifies the fingerprint, as shown in Example 3-3.

Example 3-3   *Authentication of CA Certificate and Verification of Fingerprint*

```
Device: SPOKE

r35-4-1023(config)# crypto pki authenticate ra

Enter the base 64 encoded CA certificate.
End with a blank line or the word "quit" on a line by itself

-----BEGIN CERTIFICATE-----
MIICMDCCAZmgAwIBAgIBCDANBgkqhkiG9w0BAQQFADASMRAwDgYDVQQDEwdyb290
LWNhMB4XDTA5MDEyODE2MjExOVoXDTExMDEyODE2MjExOVowEzERMA8GA1UEAxMI
cmEtc3ViY2EwgZ8wDQYJKoZIhvcNAQEBBQADgY0AMIGJAoGBAPoXSGDFGRqPiVQt
cRscN6uGG+nY1exDTzY18AUaP83laS6ylbHek1P9nzwKNZysO9Ya8+ObhG9SEHCh
XUJd4Y2DovwWnxzFEhqvWI7hVP8vkWmRFZx7EooiWlW/lTxgqrnjdg4/N9OTej0E
pmExbQfL3TN+ZAckHrVbWl8w7OH7AgMBAAGjgZQwgZEwMQYDVR0fBCowKDAmoCSg
IoYgaHR0cDovLzE3Mi4yNi4xODUuOTkvcm9vdC1jYS5jbcwwDwYDVR0TAQH/BAUw
AwEB/zALBgNVHQ8EBAMCB4AwHwYDVR0jBBgwFoAUDkMCSiWkFtEXEC4a0UrEnEV/
QdAwHQYDVR0OBBYEFOOEC8szKHCxiv4yrUtP+fgFjhTtMA0GCSqGSIb3DQEBBAUA
A4GBAF1IN0RnKRKmj2SwrygZcYdgmMPkzaXFW+9c7xEq8UWO25bG3MqKLEwEURgU
DcZ1jMgJeciGiQMO6N0kpWwYwVI1w0dJZ5Ab2Nby9ew892viw/vFWjeTdJvTkrd7
KjLtRgnnslm26gsFhA1X9uvKpXfFsDp4kLnMxZxRIPQUc8m7
-----END CERTIFICATE-----

Trustpoint 'ra' is a subordinate CA and holds a non self signed cert
Certificate has the following attributes:
        Fingerprint MD5: ECE8BE9E 9C5179A5 ABD983A2 6E5F5DE8
        Fingerprint SHA1: 0A86F03E 077E587B 2DB4644A 5BA55F0F FC57D2EF

% Do you accept this certificate? [yes/no]: yes
Trustpoint CA certificate accepted.
% Certificate successfully imported
```

```
Device: SUB-CA verify fingerprint
S-3845-ra-subca#show crypto pki certificates verbose
Certificate
  Status: Available
  Version: 3
  Certificate Serial Number (hex): 0D
  Certificate Usage: General Purpose
  Issuer:
    cn=ra-subca
  Subject:
    Name: ra-subca.cisco.com
    IP Address: 192.168.159.243
    Serial Number: FTX1111A468
    serialNumber=FTX1111A468+ipaddress=192.168.159.243+hostname=ra-subca.cisco.com
  CRL Distribution Points:
    http://172.26.185.99/ra-subca.crl
  Validity Date:
    start date: 15:26:27 EST Jul 13 2009
    end   date: 15:26:27 EST Jan 9 2010
    renew date: 15:26:27 EST Dec 4 2009
  Subject Key Info:
    Public Key Algorithm: rsaEncryption
    RSA Public Key: (512 bit)
  Signature Algorithm: MD5 with RSA Encryption
  Fingerprint MD5: 542CDC69 10C8D510 65DF5E3C 66CEF438
  Fingerprint SHA1: 5C4C6F15 E1F5E184 C4681535 3CC61012 F5D694EC
  X509v3 extensions:
    X509v3 Key Usage: A0000000
      Digital Signature
      Key Encipherment
    X509v3 Subject Key ID: 5A1CBE8B A043B0A3 651D50C7 AFB04761 B92A8862
    X509v3 Authority Key ID: E3840BCB 332870B1 8AFE32AD 4B4FF9F8 058E14ED
    Authority Info Access:
  Associated Trustpoints: ra
  Storage: nvram:ra-subca#D.cer
  Key Label: ra
  Key storage device: private config

 CA Certificate (subordinate CA certificate)
   Status: Available
   Version: 3
   Certificate Serial Number (hex): 08
   Certificate Usage: Signature
```

```
  Issuer:
    cn=root-ca
  Subject:
    cn=ra-subca
  CRL Distribution Points:
    http://172.26.185.99/root-ca.crl
  Validity Date:
    start date: 12:21:19 EST Jan 28 2009
    end   date: 12:21:19 EST Jan 28 2011
  Subject Key Info:
    Public Key Algorithm: rsaEncryption
    RSA Public Key: (1024 bit)
  Signature Algorithm: MD5 with RSA Encryption
  Fingerprint MD5: ECE8BE9E 9C5179A5 ABD983A2 6E5F5DE8
  Fingerprint SHA1: 0A86F03E 077E587B 2DB4644A 5BA55F0F FC57D2EF
  X509v3 extensions:
    X509v3 Key Usage: 80000000
      Digital Signature
    X509v3 Subject Key ID: E3840BCB 332870B1 8AFE32AD 4B4FF9F8 058E14ED
    X509v3 Basic Constraints:
        CA: TRUE
    X509v3 Authority Key ID: 0E43024A 25A416D1 17102E1A D14AC49C 457F41D0
    Authority Info Access:
  Associated Trustpoints: ra ra-subca
  Storage: nvram:root-ca#8CA.cer
```

Step 4.   The spoke makes an enrollment request, as shown in Example 3-4.

Example 3-4 *Spoke Makes Enrollment Request*

```
Device: SPOKE Generate enrollment request

r35-4-1023(config)# crypto pki enroll ra
% Start certificate enrollment ..

% The subject name in the certificate will include: r35-4-1023
% Include the router serial number in the subject name? [yes/no]: yes
% The serial number in the certificate will be: FTX1048A6EJ
% Include an IP address in the subject name? [no]:
Display Certificate Request to terminal? [yes/no]: yes
Certificate Request follows:

-----BEGIN CERTIFICATE REQUEST-----
MIIBCjCBtQIBADAvMS0wEgYDVQQFEwtGVFgxMDQ4QTZFSjAXBgkqhkiG9w0BCQIW
```

```
CnIzNS00LTEwMjMwXDANBgkqhkiG9w0BAQEFAANLADBIAkEAxcrafPm39Mmk51I+
dhnuVtkU9cYPOSHhS694b1taJG42esxtSUV8AwP4TcnQC/omIaIM1k5qIwnPe7FI
7Vic8QIDAQABoCEwHwYJKoZIhvcNAQkOMRIwEDAOBgNVHQ8BAf8EBAMCBaAwDQYJ
KoZIhvcNAQEEBQADQQBXw6esEMhzh9Jig0M3COwpX/wWMxUYQryYJK+uNDQf/PqH
n7zzC6Ii3UmfxlJKoK+Dgc6K3X87TVY6JRgMnlos
-----END CERTIFICATE REQUEST-----


Device: SUB-CA paste request generated from spoke

S-3845-ra-subca#crypto pki server ra-subca request pkcs10 terminal pem
% Enter Base64 encoded or PEM formatted PKCS10 enrollment request.
% End with a blank line or "quit" on a line by itself.
-----BEGIN CERTIFICATE REQUEST-----
MIIBCjCBtQIBADAvMS0wEgYDVQQFEwtGVFgxMDQ4QTZFSjAXBgkqhkiG9w0BCQIW
CnIzNS00LTEwMjMwXDANBgkqhkiG9w0BAQEFAANLADBIAkEAxcrafPm39Mmk51I+
dhnuVtkU9cYPOSHhS694b1taJG42esxtSUV8AwP4TcnQC/omIaIM1k5qIwnPe7FI
7Vic8QIDAQABoCEwHwYJKoZIhvcNAQkOMRIwEDAOBgNVHQ8BAf8EBAMCBaAwDQYJ
KoZIhvcNAQEEBQADQQBXw6esEMhzh9Jig0M3COwpX/wWMxUYQryYJK+uNDQf/PqH
n7zzC6Ii3UmfxlJKoK+Dgc6K3X87TVY6JRgMnlos
-----END CERTIFICATE REQUEST-----

% Enrollment request pending, reqId=2
```

Step 5.   The certificate authority grants the request, as shown in Example 3-5.

Example 3-5   *CA Grants Request*

```
Device: SUB-CA

S-3845-ra-subca# crypto pki server ra-subca grant 2
Writing 2.crt !
Writing 2.cnm !
Writing ra-subca.ser !
% Granted certificate:
-----BEGIN CERTIFICATE-----
MIIB/DCCAWWgAwIBAgIBAjANBgkqhkiG9w0BAQQFADATMREwDwYDVQQDEwhyYS1z
dWJjYTAeFw0wOTA3MjkxNTI1MzZaFw0xMDAxMjUxNTI5MzZaMC8xLTASBgNVBAUT
C0ZUWDEwNDhBNkVKMBcGCSqGSIb3DQEJAhYKcjM1LTQtMTAyMzBcMA0GCSqGSIb3
DQEBAQUAA0sAMEgCQQDFytp8+bf0yaTnUj52Ge5W2RT1xg85IeFLr3hvW1okbjZ6
zG1JRXwDA/hNydAL+iYhogzWTmojCc97sUjtWJzxAgMBAAGjgYcwgYQwMgYDVR0f
BCswKTAnoCWgI4YhaHR0cDovLzE3Mi4yNi4xODUuOTkvcmEtc3ViY2EuY3JsMA4G
A1UdDwEB/wQEAwIFoDAfBgNVHSMEGDAWgBTjhAvLMyhwsYr+Mq1LT/n4BY4U7TAd
BgNVHQ4EFgQULA4QQvFQjDDe2ZwgmND9L1MYhJIwDQYJKoZIhvcNAQEEBQADgYEA
```

```
4eyutNSNdNA2uKgqatQGT66Nxx2s6DF4fLPJY7wLMHJv+pXwrmzYzJpKqQrzf0ZL
WbaVHu6RdRvq35PFSdIm72l/whuATZSEdnHUsEU9GnGDjpvJCmAw73IAa8LDnfaZ
3N2NaAxY4CXAsxHWWtD1ea7A7utdS0R29d2aqNkvaXM=
-----END CERTIFICATE-----
```

Step 6.   Paste the spoke certificate into the terminal, as shown in Example 3-6.

Example 3-6   *Spoke Certificate Pasted into Terminal*

```
SPOKE import certificate from SUB-CA

r35-4-1023(config)# crypto pki import ra certificate

Enter the base 64 encoded certificate.
End with a blank line or the word "quit" on a line by itself

-----BEGIN CERTIFICATE-----
MIIB/DCCAWWgAwIBAgIBAjANBgkqhkiG9w0BAQQFADATMREwDwYDVQQDEwhyYS1z
dWJjYTAeFw0wOTA3MjkxNTI1MzZaFw0xMDAxMjUxNTI1MzZaMC8xLTASBgNVBAUT
C0ZUWDEwNDhBNkVKMBcGCSqGSIb3DQEJAhYKcjM1LTQtMTAyMzBcMA0GCSqGSIb3
DQEBAQUAA0sAMEgCQQDFytp8+bf0yaTnUj52Ge5W2RT1xg85IeFLr3hvW1okbjZ6
zG1JRXwDA/hNydAL+iYhogzWTmojCc97sUjtWJzxAgMBAAGjgYcwgYQwMgYDVR0f
BCswKTAnoCWgI4YhaHR0cDovLzE3Mi4yNi4xxODUuOTkvcmEtc3ViY2EuY3JsMA4G
A1UdDwEB/wQEAwIFoDAfBgNVHSMEGDAWgBTjhAvLMyhwsYr+Mq1LT/n4BY4U7TAd
BgNVHQ4EFgQULA4QQvFQjDDe2ZwgmND9L1MYhJIwDQYJKoZIhvcNAQEEBQADgYEA
4eyutNSNdNA2uKgqatQGT66Nxx2s6DF4fLPJY7wLMHJv+pXwrmzYzJpKqQrzf0ZL
WbaVHu6RdRvq35PFSdIm72l/whuATZSEdnHUsEU9GnGDjpvJCmAw73IAa8LDnfaZ
3N2NaAxY4CXAsxHWWtD1ea7A7utdS0R29d2aqNkvaXM=
-----END CERTIFICATE-----

% Router Certificate successfully imported
```

The entire process is conducted by use of terminal access. Consequently, no packet exchanges are required between the certificate authority and the end spoke.

SCEP-Based Enrollment

Adding a large number of routers in an enterprise and going through the steps for each of those would be a painful exercise for the network engineer. Consider a thousand routers. Often, engineers prefer to have a templated configuration that can be set up one time, enabling automation for subsequent certificates upon certificate expiration.

When network connections are possible between an endpoint and a certificate server, a network-based approach might be preferred because it provides the opportunity to templatize the approach, and in the future with features mentioned later, automatic addressing of certificate expiry issues. This approach is easier to implement and requires significantly less labor. Whenever possible, SCEP enrollment is the preferred solution. This approach requires minimal configuration on the router endpoints.

The use of the network-based approach has the chief benefit of improving scalability and limiting operational overhead. SCEP enables an endpoint to request a certificate or other certificate-related functions (revocation checking, and so on) remotely. SCEP runs on TCP port 80; however, it can also run on a nonstandard TCP port.

When an end device has an RSA key pair, it can make a request to the certificate authority using SCEP. That certificate request includes the public key. The CA responds with the new certificate, which is encrypted with the requestor's public key. This way, only the person making the request can decrypt it.

SCEP-based enrollment is configured in trustpoint mode. TCP port 80 is the default port used for SCEP and is configurable using the enrollment command. If a nonstandard port is used, make sure the http server configuration on the CA matches the nonstandard port. As shown in Example 3-7, the spoke is configured to use the CA or sub-CA URL for enrollment.

Example 3-7 *SCE- Based Enrollment Configuration Example*

```
r35-4-1023(config)#crypto pki trustpoint ra
r35-4-1023(ca-trustpoint)# enrollment url http://192.168.159.243:80
```

Certificate Expiration and Renewal

Certificates have a fixed lifetime. Eventually, both the root's certificate and the spoke's certificate expire. When a certificate expires, widespread connectivity issues might result so that in large scale VPN solutions, authentication in IKE would fail and connectivity could not be established. To prevent this type of failure, two mechanisms should be deployed for certificate renewal: auto-enrollment and rollover for end spokes and servers.

Auto-Enrollment

When a certificate on an end device is going to expire, auto-enrollment obtains a new certificate without disruption. By configuring auto-enrollment, the end host can request a new certificate at X time before its local certificate expires. This feature is used with SCEP, and together this provides an automated mechanism for enrollment requests prior to end node certificate expiration.

In Example 3-8, a spoke is configured to request a new certificate at 50 percent of the life time expiration, or 15 minutes into its assigned 30-minute lifetime. In the show crypto pki certificate output, notice the renew date is exactly 50 percent between the start date and end date (15 minutes).

Example 3-8 *Auto-Enrollment Example with* **show** *Command*

```
crypto pki trustpoint ra
 enrollment url http://192.168.159.243:80
 auto-enroll 50

S-3845-gm4-s-134# sh crypto pki cert
Certificate
  Status: Available
  Certificate Serial Number: 0x0DD
  Certificate Usage: General Purpose
...
  Validity Date:
    start date: 15:57:54 EST Mar 28 2008
    end   date: 16:27:54 EST Mar 28 2009
    renew date: 16:12:54 EST Sep 28 2008
  Associated Trustpoints: ra
```

The certificate authority has the option to grant requests manually or use grant auto, which is a feature that automatically grants certificate requests. This raises a classic problem in network security: availability versus security. Using grant auto makes the entire granting process more highly available and easier. However, grant auto on the CA makes it easy for any device to request and get a certificate.

Grant auto should be used with great care. Some circumstances where it might be all right are in closed systems, such as staging areas. Another situation would be in which policy controls are in place, such as a firewall, which enables only specific end hosts to access the CA, and only during windows when auto-enrollment requests occur. Also, the feature **grant auto trustpoint xxx** will only auto-grant requests signed by trustpoint xxx. Normally, xxx is the server trustpoint. Renewal requests are signed by the existing certificate. In that way, only renewal requests from clients with a valid certificate from your CA will be auto-granted.

Example 3-9 *Grant Auto to Facilitate Auto-Enrollment*

```
crypto pki server root-ca
 grant auto
```

Rollover

When a certificate on the CA server is going to expire, rollover enables the root CA to obtain a new certificate without disruption. By configuring rollover, the CA can generate a new certificate at X time before its local certificate expires. The new certificate, which is called the shadow certificate, becomes active at the precise moment the current CA certificate expires.

Notice in Example 3-10, the end date of the current certificate is exactly the same as the start date of the rollover shadow certificate.

Example 3-10   *Rollover Example on the Root CA*

```
crypto pki server root-ca
 grant auto
 auto-rollover 0 1
 database url ftp://172.26.129.252
 S-3825-root-ca# show crypto pki certificates
CA Certificate (Rollover)
  Status: Available
  Certificate Serial Number: 0x4
  Certificate Usage: Signature
  Issuer:
    cn=root L\=RTP ST\=NC C\=US
  Subject:
    Name: root L=RTP ST=NC C=US
   cn=root L\=RTP ST\=NC C\=US
  Validity Date:
    start date: 15:14:48 EST Feb 28 2008
    end   date: 15:14:48 EST Mar 1 2008
  Associated Trustpoints: root-ca

CA Certificate
  Status: Available
  Certificate Serial Number: 0x3
  Certificate Usage: Signature
  Issuer:
    cn=root L\=RTP ST\=NC C\=US
  Subject:
    cn=root L\=RTP ST\=NC C\=US
  Validity Date:
    start date: 15:14:48 EST Feb 26 2008
    end   date: 15:14:48 EST Feb 28 2008
  Associated Trustpoints: root-ca
```

Certificate Verification and Enforcement

Certificates expire. Network administrators might simply wait for a certificate to expire or use another method to remove a certificate. For example, if a router is stolen, there needs to be a way to revoke its certificate so that it can no longer participate in the network. In the case of IPsec deployments, for example, a revoked certificate would result in failure during IKE.

There are three significant approaches that use certificates. The first approach uses certificate revocation lists (CRL), which are periodically downloaded to a router and thus require lower overhead. The second approach uses OCSP, which provides real-time updates and makes a network call for each certificate that is presented. The third approach uses an AAA server and certificates together, which involves the end user performing authentication. The differences in these approaches are outlined in Table 3-1.

Table 3-1 *Certificate Verification Approaches*

	Advantages	Disadvantages
CRL	Low network profile, CRL server supported in IOS	Periodic, hours can pass between the time revocation occurs and CRL update takes effect. If lists grow long, processing time becomes a problem.
OCSP	Real-time revocations	Server feature is not available in IOS. IOS CA is not supported with OCSP. Only client checking is supported.
AAA	Real-time authorization enforcement and optional granular authorization controls	Specific certificate credentials must be entered into the AAA server. Depending on the selection criteria, this could be labor-intensive for an administrator.

Certificate Revocation Lists

Certificate revocation lists (CRL) enable devices to determine if a certificate has been revoked prior to expiration. A certificate revocation list is composed of the certificate's serial number (issued by the granting authority) and the date of revocation.

The CRL database is located on an external server (recommended) or on the CA. The CA will, by default, store the CRL locally. If the recommended practice of housing the CRL on an external server is used, the command **database url crl** points to the location where the CRL database file is stored. This is configured under cs-server sub configuration mode.

The location of the database file and where end devices or users go to access the CRL might be the same. The location can also be different (see Figure 3-1 for an example CRL stored on Windows). As a recommended practice, housing the CRL for retrieval for end devices should be in a different location than the database file actively used by the CA. This insures that end users do not have access to the source CRL database file that might pose a security risk. The command to configure the location to direct end devices and users to retrieve the CRL information is the **cdp-url** command, which is also configured in cs-server sub configuration mode. The cdp url information is given to certificate users as part of the certificate they receive. Consequently, the decision regarding the url for end user retrieval of the CRL needs to be made before certificates are issued.

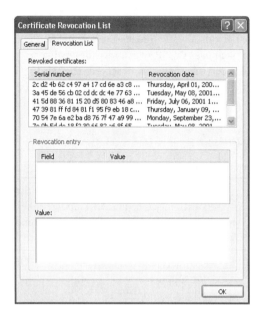

Figure 3-1 *A CRL Stored in Windows*

CRLs also have a lifetime. At a given time a CRL will expire and is valid only for an interval. When the interval is complete, a new CRL is downloaded by IOS via http. The CRL is then cached locally on the router. Consequently CRLs are not in real time. A certificate is revoked and then that information is propagated at a periodic interval.

There are two significant drawbacks to using CRLs in some environments. The first drawback is that CRLs are downloaded periodically, which means that a revoked certificate can still be authenticated before a new CRL is downloaded. The second drawback involves scalability of CRLs. If CRLs are deployed, the choice to revoke a certificate should be done with great care (that is, not add entries for administration or testing purposes). The lookup routers do against the CRL when verifying a peers certificate is linear; that is, it is line by line. As lists become longer, this takes up that much more CPU resources. Consequently, this can slow down and even timeout during IKE negotiations.

Example 3-11 shows a certificate being revoked.

Example 3-11 *Revoking a Certificate*

```
s-3845-ra-subca# crypto pki server ra-subca revoke 0x50
Writing ra-subca.crl !
% Certificate 0x50 successfully revoked.
```

The **Crypto pki server {name} revoke {serial number}** is executed on the granting certificate authority. Serial numbers are used to track certificates. After the certificate is revoked, the information will not be updated until the CRL expires, which might be many hours from the time of expiration. The CR lifetime can be changed. Example 3-12 illustrates shortening the CRL lifetime from the default of 24 hours.

Example 3-12   *CRL Lifetime Configuration*

```
3845-root-ca# Show run
...
crypto pki server root-ca
 database archive pkcs12 password 7 843595F
 grant auto rollover ca-cert
 grant auto
 lifetime crl 0 10
 cdp-url http://www.crl.cisco.com/ca.crl
 database url crl ftp://172.26.129.252
```

Figure 3-2 illustrates a possible design for handling CRLs.

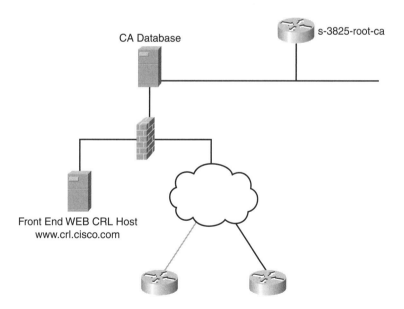

Figure 3-2   *CRL Server Architecture*

As shown in the figure, the end routers would have the frontend web server's URL included in their certificates for the CRL distribution point. The frontend server can get data from the backend server's database. This can be done via ftp and crontab or other methods. The firewall can provide a separation between the vulnerable frontend server and backend database by enabling only the minimal traffic to pass between the frontend service layer and backend server in the datacenter's access layer.

Online Certificate Status Protocol

A major disadvantage of CRL checking is the timeliness of updates for end hosts. The chief advantage of Online Certificate Status Protocol (OCSP) is that it provides a real-time update to end users. OCSP's disadvantage is that it relies on third-party software. A router cannot act as an OCSP server. Also, IOS CA is not officially supported with OCSP servers at the time of this writing. OCSP as a method of revocation checking is supported for end spokes.

An OCSP server has two methods to obtain information about the validity of a certificate. It can receive periodic updates from a CA by means of a "push" from the CA, or it can periodically poll a CRL distribution point (see Figure 3-3). This approach is still periodic in nature. The periods are much smaller than with a traditional CRL approach, and simple exchanges occur between a CRL distribution point and the OCSP server.

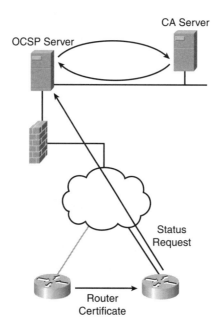

Figure 3-3   *OCSP Devices*

When an end host requests the validity of a certificate, it submits a query to the OCSP server, which contains the certificate's serial number. The OCSP server can provide a response to the query with a status for that certificate. The status response can be good, unknown, or revoked. The response from the OCSP server can be used immediately and consequently does not require local storage space on the router. Example 3-13 shows how to configure OCSP in IOS.

Example 3-13 *OCSP Configuration*

```
Router(ca-trustpoint)# ocsp url http://ocspserver.cisco.com:80
Router(ca-trustpoint)# revocation-check ocsp
```

OCSP service can function like a "cloud" service, using a push model between the CA server and the OCSP server. Also the OCSP server can have a certificate issued by the CA to verify its identity to others who make requests.

PKI Integration with AAA

Authentication, authorization, and accounting (AAA) servers are common in enterprise infrastructures. The Cisco AAA server is Cisco Secure Access Control System (ACS). AAA integration provides a mechanism for authorization. A certificate can provide authentication; when combined with an AAA server, the AAA server can provide authorization for the end host.

Fields in the certificate (such as **subject** and **serial number**) can be passed back to a RADIUS server or TACACS server. The server can check the credentials provided to it by the authorizing router to determine if the device is authorized for network access.

The advantage of using AAA as a solution is that it enables authorization in addition to authentication. The moment an administrator decides a certificate is no longer authorized, the administrator can make the change in the AAA server, and it is immediately effective. The disadvantage of the solution is that it requires manual entry of certificate credentials and authorization in the AAA server.

The leading practice for this approach uses an ACS RADIUS server. The credentials recommended to pass back are several Cisco AV pairs. The Cisco AV pairs recommended are **avpair=pki:cert-application=all**, which announces this is a certificate, and **cisco-avpair=pki:cert-trustpoint={trust point name}**, which announces the trustpoint associated with the certificate. Lastly, user level credentials are passed back. The recommended credential is the subject name as it appears in the certificate, which is the FQDN provided to the CA by the router requesting a certificate.

The ACS server would reside local to the server performing the authorization. Often, the authorizing router can be a central or hub gateway to a central location. Cisco AV pairs that are commonly passed to a RADIUS server are **cisco-avpair=pki:cert-application=all**, **cisco-avpair=pki:cert-trustpoint={trust point name}**, and **cisco-avpair=pki:cert-serial={serial number}**.

Although these AV pairs are often used, the drawback is every time a new certificate is issued the serial number and potentially other information would need to be re-entered. A simpler approach would be to use the Fully Qualified Domain Name (FQDN) of the router, which would be included in the certificate. Then the only AV pair should be associated with the CA at the group level, as will be shown in the example. The AV pair associated with the CA is combined with the FQDN taken from the certificate's subject name field will provide all the credentials for authorization.

Upon disabling authorization for that router, the fully qualified domain name of that router can be removed as a user on the AAA server to deny authorization. This reduces the overall administrative overhead in keeping up with the changing fields in certificates (such as serial number). Example 3-14 illustrates how to configure a router to use AAA.

Example 3-14   *Configuring the Authorizing Router for AAA Using RADIUS*

```
aaa authentication login no-auth none
aaa authorization exec dmvpn-pki group radius
aaa authorization network dmvpn-pki group radius
!
crypto pki trustpoint ra
 enrollment url http://192.168.159.243:12345
 serial-number
 ip-address 192.168.159.242
 revocation-check crl
 rsakeypair hub-keys
 auto-enroll 70 regenerate
 authorization list dmvpn-pki
 authorization username subjectname unstructuredname
! above line will not appear in show run since it is a default !
```

On the ACS configuration, screen captures can be found in Figure 3-4 and Figure 3-5. The PKI group is created with the appropriate AV pairs. Then a user with the FQDN is named and added to that group.

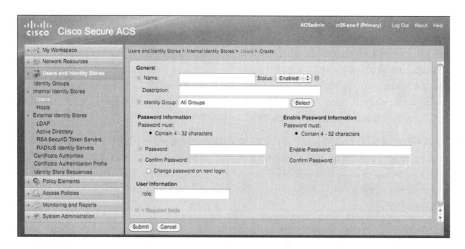

Figure 3-4   *ACS AAA Server Configuration for PKI Integration*

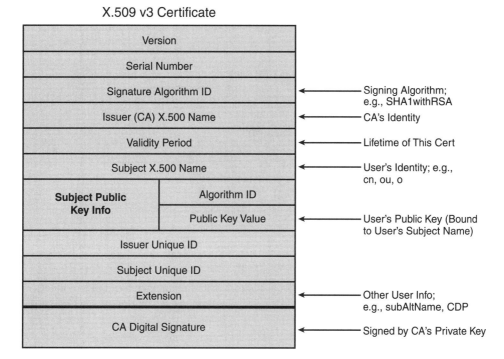

Figure 3-5 *X.509 Certificate Structure*

PKI Resiliency

Sometimes, routers experience hardware failures, or an administrator might accidentally lose information on a router. If this router is the certificate authority, a key part of the network infrastructure is compromised. Consequently, a method should exist to recover from such events without resulting in a catastrophic failure.

Certificate Authority Resiliency

The certificate authority is the key piece to consider for a resilient PKI. There are several files on a CA server to consider, including the following:

■ **Database** file contains the RSA keys and local certificate.

■ The **.Ser** file has the last serial number issued by the CA.

■ The **.CRL** file contains the list certificates that have been revoked.

The default location for file storage is on the local NVRAM. For maximum resiliency, it is considered best practice to use an external FTP server to store these files. This external server should not be used for anything else and should have reachability only from the CA servers. Resiliency practices for mission critical servers should be applied to this server. Example 3-15 shows optionally placing the CRL file in a different location than the URL file. The CRL file by default would be stored in the same location as the database file.

Example 3-15   *Configuring an External FTP Server*

```
3845-root-ca# show run
crypto pki server root-ca
 database archive pkcs12 password {password}
 database url ftp://172.26.129.252
 database url crl ftp://172.26.129.252
```

If a router fails, a new router should be available to become the new CA. The steps to restore are simple:

Step 1.   Import the database file using the command **crypto pki import** {*root-ca name*} **pkcs12 ftp://**{*x.y.z.w*} {*password*}.

Step 2.   Paste the configuration that is a common and recommended standard practice to be backed up regularly. Using this method the restoration process is simple and straight forward.

Summary

Many processes need to occur in the background of a PKI for things to run smoothly. Some considerations are enrollment, certificate renewal, certificate verification and enforcement, and resiliency. This chapter discussed manual enrollment and SCEP, which is a network-based enrollment process and is preferred where ever possible because enrollment over the network is much simpler to implement.

For certificate renewal, consider two elements: the CA certificate expiring and the spoke certificate expiring. To renew the CA certificate, the IOS feature rollover is used that creates a shadow certificate on the CA server that is valid at the moment of the current certificate's expiration. For the spoke, an auto-enrollment certificate renewal feature is used. At a time in which is a certain percentage "X" of the lifetime has passed, the spoke requests a new certificate.

Certificate verification and enforcement is required to make sure certificates presented during authentication are valid. Two principal methods are used for this enforcement, plus a third authorization-based method that is adapted to provide similar functionality. The approaches are CRL, OCSP, and AAA integration. CRL lists provide a list of revoked certificates and is supported by IOS CA. However, CRLs are not real time and may take many hours for information to be propagated about the expiration of a certificate. OCSP is real time, however, is not supported on IOS CA and requires third-party servers. Integration with AAA provides a method of authorization that is real time.

Authentication occurs as usual, and authorization enforcement can determine if network access is permitted. The disadvantage of this approach is that the AAA server needs to have information for all certificates in the network.

Another important process for any network device is what to do if a device must be restored. If you follow leading practices that dictate using an external FTP server to store the database, restoring an IOS CA is straightforward. The steps involved in restoration are twofold; import the database file and copy-paste the old configuration on to the new IOS CA server.

Chapter 4

Troubleshooting

This chapter focuses on the steps you can use to troubleshoot a PKI-related problem. The intent is not to provide an exhaustive list of possible issues, but rather to teach you how to approach the problem and narrow down the possible failure cause. In some instances, assistance from Cisco TAC is ultimately be required, but by identifying failure points as precisely as possible, you might resolve issues without assistance.

This chapter is divided into three sections that map the lifetime of the certificate:

■ Keying Material Generation

■ Enrollment Process

■ Certificate Use and Validation

The examples are given for Cisco IOS-based devices but are applicable to other components such as Cisco ASA Firewalls.

Keying Material Generation

Although the key generation process on the device is straightforward and should not cause any problems, you need to pay attention to several parameters or options that must be selected at generation time and cannot be changed later; such changes would require the operator to perform the entire enrollment process again.

Key Sizes

Key size defines the level of security attached to the key. A larger key size is always more secure; the drawback, however, is that it requires more computing resources not only at generation time, but also for every operation (signature generation, verification, and so on) involving the key. In a large scale deployment with hub-and-spoke topology, for example, the load on the hub can potentially increase significantly when larger keys are used.

The key size ranges from 360 bits to 4096 bits, depending on the platform. The size to use might be dictated by your security policy. Currently, a minimum of 1024 bits for normal operations and 2048 bits for increased security (for example, the certificate server) is recommended. Because 4096 bits is not supported on all platforms, carefully evaluate the complete solution before adopting such settings.

Label

The label is a name that you give to the key pair. This is only locally significant because it is stored only on the device and will never be used as part of any PKI process.

By default, the label is the FQDN (hostname.domain-name) of the device.

In latest Cisco IOS releases, the keys will be renamed if you change the device name after the keys have been generated, as shown in Example 4-1.

Example 4-1   *Automatic Update of Key Label*

```
router871(config)#hostname router872
router872(config)#^Z


*Dec 11 06:02:16.406: CRYPTO: Renamed keypair router871.cisco.com to
   router872.cisco.com
*Dec 11 06:02:16.406: CRYPTO: Renamed keypair router871.cisco.com.server to
   router872.cisco.com.server
```

Note   For the last console output, although only one key pair was manually generated through the CLI, an additional key pair with a name ending with .server has been automatically created. This key is a temporary key, regenerated every hour, used by SSHv1 server as an additional security measure, completing the host key that is permanent and enabling the authentication of the server by the client. If only SSHv2 is enabled, the server key will exist but will not be refreshed hourly.

The label becomes important when the device has multiple key pairs simultaneously; for example, if it must be enrolled to more than one certification authority, you might want to use a different key pair for security reasons. (Although this is not mandatory.) In that case, it is a good practice to specify a meaningful label for each key pair created (or imported). The label can be referenced later in the trustpoint configuration section.

Exportable Keys

An exportable key pair means that you can take a copy of both private and public keys. This is mostly useful for backup purposes. By default, private keys are not exportable as this is the most secure option. If you choose to mark the keys "exportable," be aware that the private key can now be duplicated for both good and bad intents. Access to the original device must therefore be secured accordingly. The exportable flag can be set only at generation time. In latest Cisco IOS releases, the flag can be later changed from exportable to non-exportable, as shown in Example 4-2, but not from non-exportable to exportable.

Example 4-2   *Changing Exportable Setting on Key Pair*

```
myrouter(config)#crypto key generate rsa label testkey modulus 1024 exportable
The name for the keys will be: testkey


% The key modulus size is 1024 bits
% Generating 1024 bit RSA keys, keys will be exportable...



myrouter(config)#

*Dec 11 07:00:47.046: %SSH-5-ENABLED: SSH 1.99 has been enabled

myrouter(config)#do show crypto key mypubkey rsa
% Key pair was generated at: 07:00:47 UTC Dec 11 2006
Key name: testkey
 Storage Device: not specified
 Usage: General Purpose Key
 Key is exportable.
 Key Data:
  30819F30 0D06092A 864886F7 0D010101 05000381 8D003081 89028181 009DFA1B
  ...
  4DFD330F F72D6DBE D4E8E707 4DD90758 ED07DA8A A6C0D264 A4FD7FE6 31020301 0001


myrouter(config)#crypto key move rsa testkey non-exportable
myrouter(config)#do show crypto key mypubkey rsa
% Key pair was generated at: 07:00:47 UTC Dec 11 2006
Key name: testkey
 Storage Device: not specified
 Usage: General Purpose Key
```

```
Key is not exportable.
Key Data:
 30819F30 0D06092A 864886F7 0D010101 05000381 8D003081 89028181 009DFA1B
...
 4DFD330F F72D6DBE D4E8E707 4DD90758 ED07DA8A A6C0D264 A4FD7FE6 31020301 0001
```

With this capability in mind, the following process is recommended:

■ Always generate your keys as exportable.

■ Make a backup of the keys if necessary.

■ Modify the key setting to non-exportable to increase security.

During the export process, you can (highly recommended) use an additional password to encrypt the private key.

Issues When Importing Key Pairs

In addition to generating the keys locally on the device, you can import keys into the device. Those keys can either be a backup of previous keys (generated on the same or a different Cisco IOS device) or keys that have been generated by a third-party PKI solution (OpenSSL, Certification Authority, and so on). In those cases, the security of those key pairs must be verified to ensure that only intended use of them can be guaranteed. By security, you mainly need to verify who else has access to the private key.

During the import process, either through TFTP or CLI, Cisco IOS Software performs a few verifications to ensure that the key pair is correctly formatted and can be used later. Failure to pass those checks results in an error message being displayed. The command parser is typically not verbose during the import process, so it is not straightforward to determine the exact failure cause. A few of those will be listed.

A first scenario in which a Cisco IOS device fails to import the key is when the size of the key is larger than the maximum supported one on the device. Example 4-3 tries to import a 4096-bit key while the device limit is 2048 bits.

Example 4-3 *Importing Too Large Key*

```
router(config)#crypto key import rsa key4096 pem terminal
% Enter PEM-formatted public General Purpose key or certificate.
% End with a blank line or "quit" on a line by itself.
-----BEGIN PUBLIC KEY-----
MIICIjANBgkqhkiG9w0BAQEFAAOCAg8AMIICCgKCAgEA3JbUeKLnDVNBV4vZaTm3
...
cAGCu64rksK/YKRXWWvzGneWmzXIcwrxmYGPTXMzSUB5BbyQyu9RKoy5wLEMo52h
BMnRFZffW/Wu/12GJ6hEIOECAwEAAQ==
-----END PUBLIC KEY-----
```

```
% Enter PEM-formatted encrypted private General Purpose key.
% End with "quit" on a line by itself.
-----BEGIN RSA PRIVATE KEY-----
MIIJKwIBAAKCAgEA3JbUeKLnDVNBV4vZaTm3+uh8hXeo8QFO1+FmjwlXeG5icmiI
...
6wcGLkTvAWv3jeS3xtJiMitQb5MWuvI3qnK2Q5chKunhrjK7kawsOdMF3C9gwhg=
-----END RSA PRIVATE KEY-----
quit
% Key pair import failed.
```

Another case of failure can occur when trying to import a password protected key. This is a common scenario because it is dangerous to carry a private key in a nonencrypted format. When importing such a key, you need to have the proper associated password; otherwise, import will fail.

Example 4-4 uses an incorrect password.

Example 4-4   *Using Incorrect Password When Importing Key*

```
router(config)#crypto key import rsa imported-key pem terminal cisco12
% Enter PEM-formatted public General Purpose key or certificate.
% End with a blank line or "quit" on a line by itself.
-----BEGIN PUBLIC KEY-----
MIGfMA0GCSqGSIb3DQEBAQUAA4GNADCBiQKBgQCtX9I2A+lKu93+S4iqkGm4k7Kx
...
QLyeEP7LtZDJYKa5I7LZ3RBxhxVQ0TWybe7ZphvIvb5MLWzFmSslcqHSBVWIqWvc
kdV+s4AxqATHbGEmTwIDAQAB
-----END PUBLIC KEY-----

% Enter PEM-formatted encrypted private General Purpose key.
% End with "quit" on a line by itself.
-----BEGIN RSA PRIVATE KEY-----
Proc-Type: 4,ENCRYPTED
DEK-Info: DES-EDE3-CBC,1311ACC62D001F7E

NETZmF6DeUYAcmujo2AaDoT4pQqgQD3tlJ5f3fs00Psb7t/fJmE2hmS0hkqV75wU
...
JN0JjgnEq7AVIOp6Umt8QPTp1sGemBpoD8hToJ+x7hyJXpC3Tf6ol8lrKhC7f2FR
8952q5gFcwoVbZb3yVaXWCo72a/r4V4V+rrnfLiCOWPg165d/Cd5SQ==
-----END RSA PRIVATE KEY-----
quit
% Key pair import failed.
```

Example 4-5 uses the correct cisco123 password.

Example 4-5 *Importing Key with Correct Password*

```
router(config)#crypto key import rsa imported-key pem terminal cisco123
% Enter PEM-formatted public General Purpose key or certificate.
% End with a blank line or "quit" on a line by itself.
-----BEGIN PUBLIC KEY-----
MIGfMA0GCSqGSIb3DQEBAQUAA4GNADCBiQKBgQCtX9I2A+lKu93+S4iqkGm4k7Kx
...
kdV+s4AxqATHbGEmTwIDAQAB
-----END PUBLIC KEY-----

% Enter PEM-formatted encrypted private General Purpose key.
% End with "quit" on a line by itself.
-----BEGIN RSA PRIVATE KEY-----
Proc-Type: 4,ENCRYPTED
DEK-Info: DES-EDE3-CBC,1311ACC62D001F7E

NETZmF6DeUYAcmujo2AaDoT4pQqgQD3tlJ5f3fs00Psb7t/fJmE2hmS0hkqV75wU
...
JN0JjgnEq7AVIOp6Umt8QPTp1sGemBpoD8hToJ+x7hyJXpC3Tf6ol8lrKhC7f2FR
8952q5gFcwoVbZb3yVaXWCo72a/r4V4V+rrnfLiCOWPg165d/Cd5SQ==
-----END RSA PRIVATE KEY-----
quit
% Key pair import succeeded.
```

Correct data formatting is important when importing keys and for other PKI interactions through CLI. As shown in Example 4-6, Cisco IOS always uses the PEM format for export and import of keys; you must use the proper headers and trailer when pasting the data.

Example 4-6 *Using PEM Headers*

```
router(config)#crypto key import rsa imported-key pem terminal cisco123
% Enter PEM-formatted public General Purpose key or certificate.
% End with a blank line or "quit" on a line by itself.
-----BEGIN PUBLIC KEY-----
...
-----END PUBLIC KEY-----

% Enter PEM-formatted encrypted private General Purpose key.
% End with "quit" on a line by itself.
-----BEGIN RSA PRIVATE KEY-----
...
-----END RSA PRIVATE KEY-----
```

Those headers have a standard definition, and the correct header must be used for each purpose.

Enrollment Process

When the keying material has been generated or imported, the next step is to get the device enrolled with a Certification Authority (CA); the aim is to have a certificate installed.

Although different enrollment methods are available, the focus is on the most current method through CLI (terminal) and through Simple Certificate Enrollment Protocol (SCEP). The first relies on copy-paste, whereas the second is networked-based over HTTP.

Before proceeding to the enrollment phase, you need to authenticate the certification authority by importing the corresponding CA certificate. This step can also be performed both through CLI or SCEP. As a safeguard, you should always verify that the imported CA certificate is the correct one, through comparison of the displayed hash.

A CA certificate also contains special values or fields that differentiate it from a user certificate. For example, as described in the "Basic Constraints" section in Chapter 2, "Understanding PKI Building Blocks," the CA field must be set to *true*. An optional field (also described in the "Basic Constraints" section) is the Path Length Constraint that indicates the maximum number of CA certificates that might follow (that is, not including the current CA) in the certification path.

When working with certificates, OpenSSL is an amazingly valuable tool because it enables you to display the certificate content in a human-readable format. Example 4-7 shows a CA certificate with the attributes previously discussed.

Example 4-7   *Using OpenSSL to Display Certificate Content*

```
openssl x509 -in BelgiumCA.pem -text -noout
Certificate:
    Data:
        Version: 3 (0x2)
        Serial Number:
            6c:85:9f:47:73:14:38:15:01:a2:52:6d:e0:23:d2:c4
        Signature Algorithm: sha1WithRSAEncryption
        Issuer: C=BE, CN=Belgium Root CA2
        Validity
            Not Before: Oct  4 12:00:00 2007 GMT
            Not After : Jun  4 12:00:00 2014 GMT
        Subject: C=BE, CN=Government CA/serialNumber=2008
        Subject Public Key Info:
            Public Key Algorithm: rsaEncryption
            RSA Public Key: (2048 bit)
```

```
                    Modulus (2048 bit):
                        00:d7:d1:79:00:cb:fe:b8:32:ca:bb:52:ba:68:68:
                        ...
                        77:cf:ae:1c:6a:a6:a1:48:f8:ef:07:96:75:14:50:
                        68:2b
                    Exponent: 65537 (0x10001)
            X509v3 extensions:
                X509v3 Key Usage: critical
                    Certificate Sign, CRL Sign
                X509v3 Basic Constraints: critical
                    CA:TRUE, pathlen:0
                X509v3 Certificate Policies:
                    Policy: 2.16.56.9.1.1.3
                      CPS: http://repository.pki.belgium.be

                X509v3 Subject Key Identifier:
                    95:F5:D7:EB:D3:97:EC:28:16:38:0D:D5:90:F9:1A:AB:83:DB:8D:22
                X509v3 CRL Distribution Points:
                    URI:http://crl.pki.belgium.be/belgium2.crl

                Netscape Cert Type:
                    SSL CA, S/MIME CA, Object Signing CA
                X509v3 Authority Key Identifier:
                    keyid:85:8A:EB:F4:C5:BB:BE:0E:59:03:94:DE:D6:80:01:15:E3:10:9C:39

    Signature Algorithm: sha1WithRSAEncryption
        66:15:56:d8:79:55:22:1e:07:07:56:70:3f:89:bd:ac:bc:23:
        ...
        84:9d:45:24:4c:d9:02:aa:83:64:eb:a0:89:6b:2f:47:ec:b9:
        77:2b:60:76
```

A user certificate will not have the CA:true constraint option. (It will have either CA:false or no such option at all.) Now try to import a user certificate as CA, and look at the CLI output in Example 4-8.

Example 4-8 *Importing a Non-CA Certificate During Trustpoint Authentication*

```
crypto pki trustpoint TestCA
 enrollment terminal
 revocation-check crl

myrouter(config)#crypto pki authenticate TestCA

Enter the base 64 encoded CA certificate.
```

```
End with a blank line or the word "quit" on a line by itself

MIIDMzCCAhugAwIBAgIBBzANBgkqhkiG9w0BAQQFADBAMQwwCgYDVQQKEwNDb20x
...
f+IFwh673ovMqcUvqHtXObmdop8hPIe6h4dybUPMkxxuSdvag2tcSUxsG7lv+ND2
3SzkEHyxJQ==

Trustpoint 'TestCA' is a subordinate CA and holds a non self signed cert
Trustpoint 'TestCA' is a subordinate CA.
but certificate is not a CA certificate.
Manual verification required
Certificate has the following attributes:
        Fingerprint MD5: 71BFFB89 96E5E175 CD316382 82D06238
        Fingerprint SHA1: 94E417B4 64E61FC5 243ACB04 B92AD391 722D500F

% Do you accept this certificate? [yes/no]: yes
Trustpoint CA certificate accepted.
% Certificate successfully imported

myrouter(config)#
```

Although the messages are confusing, a warning displays to inform the user that the imported certificate is not a CA certificate.

In the example, the trustpoint is configured to use terminal enrollment, where you will be required to paste the CA certificate through the CLI. Because there is a failure message, it is retried in Example 4-9 with **debug crypto pki transactions** enabled.

Example 4-9   *CA Authentication with* **debug** *Enabled*

```
router(config)#crypto pki authenticate MyCA

Enter the base 64 encoded CA certificate.
End with a blank line or the word "quit" on a line by itself

MIID3zCCAsegAwIBAgIQbIWfR3MUOBUBolJt4CPSxDANBgkqhkiG9w0BAQUFADAo
...
HWhPy6NOVyZlHHsuYvNu7SGRXXumZn/5SvbafxjAn+QnXH988JiiLtXQBq/oRDBV
A+kBNoxBQIYbnc1IlISdRSRM2QKqg2TroIlrL0fsuXcrYHY=
quit
% Error in saving certificate: status = FAIL

router(config)#
```

```
*Dec 11 15:11:38.381: Read 995 bytes as CA certificate:
*Dec 11 15:11:38.393: CRYPTO_PKI: crypto_pki_authenticate_tp_cert()


*Dec 11 15:11:38.393: CRYPTO_PKI: trustpoint MyCA authentication status = 0
%CRYPTO_PKI: Cert not yet valid or is expired -
    start date: 12:00:00 UTC Oct 4 2007
    end   date: 12:00:00 UTC Jun 4 2014


*Dec 11 15:11:38.397: CRYPTO_PKI: status = 65535: failed to insert CA cert
```

You can immediately see that the problem is related to the clock of the router. NTP is not configured, so the router clock is far behind, and therefore the CA certificate is not considered as valid.

In Example 4-10, the * character in the **show clock** output indicates an unsynchronized clock. The proper solution is to configure Network Time Protocol (NTP) on the router to have its clock synchronized with an accurate external time source. It can take a few minutes for NTP associations to synchronize and have the router clock adjusted. The **show ntp status** and **show ntp associations** commands are useful to verify the actual status.

Example 4-10 *Device Clock Is Not Synchronized*

```
router#show clock
*15:12:11.965 UTC Mon Dec 11 2006
router#show ntp status
%NTP is not enabled.
```

Note If you don't have an NTP server available within the perimeter of your organization, you can use one of the publicly available time sources. You can find more information at the following URL: http://www.pool.ntp.org/en/.

Using an uncontrolled NTP server can open some security risks. It is therefore advised to use a trusted time source when possible and to enable authentication when available.

Example 4-11 *Adding and Verifying NTP Configuration*

```
router(config)#ntp server ntp1.cisco.com
router(config)#ntp server ntp2.cisco.com


# Synchronization is not immediate


router(config)#show ntp status
Clock is unsynchronized, stratum 16, no reference clock
nominal freq is 250.0000 Hz, actual freq is 249.9977 Hz, precision is 2**24
```

```
reference time is D03B04B8.D251DB21 (15:13:20.821 UTC Mon Dec 11 2006)
clock offset is 0.0000 msec, root delay is 0.00 msec
root dispersion is 0.00 msec, peer dispersion is 0.00 msec
loopfilter state is 'CTRL' (Normal Controlled Loop), drift is 0.000009207 s/s
system poll interval is 64, last update was 33 sec ago.

router(config)#show ntp associations

  address           ref clock        st   when  poll reach  delay  offset   disp
 ~192.168.10.1      .INIT.           16    -     64     0  0.000   0.000 15937.
 ~192.168.10.2      .INIT.           16    -     64     0  0.000   0.000 15937.
 * sys.peer, # selected, + candidate, - outlyer, x falseticker, ~ configured

# After a few minutes

router#show ntp status
Clock is synchronized, stratum 2, reference is 192.168.10.2
nominal freq is 250.0000 Hz, actual freq is 249.9976 Hz, precision is 2**24
reference time is D03B104F.D96E1055 (18:32:47.849 UTC Wed Feb 17 2010)
clock offset is 0.0083 msec, root delay is 0.00 msec
root dispersion is 0.01 msec, peer dispersion is 0.00 msec
loopfilter state is 'CTRL' (Normal Controlled Loop), drift is 0.000009283 s/s
system poll interval is 128, last update was 325 sec ago.


router#show ntp associations

  address           ref clock        st   when  poll reach  delay  offset   disp
+~192.168.10.1      .GPS.            1    48    128   377  0.000   8.500  4.881
*~192.168.10.2      .GPS.            1    50    128   377  0.000   8.361  7.104
 * sys.peer, # selected, + candidate, - outlyer, x falseticker, ~ configured

# The clock is now updated
router#show clock
18:34:37.322 UTC Wed Feb 17 2010
```

Note The time displayed in Example 4-11 uses Coordinated Universal Time (UTC), which can differ from your actual time zone. Certificates use the same reference time. To have the router display the correct time for your location, you might want to configure the timezone using the command **clock timezone <timezone-name> <offset-from-UTC>**, for example, **clock timezone CEST 2** for Central Europe Summer Time. You need to understand that time zone configuration affects only the display and not the actual router clock.

Now you can import the certificate without a problem.

Example 4-12   *Successful CA Authentication After Clock Has Been Synchronized*

```
router(config)#crypto pki authenticate MyCA

Enter the base 64 encoded CA certificate.
End with a blank line or the word "quit" on a line by itself

-----BEGIN CERTIFICATE-----
MIID3zCCAsegAwIBAgIQbIWfR3MUOBUBolJt4CPSxDANBgkqhkiG9w0BAQUFADAo
...
HWhPy6NOVyZlHHsuYvNu7SGRXXumZn/5SvbafxjAn+QnXH988JiiLtXQBq/oRDBV
A+kBNoxBQIYbnc1IlISdRSRM2QKqg2TroIlrL0fsuXcrYHY=
-----END CERTIFICATE-----
quit
Trustpoint 'MyCA' is a subordinate CA and holds a non self signed cert
Certificate has the following attributes:
        Fingerprint MD5: E4BC675E 86AB1F67 1C5E890F C61CA35F
        Fingerprint SHA1: 156C24D1 3257B076 01E19ECF 68AF63D3 7370F4FB

% Do you accept this certificate? [yes/no]: yes
Trustpoint CA certificate accepted.
% Certificate successfully imported
```

Following are two comments about the process:

■   The first attempt does not include the PEM headers, whereas they were pasted in the second try. Both scenarios are accepted: The *pem* keyword in the configuration is targeted for the CLI output, as you see later in the Certificate Signing Request (CSR). This helps you so that you don't need to manually add those headers when pasting into your CA GUI, for example.

■   During the authentication process, there was a prompt to verify the CA fingerprint to validate that it is correct. There was also a notification that the CA was actually a subordinate CA (that is, not a root CA); therefore, a complete verification chain was not installed.

To validate the entire certification path, you should ideally install all the CA certificates up to the Root CA. However this is not mandatory, and Cisco IOS enables you to install and trust only the bottom part of a certification tree. Obviously, only the certificates issued by a trusted CA (or trusted subordinate CA) will be considered valid; therefore, you should pay attention to that point when working with complex PKIs involving multiple subtrees. Always ensure that the common point is installed as a trusted CA.

After the CA (trustpoint) certificate has been installed, you can proceed with the enrollment phase. This is a two-step process. The first step is to generate a CSR enrollment request. The second step is to have the actual certificate issued by the CA and communicated back, in some way, to the requester.

To create the CSR, the Cisco device uses the trustpoint configuration section to determine which fields must be included in the request. Selectable fields are FQDN, IP address, serial number, and subject distinguished name (DN). Select the appropriate ones based on what information you consider relevant for identification purposes and therefore you would like to see included in the certificate. Depending on the CA, the authority has the capability to modify that information (for example, through templates) by adding or removing some fields. This is entirely dependent on the CA implementation and the way it is configured and operated.

When using enrollment via CLI (terminal), the CSR is displayed on the terminal (as shown in Example 4-13) and must be copied and pasted to the CA.

Example 4-13 *CSR Is Displayed on Terminal Console*

```
router(config)#crypto pki enroll MyCA
% Start certificate enrollment ..

% The subject name in the certificate will include: CN=router,OU=lab,O=cisco,O=com
% The subject name in the certificate will include: router.cisco.com
% Include an IP address in the subject name? [no]: no
Display Certificate Request to terminal? [yes/no]: yes
Certificate Request follows:

-----BEGIN CERTIFICATE REQUEST-----
MIICxDCCAawCAQAwXjEMMAoGA1UEChMDY29tMQ4wDAYDVQQKEwVjaXNjbzEMMAoG
A1UECxMDbGFiMQ8wDQYDVQQDEwZyb3V0ZXIxHzAdBgkqhkiG9w0BCQIWEHJvdXRl
...
VZDCFrxKerRA5Yss3OGbEA4YRtseI1jVC4mv/45Obs4/TdBwJG8XtwbMBX8t523e
71WpFDcBNGLNwVNLAnKOKTKGNmFWkM1j/+h/2HXBE86CLZOyWML8dg==
-----END CERTIFICATE REQUEST-----
---End - This line not part of the certificate request---
```

If the trustpoint does not contain configuration settings for all options, you are prompted to include them in the request. The example did not determine whether the IP address should be included. You can clearly see that the PEM headers have been displayed as per the configuration in Example 4-14.

Example 4-14 *Trustpoint Configuration References PEM Header Use*

```
crypto pki trustpoint MyCA
 enrollment terminal pem
 serial-number none
 fqdn router.cisco.com
```

```
subject-name CN=router,OU=lab,O=cisco,O=com
revocation-check crl
```

Using OpenSSL, you can visualize the content of the CSR, as shown in Example 4-15.

Example 4-15 *Using OpenSSL to Visualize CSR Content*

```
$ openssl req -in req.pem -text -noout
Certificate Request:
    Data:
        Version: 0 (0x0)
        Subject: O=com, O=cisco, OU=lab,
CN=router/unstructuredName=router.cisco.com
        Subject Public Key Info:
            Public Key Algorithm: rsaEncryption
            RSA Public Key: (2048 bit)
                Modulus (2048 bit):
                    00:c0:d3:76:94:ed:ea:cf:9a:13:31:6f:f1:8e:32:
                    ...
                    9b:a8:5b:07:7d:0b:e7:b6:4c:70:ca:55:0d:dd:7f:
                    24:cf
                Exponent: 65537 (0x10001)
        Attributes:
        Requested Extensions:
            X509v3 Key Usage: critical
                Digital Signature, Key Encipherment
    Signature Algorithm: md5WithRSAEncryption
        99:20:59:02:f7:8f:5d:3e:bd:b3:ea:15:df:f2:6f:70:03:cd:
    ...
        36:61:56:90:cd:63:ff:e8:7f:d8:75:c1:13:ce:82:2d:93:b2:
        58:c2:fc:76
```

As expected, you have only FQDN and DN in the request. The CSR must then be processed by the CA and, if granted, a certificate will be returned. When the certificate is available, it must be imported into the Cisco IOS device. The complete process must be performed using the same method (either terminal or SCEP), unless you change the trust-point configuration in between.

Example 4-16 tries to import a certificate (for enrollment) corresponding to the CSR of *another* router. (Router-A and router-B are mixed up by mistake.)

Example 4-16 *Importing a Certificate Not Matching CSR*

```
router-B(config)#crypto pki import CA-server certificate

Enter the base 64 encoded certificate.
```

```
End with a blank line or the word "quit" on a line by itself

MIIDNjCCAh6gAwIBAgIBAzANBgkqhkiG9w0BAQQFADBAMQwwCgYDVQQKEwNDb20x
...
+Vl3XMxBXBqbbxycO4ARmPQZlOtLZ8OHCFzHx4gHQPvs5am0gZLcv5Dz02qoqiFV
SoKZnwDF/esKCA==

Cannot import certificate -
   Certificate does not contain router's General Purpose public key
   for trust point CA-server

% Failed to parse or verify imported certificate

router-B(config)#
```

As displayed, the router cannot find the corresponding key pair, so it rejects the certificate. If SCEP is used as enrollment mechanism, it is more difficult to see the content transmitted at each step because part of it is encrypted.

Note   For complete details about the protocol, SCEP is defined in an IETF draft. The current version is draft-nourse-scep-21.txt and can be found at http://tools.ietf.org/html/draft-nourse-scep-21.

The steps are the same: authentication, enrollment request, and then certificate installation, which are summarized in two Cisco IOS CLI commands shown in Example 4-17.

Example 4-17   *CLI Commands Required to Complete Enrollment*

```
crypto pki authenticate <trustpoint>
crypto pki enroll <trustpoint>
```

Both commands initiate an HTTP connection to the URL specified in the trustpoint configuration. You should therefore ensure that the connection can be established; routing, firewalls, or access-lists must all be properly configured. A good test is to initiate a telnet from the device toward the CA server, on port 80. Use the correct source interface (as configured under the trustpoint config section) and the destination IP address and port number. If DNS is used, ensure that the name can be resolved correctly (and in the proper VRF) first. The corresponding test CLI would be

```
telnet <CA-server> 80 /source-interface selected-source-interface.
```

When launching the authentication command, the URL shown in Example 4-18 will be fetched.

Example 4-18   *SCEP URL to Retrieve CA Certificate*

```
<CONFIGURED-ENROLLMENT-URL>/cgi-
bin/pkiclient.exe?operation=GetCACert&message=<TRUSTPOINT-NAME>
```

This returns the CA certificate. You can actually try to connect to the same URL using a Web browser, and you can download and view the content of the CA certificate. If you enable PKI debugs (*transaction*, *calls*, *messages*), you can see the exact URL fetched and the response from the SCEP CA server. If this step fails, check connectivity and the clock as previously explained. After authenticated, the CA server appears in the list of installed certificates, which you can display through the command in Example 4-19.

Example 4-19   *Displaying Certificates Installed on the Device*

```
router877#show crypto pki certificates verbose
CA Certificate
  Status: Available
  Version: 3
  Certificate Serial Number (hex): 01
  Certificate Usage: Signature
  Issuer:
    cn=CA-Server
    ou=LAB
    o=Cisco
    o=Com
  Subject:
    cn=CA-Server
    ou=LAB
    o=Cisco
    o=Com
  Validity Date:
    start date: 12:16:03 CET Feb 20 2010
    end   date: 12:16:03 CET Feb 20 2030
  Subject Key Info:
    Public Key Algorithm: rsaEncryption
    RSA Public Key: (2048 bit)
  Signature Algorithm: SHA256 with RSA Encryption
  Fingerprint MD5: 2D4D9AE7 5A424899 1A7C7BDC B09D606C
  Fingerprint SHA1: 7E5B1F58 DA685192 8CF7D1ED AAF0810F 0E46C7D5
  X509v3 extensions:
    X509v3 Key Usage: 86000000
      Digital Signature
      Key Cert Sign
```

```
      CRL Signature
    X509v3 Subject Key ID: FBFE47A0 92D27CAF F9E3D002 BFD62EC8 6A0F11E7
    X509v3 Basic Constraints:
        CA: TRUE
    X509v3 Authority Key ID: FBFE47A0 92D27CAF F9E3D002 BFD62EC8 6A0F11E7
    Authority Info Access:
  Associated Trustpoints: CA-Server
```

You can now proceed to the enrollment phase, as shown in Example 4-20.

Example 4-20   *Device Enrollment*

```
router877(config)#crypto pki enroll CA-Server
%
% Start certificate enrollment ..
% Create a challenge password. You will need to verbally provide this
   password to the CA Administrator in order to revoke your certificate.
   For security reasons your password will not be saved in the configuration.
   Please make a note of it.


Password:
Re-enter password:


% The subject name in the certificate will include:
CN=router877,OU=Lab,O=Cisco,O=Com
% The subject name in the certificate will include: router877.cisco.com
Request certificate from CA? [yes/no]: yes


% Certificate request sent to Certificate Authority
% The 'show crypto pki certificate verbose CA-Server' commandwill show the
  fingerprint.



router877#show crypto pki certificate verbose CA-Server


Certificate
  Subject:
    Name: router877.cisco.com
  Status: Pending
  Key Usage: General Purpose
    Certificate Request Fingerprint MD5: 68EBD5B1 72E88D5A 57308341 66911D36
    Certificate Request Fingerprint SHA1: AFFA85FA E3923224 87600F91 905D1050
7BD96602
    Associated Trustpoint: CA-Server
```

The request is now pending on the CA server. Using the preceding command, you can verify the fingerprint of your request so that it can be matched during the verification process with the CA.

When using SCEP, the Cisco IOS device periodically polls the CA server to see whether the request has already been processed and returns **granted** or **rejected**. You can view when the next attempt will be triggered, using the **show crypto pki timers** command, as shown in Example 4-21.

Example 4-21   *Displaying Pending PKI Actions (Time-Based)*

```
router877#show crypto pki timers
PKI Timers
|         4:12.341
   |         4:12.341  POLL CA-Server
```

In Example 4-20, the router retries in 4 minutes and 12 seconds. The time counter should be decreasing as you repeat the command. The request must now be processed on the CA side, as previously described in Chapter 3, "PKI Processes and Procedures."

At the next poll, two cases are possible:

■   If the request has been rejected, the following message will be displayed, as shown in Example 4-22.

Example 4-22   *Log Message When Enrollment Request Has Been Rejected by CA*

```
%PKI-6-CERTREJECT: Certificate enrollment request was rejected by Certificate
Authority
```

■   If the request has been granted, and the certificate signed by the CA, the router notifies through the following log message, as shown in Example 4-23.

Example 4-23   *Log Message When Certificate Has Been Granted by CA*

```
%PKI-6-CERTRET: Certificate received from Certificate Authority
```

There will now be installed certificates for the CA and the router, as shown in Example 4-24.

Example 4-24   *Displaying Installed Certificates: Both CA and Device Certificates*

```
router877#show crypto pki certificates
Certificate
  Status: Available
```

```
Certificate Serial Number (hex): 02
Certificate Usage: General Purpose
Issuer:
  cn=CA-Server
  ou=LAB
  o=Cisco
  o=Com
Subject:
  Name: router877.cisco.com
  hostname=router877.cisco.com
  cn=router877
  ou=Lab
  o=Cisco
  o=Com
CRL Distribution Points:
  http://10.3.1.5/crl.pem
Validity Date:
  start date: 14:50:26 CET Feb 20 2010
  end   date: 14:50:26 CET Feb 20 2011
Associated Trustpoints: CA-Server

CA Certificate
Status: Available
Certificate Serial Number (hex): 01
Certificate Usage: Signature
Issuer:
  cn=CA-Server
  ou=LAB
  o=Cisco
  o=Com
Subject:
  cn=CA-Server
  ou=LAB
  o=Cisco
  o=Com
Validity Date:
  start date: 12:16:03 CET Feb 20 2010
  end   date: 12:16:03 CET Feb 20 2030
Associated Trustpoints: CA-Server
```

The certificate setup process is now complete and ready to be used.

Certificate Use and Validation

To explain the certificate use and validation process, consider the example of the analysis of the complete debug output during the initiation of an IKE/IPsec tunnel between two Cisco IOS routers.

Following is the scenario:

- Two routers (A and B) enrolled using SCEP to CA-server.

- Router-A is also part of another PKI infrastructure used for other purposes (enrolled to OtherCA-server).

- CRL checking is enabled on all devices, and the CRL file is provided over HTTP by HTTP-server host.

The IP addressing scheme follows:

- Router-A: 10.3.1.11

- Router-B: 10.3.1.12

- CA-server: 10.3.1.1

- OtherCA-server: 10.3.1.2

- HTTP-server: 10.3.1.1 (same as CA-server in the example but could be different)

The lab troubleshooting setup is shown in Figure 4-1. CA and OtherCA are the hostnames of the devices, whereas CA-server and OtherCA-server are the names given to the Certificate Server processes configured on the respective devices.

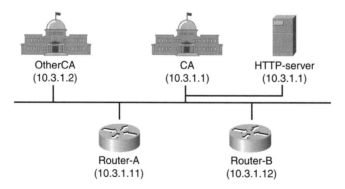

Figure 4-1   *PKI Troubleshooting Lab Setup*

To watch the IKE authentication process including PKI, the debug output on Router-A and Router-B has been enabled, as shown in Example 4-25.

Example 4-25 *Useful* debug *Output to Enable*

```
router-B# debug crypto isakmp
Crypto ISAKMP debugugging is on

router-B# debug crypto pki transactions
Crypto PKI Trans debugugging is on

router-B# debug crypto pki callbacks
Crypto PKI callbacks debugugging is on

router-B# debug crypto pki messages
Crypto PKI Msg debugugging is on
```

Router-A is initiating the IPsec connection, as shown in Example 4-26.

Example 4-26 *Initiation of ISAKMP Connection*

```
router-B#
*Feb 28 17:10:13.727: ISAKMP (0): received packet from 10.3.1.11 dport 500 sport
  500 Global (N) NEW SA
*Feb 28 17:10:13.727: ISAKMP: Created a peer struct for 10.3.1.11, peer port 500
*Feb 28 17:10:13.727: ISAKMP: New peer created peer = 0x5C28020 peer_handle =
  0x80000040
*Feb 28 17:10:13.727: ISAKMP: Locking peer struct 0x5C28020, refcount 1 for
  crypto_isakmp_process_block
*Feb 28 17:10:13.727: ISAKMP: local port 500, remote port 500
*Feb 28 17:10:13.727: ISAKMP:(0):insert sa successfully sa = 5C45420
*Feb 28 17:10:13.727: ISAKMP:(0):Input = IKE_MESG_FROM_PEER, IKE_MM_EXCH
*Feb 28 17:10:13.727: ISAKMP:(0):Old State = IKE_READY  New State = IKE_R_MM1


*Feb 28 17:10:13.727: ISAKMP:(0): processing SA payload. message ID = 0
*Feb 28 17:10:13.727: ISAKMP:(0): processing vendor id payload
*Feb 28 17:10:13.727: ISAKMP:(0): vendor ID seems Unity/DPD but major 69 mismatch
*Feb 28 17:10:13.727: ISAKMP (0): vendor ID is NAT-T RFC 3947
*Feb 28 17:10:13.727: ISAKMP:(0): processing vendor id payload
*Feb 28 17:10:13.727: ISAKMP:(0): vendor ID seems Unity/DPD but major 245 mismatch
*Feb 28 17:10:13.727: ISAKMP (0): vendor ID is NAT-T v7
*Feb 28 17:10:13.727: ISAKMP:(0): processing vendor id payload
*Feb 28 17:10:13.727: ISAKMP:(0): vendor ID seems Unity/DPD but major 157 mismatch
*Feb 28 17:10:13.727: ISAKMP (0): vendor ID is NAT-T v3
*Feb 28 17:10:13.727: ISAKMP:(0): processing vendor id payload
*Feb 28 17:10:13.727: ISAKMP:(0): vendor ID seems Unity/DPD but major 123 mismatch
*Feb 28 17:10:13.727: ISAKMP:(0): vendor ID is NAT-T v2
*Feb 28 17:10:13.727: ISAKMP : Scanning profiles for xauth ...
*Feb 28 17:10:13.727: ISAKMP:(0):Checking ISAKMP transform 1 against priority 10
  policy
```

```
*Feb 28 17:10:13.727: ISAKMP:          encryption AES-CBC
*Feb 28 17:10:13.727: ISAKMP:          keylength of 256
*Feb 28 17:10:13.727: ISAKMP:          hash SHA
*Feb 28 17:10:13.727: ISAKMP:          default group 1
```

Certificates (RSA signatures) are used for ISAKMP authentication, as shown in Example 4-27.

Example 4-27   *RSA Signature (Certificate) Authentication in Use*

```
router-B#
*Feb 28 17:10:13.727: ISAKMP:          auth RSA sig
*Feb 28 17:10:13.727: ISAKMP:          life type in seconds
*Feb 28 17:10:13.727: ISAKMP:          life duration (VPI) of  0x0 0x1 0x51 0x80
*Feb 28 17:10:13.727: ISAKMP:(0):atts are acceptable. Next payload is 0
*Feb 28 17:10:13.727: ISAKMP:(0):Acceptable atts:actual life: 0
*Feb 28 17:10:13.727: ISAKMP:(0):Acceptable atts:life: 0
*Feb 28 17:10:13.727: ISAKMP:(0):Fill atts in sa vpi_length:4
*Feb 28 17:10:13.727: ISAKMP:(0):Fill atts in sa life_in_seconds:86400
*Feb 28 17:10:13.727: CRYPTO_PKI: Identity not specified for session 10079
*Feb 28 17:10:13.727: ISAKMP:(0):Returning Actual lifetime: 86400
*Feb 28 17:10:13.727: ISAKMP:(0)::Started lifetime timer: 86400.

*Feb 28 17:10:13.727: ISAKMP:(0): processing vendor id payload
*Feb 28 17:10:13.727: ISAKMP:(0): vendor ID seems Unity/DPD but major 69 mismatch
*Feb 28 17:10:13.727: ISAKMP (0): vendor ID is NAT-T RFC 3947
*Feb 28 17:10:13.727: ISAKMP:(0): processing vendor id payload
*Feb 28 17:10:13.727: ISAKMP:(0): vendor ID seems Unity/DPD but major 245 mismatch
*Feb 28 17:10:13.727: ISAKMP (0): vendor ID is NAT-T v7
*Feb 28 17:10:13.727: ISAKMP:(0): processing vendor id payload
*Feb 28 17:10:13.727: ISAKMP:(0): vendor ID seems Unity/DPD but major 157 mismatch
*Feb 28 17:10:13.727: ISAKMP:(0): vendor ID is NAT-T v3
*Feb 28 17:10:13.727: ISAKMP:(0): processing vendor id payload
*Feb 28 17:10:13.727: ISAKMP:(0): vendor ID seems Unity/DPD but major 123 mismatch
*Feb 28 17:10:13.727: ISAKMP:(0): vendor ID is NAT-T v2
*Feb 28 17:10:13.727: ISAKMP:(0):Input = IKE_MESG_INTERNAL, IKE_PROCESS_MAIN_MODE
*Feb 28 17:10:13.727: ISAKMP:(0):Old State = IKE_R_MM1  New State = IKE_R_MM1

*Feb 28 17:10:13.727: ISAKMP:(0): constructed NAT-T vendor-rfc3947 ID
*Feb 28 17:10:13.727: ISAKMP:(0): sending packet to 10.3.1.11 my_port 500
  peer_port 500 (R) MM_SA_SETUP
*Feb 28 17:10:13.727: ISAKMP:(0):Sending an IKE IPv4 Packet.
*Feb 28 17:10:13.727: ISAKMP:(0):Input = IKE_MESG_INTERNAL, IKE_PROCESS_COMPLETE
*Feb 28 17:10:13.727: ISAKMP:(0):Old State = IKE_R_MM1  New State = IKE_R_MM2
```

```
*Feb 28 17:10:13.731: ISAKMP (0): received packet from 10.3.1.11 dport 500 sport
  500 Global (R) MM_SA_SETUP
*Feb 28 17:10:13.731: ISAKMP:(0):Input = IKE_MESG_FROM_PEER, IKE_MM_EXCH
*Feb 28 17:10:13.731: ISAKMP:(0):Old State = IKE_R_MM2  New State = IKE_R_MM3


*Feb 28 17:10:13.731: ISAKMP:(0): processing KE payload. message ID = 0
*Feb 28 17:10:13.743: ISAKMP:(0): processing NONCE payload. message ID = 0
```

A certificate request (CERT_REQ) is received from router-A, as shown in Example 4-28.

Example 4-28 *Receiving Certificate Request from Peer*

```
router-B#
*Feb 28 17:10:13.743: ISAKMP:(1061): processing CERT_REQ payload. message ID = 0
*Feb 28 17:10:13.743: ISAKMP:(1061): peer wants a CT_X509_SIGNATURE cert
```

Router-A indicates which CA it trusts: *OtherCA-server*, as shown in Example 4-29.

Example 4-29 *Decoding the CERT_REQ Payload*

```
router-B#
*Feb 28 17:10:13.743: ISAKMP:(1061): peer wants cert issued by cn=OtherCA-
  server,ou=Lab,o=Cisco,o=Com
*Feb 28 17:10:13.743: CRYPTO_PKI: crypto_pki_get_cert_record_by_subject()
*Feb 28 17:10:13.743: CRYPTO_PKI: Found a subject match
*Feb 28 17:10:13.743: CRYPTO_PKI: crypto_pki_get_cert_record_by_subject()
*Feb 28 17:10:13.743: CRYPTO_PKI: Found a subject match
```

However, router-B is not enrolled with OtherCA-server, so it is impossible to provide a suitable certificate, as shown in Example 4-30.

Example 4-30 *Unable to Satisfy the Request*

```
router-B#
*Feb 28 17:10:13.743: ISAKMP:(1061): issuer name is not a trusted root.
```

The request from router-A actually contains multiple CERT_REQ payloads, so router-B processes the next one, as shown in Example 4-31.

Example 4-31 *Processing the Next CERT_REQ Payload*

```
router-B#
*Feb 28 17:10:13.743: ISAKMP:(1061): processing CERT_REQ payload. message ID = 0
*Feb 28 17:10:13.743: ISAKMP:(1061): peer wants a CT_X509_SIGNATURE cert
```

Router-A also indicates that it trusts CA-server, as shown in Example 4-32.

Example 4-32   *Decoding the Next CERT_REQ Payload*

```
router-B#
*Feb 28 17:10:13.743: ISAKMP:(1061): peer wants cert issued by cn=CA-
  server,ou=Lab,o=Cisco,o=Com
```

This is a CA that router-B also trusts and is enrolled with. You can therefore choose that trustpoint for your authentication process, as shown in Example 4-33.

Example 4-33   *Finding an Appropriate Trustpoint to Answer*

```
router-B#
*Feb 28 17:10:13.743: CRYPTO_PKI: Trust-Point CA-server picked up
*Feb 28 17:10:13.743: CRYPTO_PKI: Identity selected (CA-server) for session 2007A
*Feb 28 17:10:13.743:  Choosing trustpoint CA-server as issuer
*Feb 28 17:10:13.743: CRYPTO_PKI: unlocked trustpoint CA-server, refcount is 0
*Feb 28 17:10:13.743: CRYPTO_PKI: locked trustpoint CA-server, refcount is 1
*Feb 28 17:10:13.743: CRYPTO_PKI: Identity bound (CA-server) for session 10079

*Feb 28 17:10:13.743: ISAKMP:(1061): processing vendor id payload
*Feb 28 17:10:13.743: ISAKMP:(1061): vendor ID is DPD
*Feb 28 17:10:13.743: ISAKMP:(1061): processing vendor id payload
*Feb 28 17:10:13.743: ISAKMP:(1061): speaking to another IOS box!
*Feb 28 17:10:13.743: ISAKMP:(1061): processing vendor id payload
*Feb 28 17:10:13.743: ISAKMP:(1061): vendor ID seems Unity/DPD but major 22
  mismatch
*Feb 28 17:10:13.743: ISAKMP:(1061): vendor ID is XAUTH
*Feb 28 17:10:13.743: ISAKMP:received payload type 20
*Feb 28 17:10:13.743: ISAKMP (1061): His hash no match - this node outside NAT
*Feb 28 17:10:13.743: ISAKMP:received payload type 20
*Feb 28 17:10:13.743: ISAKMP (1061): No NAT Found for self or peer
*Feb 28 17:10:13.743: ISAKMP:(1061):Input = IKE_MESG_INTERNAL,
  IKE_PROCESS_MAIN_MODE
*Feb 28 17:10:13.743: ISAKMP:(1061):Old State = IKE_R_MM3  New State = IKE_R_MM3
```

It is now your turn to send a certificate request (CERT_REQ) to router-A. You can trust only CA-server, therefore, your request needs to contain only one such payload, as shown in Example 4-34.

Example 4-34   *Preparing Our Own Certificate Request*

```
router-B#
*Feb 28 17:10:13.755: ISAKMP (1061): constructing CERT_REQ for issuer cn=CA-
  server,ou=Lab,o=Cisco,o=Com
```

```
*Feb 28 17:10:13.755: ISAKMP:(1061): sending packet to 10.3.1.11 my_port 500
  peer_port 500 (R) MM_KEY_EXCH
*Feb 28 17:10:13.755: ISAKMP:(1061):Sending an IKE IPv4 Packet.
*Feb 28 17:10:13.755: ISAKMP:(1061):Input = IKE_MESG_INTERNAL, IKE_PROCESS_COMPLETE
*Feb 28 17:10:13.755: ISAKMP:(1061):Old State = IKE_R_MM3  New State = IKE_R_MM4


*Feb 28 17:10:13.811: ISAKMP (1061): received packet from 10.3.1.11 dport 500
  sport 500 Global (R) MM_KEY_EXCH
*Feb 28 17:10:13.811: ISAKMP:(1061):Input = IKE_MESG_FROM_PEER, IKE_MM_EXCH
*Feb 28 17:10:13.811: ISAKMP:(1061):Old State = IKE_R_MM4  New State = IKE_R_MM5


*Feb 28 17:10:13.811: ISAKMP:(1061): processing ID payload. message ID = 0
*Feb 28 17:10:13.811: ISAKMP (1061): ID payload
        next-payload : 6
        type         : 2
        FQDN name    : router.A.cisco.com
        protocol     : 17
        port         : 500
        length       : 26
*Feb 28 17:10:13.811: ISAKMP:(0):: peer matches *none* of the profiles
```

Router-A sent you its certificate (CERT) and an associated signature (to prove that it has the corresponding private key), as shown in Example 4-35.

Example 4-35 *Receiving the Certificate from Peer Router*

```
router-B#
*Feb 28 17:10:13.811: ISAKMP:(1061): processing CERT payload. message ID = 0
*Feb 28 17:10:13.811: ISAKMP:(1061): processing a CT_X509_SIGNATURE cert
*Feb 28 17:10:13.811: CRYPTO_PKI: Added x509 peer certificate - (823) bytes
```

A frequent problem occurs when the sending router displays a message that the certificate is sent but no corresponding entry is seen on the receiving device. IKE packets containing certificates are usually large IP packets (the size increases with the key length), often causing fragmentation to occur. Because some intermediate devices (firewalls, for example) do not handle IP fragments correctly, the certificate packet (or part of it) can be dropped in transit. Testing with varying key sizes usually confirms such problem; although logs on intermediate device, if available, can also show the drops.

If an error occurs during the processing of the certificate payload, the most frequent reasons are as follows:

■ Encoding issue caused by the use of special characters, for example

■ Structure issue because of the presence of some unusual or nonstandard fields

■ Unusual key length or algorithm

For those cases, the most efficient approach is to obtain a copy of the certificate and parse it through the OpenSSL tool to visualize its content in a human readable format and compare it with known-to-work certificates.

Back to the scenario, you have not seen this certificate recently (it is not cached), so you need to perform the complete validation process for it, as shown in Example 4-36.

Example 4-36   *Received Certificate Is Unknown (Not Cached)*

```
router-B#
*Feb 28 17:10:13.811: ISAKMP:(1061): peer's pubkey isn't cached
*Feb 28 17:10:13.811: CRYPTO_PKI: crypto_pki_get_cert_record_by_subject()
*Feb 28 17:10:13.811: CRYPTO_PKI: Found a subject match
```

The validation path has only one certificate (directly the root CA), as shown in Example 4-37.

Example 4-37   *Starting the Validation Process*

```
router-B#
*Feb 28 17:10:13.811: CRYPTO_PKI: validation path has 1 certs
*Feb 28 17:10:13.811: CRYPTO_PKI(Cert Lookup) issuer="cn=CA-
  server,ou=Lab,o=Cisco,o=Com" serial number= 07
```

Router-B uses different criteria to find the corresponding CA certificate to use during the verification. In the present case, the issuer name lookup is successful, as shown in Example 4-38.

Example 4-38   *Finding the Appropriate CA to Use for Validation*

```
router-B#
*Feb 28 17:10:13.811: CRYPTO_PKI: looking for cert in handle=59496E4, digest=
 0B B3 D3 0D 96 B0 AF 6E 95 52 BA 83 62 F3 07 7C
*Feb 28 17:10:13.811: CRYPTO_PKI: Cert record not found, returning E_NOT_FOUND
*Feb 28 17:10:13.811: CRYPTO_PKI: crypto_pki_get_cert_record_by_issuer()
*Feb 28 17:10:13.811: CRYPTO_PKI: Found a issuer match
*Feb 28 17:10:13.811: CRYPTO_PKI: Using CA-server to validate certificate
*Feb 28 17:10:13.811: CRYPTO_PKI(make trusted certs chain)
*Feb 28 17:10:13.811: P11:C_CreateObject:
*Feb 28 17:10:13.811:   CKA_CLASS: PUBLIC KEY
*Feb 28 17:10:13.811:   CKA_KEY_TYPE: RSA
*Feb 28 17:10:13.811:   CKA_MODULUS:
     B2 E6 71 8A 3D B6 62 4F 6F 04 AF 34 F3 5A A5 F7
...
     D3 57 08 4A 20 02 D7 9B 58 A3 9B 14 2D 54 8B 09
```

```
*Feb 28 17:10:13.811:   CKA_PUBLIC_EXPONENT:   01 00 01
*Feb 28 17:10:13.811:   CKA_VERIFY_RECOVER:   01


*Feb 28 17:10:13.811: P11:C_CreateObject: 84709972
*Feb 28 17:10:13.811: P11:C_GetMechanismInfo slot 1 type 3 (invalid mechanism)
*Feb 28 17:10:13.811: P11:C_GetMechanismInfo slot 1 type 1
*Feb 28 17:10:13.811: P11:C_VerifyRecoverInit - 131138
*Feb 28 17:10:13.811: P11:C_VerifyRecover - 131138
*Feb 28 17:10:13.811: P11:found pubkey in cache using index = 66
*Feb 28 17:10:13.811: P11:public key found is :
     30 82 01 22 30 0D 06 09 2A 86 48 86 F7 0D 01 01
...
     F6 D3 57 08 4A 20 02 D7 9B 58 A3 9B 14 2D 54 8B
     09 02 03 01 00 01


*Feb 28 17:10:13.835: P11:CEAL:CRYPTO_NO_ERR
*Feb 28 17:10:13.835: P11:C_DestroyObject 5A3CC28:20042
```

If an error occurred here, it is possible that despite the issuer name match, the actual CA certificate is not the one that issued the certificate. How is that possible? Anybody can create a CA certificate with the name of its choice. However, the key pair used to sign certificates is unique and cannot be re-created. Using an incorrect key pair can cause verification operations to fail.

Now verify that the certificate provided by router-A has not been revoked (listed in the CRL), as shown in Example 4-39.

Example 4-39   *Starting Certificate Validation Against CRL*

```
router-B#
*Feb 28 17:10:13.835: CRYPTO_PKI: Starting CRL revocation
*Feb 28 17:10:13.835: CRYPTO_PKI: Select crl(cn=CA-server,ou=Lab,o=Cisco,o=Com)
```

In your setup, the CRL location (CRL Distribution Point - CDP) is referenced in the certificate itself through a CDP URL: http://10.3.1.1/cgi-bin/pkiclient.exe?operation=GetCRL. (See Example 4-40.)

Note   For demonstration purposes, the same URL was used as the one automatically used in the SCEP protocol. However, the URL could be anything that points to the correct CRL file on the HTTP server.

Example 4-40   *Retrieving CRL*

```
router-B#
*Feb 28 17:10:13.835: CRYPTO_PKI: Retreive CRL using HTTP URI
*Feb 28 17:10:13.835: CRYPTO_PKI: pki request queued properly
*Feb 28 17:10:13.835: CRYPTO_PKI: status = 0: poll CRL
*Feb 28 17:10:13.835: CRYPTO_PKI: Capabilites already obtained 80000000
*Feb 28 17:10:13.835: CRYPTO_PKI: Requesting CRL at http://10.3.1.1/cgi-bin/
  pkiclient.exe?operation=GetCRL:

*Feb 28 17:10:13.835: CRYPTO_PKI: locked trustpoint CA-server, refcount is 1
*Feb 28 17:10:13.835: CRYPTO_PKI: http connection opened
*Feb 28 17:10:13.835: CRYPTO_PKI: Sending HTTP message

*Feb 28 17:10:13.835: CRYPTO_PKI: Reply HTTP header:
HTTP/1.0
Host: 10.3.1.1


*Feb 28 17:10:13.835: CRYPTO_PKI: unlocked trustpoint CA-server, refcount is 0
*Feb 28 17:10:13.835: CRYPTO_PKI: Send HTTP header:
GET /cgi-bin/pkiclient.exe?operation=GetCRL HTTP/1.0
Host: 10.3.1.1


*Feb 28 17:10:13.835: CRYPTO_PKI: HTTP data
     47 45 54 20 2F 63 67 69 2D 62 69 6E 2F 70 6B 69
     ...
     00 00 00 00 00 00 00 00 00

*Feb 28 17:10:13.835: CRYPTO_PKI: locked trustpoint CA-server, refcount is 1
*Feb 28 17:10:13.855: CRYPTO_PKI: unlocked trustpoint CA-server, refcount is 0
router-B#
```

Your HTTP GET is successful, and you receive the CRL file in reply. If you suspect a problem at this step, you can always fetch the CRL from a web browser using the displayed URL. The file can be processed by OpenSSL.

The path between your router and the CRL server might be different than the path between your computer and the CRL server: access-lists and firewalls must be opened accordingly. The most common protocols for CRL retrieving are HTTP (either through SCEP or a direct file download) and LDAP.

If a proxy is used to offload the web servers, it is possible that a cached, expired CRL file is returned to the requester (see Example 4-41.)

Example 4-41 *Receiving CRL from Server*

```
router-B#
*Feb 28 17:10:13.855: CRYPTO_PKI: Reply HTTP header:
HTTP/1.1 200 OK
Date: Sun, 28 Feb 2010 17:10:13 GMT
Server: cisco-IOS
Content-Type: application/pkix-crl
Expires: Sun, 28 Feb 2010 17:10:13 GMT
Last-Modified: Sun, 28 Feb 2010 17:10:13 GMT
Cache-Control: no-store, no-cache, must-revalidate
Pragma: no-cache
Accept-Ranges: none


*Feb 28 17:10:13.855: CRYPTO_PKI: FETCH IO data
     30 82 01 85 30 6F 30 0D 06 09 2A 86 48 86 F7 0D
...
     A2 23 91 08 81 2D D9 0A F9


*Feb 28 17:10:13.859: P11:C_CreateObject:
*Feb 28 17:10:13.859:   CKA_CLASS: PUBLIC KEY
*Feb 28 17:10:13.859:   CKA_KEY_TYPE: RSA
*Feb 28 17:10:13.859:   CKA_MODULUS:
     B2 E6 71 8A 3D B6 62 4F 6F 04 AF 34 F3 5A A5 F7
...
     D3 57 08 4A 20 02 D7 9B 58 A3 9B 14 2D 54 8B 09


*Feb 28 17:10:13.859:   CKA_PUBLIC_EXPONENT:   01 00 01


*Feb 28 17:10:13.859:   CKA_VERIFY_RECOVER:   01


*Feb 28 17:10:13.859: P11:C_CreateObject: 84711772
*Feb 28 17:10:13.859: P11:C_GetMechanismInfo slot 1 type 3 (invalid mechanism)
*Feb 28 17:10:13.859: P11:C_GetMechanismInfo slot 1 type 1
*Feb 28 17:10:13.859: P11:C_VerifyRecoverInit - 131139
*Feb 28 17:10:13.859: P11:C_VerifyRecover - 131139
*Feb 28 17:10:13.859: P11:found pubkey in cache using index = 67
*Feb 28 17:10:13.859: P11:public key found is :
     30 82 01 22 30 0D 06 09 2A 86 48 86 F7 0D 01 01
...
     09 02 03 01 00 01


*Feb 28 17:10:13.875: P11:CEAL:CRYPTO_NO_ERR
*Feb 28 17:10:13.875: P11:C_DestroyObject 5A3CC28:20043
*Feb 28 17:10:13.875: CRYPTO_PKI: inserting CRL
```

Every CRL has a lifetime, set by the CA when signing it. (see Example 4-42).

Example 4-42   *Not Caching CRL (as Per Configuration)*

```
router-B#
*Feb 28 17:10:13.875: CRYPTO_PKI: CRL not cached
*Feb 28 17:10:13.875: CRYPTO_PKI: the current router time: 17:10:13 CET Feb 28 2010

*Feb 28 17:10:13.875: CRYPTO_PKI: the last CRL update time: 14:58:06 CET
  Feb 28 2010
*Feb 28 17:10:13.875: CRYPTO_PKI: the next CRL update time: 20:58:06 CET
  Feb 28 2010
```

For the test, you have configured router-B not to store (cache) the retrieved CRL files. By default, the router would cache it until the next CRL update time, as shown in Example 4-43.

Example 4-43   *Validating Certificate Against CRL*

```
router-B#
*Feb 28 17:10:13.875: CRYPTO_PKI: CRL not cached
*Feb 28 17:10:13.875: CRYPTO_PKI: transaction Unknown completed
*Feb 28 17:10:13.875: CRYPTO_PKI: Poll CRL callback
*Feb 28 17:10:13.875: CRYPTO_PKI: status = 105: Blocking chain verification
  callback received status
*Feb 28 17:10:13.875: CRYPTO_PKI: Using CA-server to validate certificate
*Feb 28 17:10:13.875: CRYPTO_PKI: Starting CRL revocation
*Feb 28 17:10:13.875: CRYPTO_PKI: Select crl(cn=CA-server,ou=Lab,o=Cisco,o=Com)
*Feb 28 17:10:13.875: P11:C_CreateObject:
*Feb 28 17:10:13.875:   CKA_CLASS: PUBLIC KEY
*Feb 28 17:10:13.875:   CKA_KEY_TYPE: RSA
*Feb 28 17:10:13.875:   CKA_MODULUS:
     B2 E6 71 8A 3D B6 62 4F 6F 04 AF 34 F3 5A A5 F7
...
     D3 57 08 4A 20 02 D7 9B 58 A3 9B 14 2D 54 8B 09

*Feb 28 17:10:13.875:   CKA_PUBLIC_EXPONENT:  01 00 01

*Feb 28 17:10:13.875:   CKA_VERIFY_RECOVER:  01
*Feb 28 17:10:13.875: P11:C_CreateObject: 84707380
*Feb 28 17:10:13.875: P11:C_GetMechanismInfo slot 1 type 3 (invalid mechanism)
*Feb 28 17:10:13.875: P11:C_GetMechanismInfo slot 1 type 1
*Feb 28 17:10:13.875: P11:C_VerifyRecoverInit - 131140
```

```
*Feb 28 17:10:13.875: P11:C_VerifyRecover - 131140
*Feb 28 17:10:13.875: P11:found pubkey in cache using index = 68
*Feb 28 17:10:13.875: P11:public key found is :
      30 82 01 22 30 0D 06 09 2A 86 48 86 F7 0D 01 01
...
      09 02 03 01 00 01

*Feb 28 17:10:13.875: P11:CEAL:CRYPTO_NO_ERR
*Feb 28 17:10:13.875: P11:C_DestroyObject 5A3CC28:20044
```

The certificate has been validated, so you can continue the IKE authentication process, as shown in Example 4-44.

Example 4-44 *Successful Validation*

```
router-B#
*Feb 28 17:10:13.875: CRYPTO_PKI: Certificate validated
*Feb 28 17:10:13.875: CRYPTO_PKI: Selected AAA username: 'router-A.cisco.com'
*Feb 28 17:10:13.875: CRYPTO_PKI: Selected AAA username: 'router-A.cisco.com'
```

Verify that the key-usage mentioned in the certificate is adequate for your purpose (here ISAKMP authentication, which requires digital signature). (See Example 4-45.)

Example 4-45 *Verifying Certificate Key Usage*

```
router-B#
*Feb 28 17:10:13.875: PKI: Cert key-usage: Digital-Signature, Key-Encipherment
```

If an error occurs here, it is possible that the certificate contains some unusual or unknown settings for key usage. You get the final status of the certificate validation process, as shown in Example 4-46.

Example 4-46 *Final Validation Status (Successful)*

```
router-B#
*Feb 28 17:10:13.875: CRYPTO_PKI: chain cert was anchored to
  trustpoint CA-server, and chain validation result was:
  CRYPTO_VALID_CERT
*Feb 28 17:10:13.883: CRYPTO_PKI: Validation TP is CA-server
```

Some attributes from the certificate could be used (in a certificate map) as match criteria for mapping to a given ISAKMP profile. This is not used here (see Example 4-47).

Example 4-47   *Looking for Matching ISAKMP Profiles (Not Used Here)*

```
router-B#
*Feb 28 17:10:13.883: ISAKMP:(0):: peer matches *none* of the profiles
*Feb 28 17:10:13.883: CRYPTO_PKI(Cert Lookup) issuer="cn=CA-server,ou=Lab,
  o=Cisco,o=Com" serial number= 08


*Feb 28 17:10:13.883: CRYPTO_PKI: looking for cert in handle=59496E4, digest=
  A2 C5 9E 34 31 71 F1 65 F9 90 DD BC FD 15 26 EB


*Feb 28 17:10:13.883: ISAKMP:(1061): processing SIG payload. message ID = 0
*Feb 28 17:10:13.883: ISAKMP:(1061): processing NOTIFY INITIAL_CONTACT protocol 1
      spi 0, message ID = 0, sa = 5C45420
*Feb 28 17:10:13.883: ISAKMP:(1061):SA authentication status:
        authenticated
*Feb 28 17:10:13.883: ISAKMP:(1061):SA has been authenticated with 10.3.1.11
*Feb 28 17:10:13.883: ISAKMP:(1061):SA authentication status:
        Authenticated
*Feb 28 17:10:13.883: ISAKMP:(1061): Process initial contact,
bring down existing phase 1 and 2 SA's with local 10.3.1.12 remote 10.3.1.11
remote
  port 500
*Feb 28 17:10:13.883: ISAKMP:(0):received initial contact, deleting SA
*Feb 28 17:10:13.883: ISAKMP:(0):peer does not do paranoid keepalives.


*Feb 28 17:10:13.883: ISAKMP:(0):deleting SA reason "Receive initial contact"
state
  (I) MM_NO_STATE (peer 10.3.1.11)
*Feb 28 17:10:13.883: ISAKMP: Trying to insert a peer 10.3.1.12/10.3.1.11/500/,
  and inserted successfully 5C28020.
*Feb 28 17:10:13.883: ISAKMP:(1061):Input = IKE_MESG_INTERNAL,
  IKE_PROCESS_MAIN_MODE
*Feb 28 17:10:13.883: ISAKMP:(1061):Old State = IKE_R_MM5  New State = IKE_R_MM5


*Feb 28 17:10:13.887: ISAKMP:(0):deleting SA reason "Receive initial contact"
state
  (I) MM_NO_STATE (peer 10.3.1.11)
*Feb 28 17:10:13.887: ISAKMP: Unlocking peer struct 0x5C464F0 for
  isadb_mark_sa_deleted(), count 0
*Feb 28 17:10:13.887: ISAKMP: Deleting peer node by peer_reap for 10.3.1.11:
  5C464F0
*Feb 28 17:10:13.887: ISAKMP:(0):deleting node 2033960603 error FALSE reason
"IKE
  deleted"
*Feb 28 17:10:13.887: ISAKMP:(0):Input = IKE_MESG_INTERNAL, IKE_PHASE1_DEL
*Feb 28 17:10:13.887: ISAKMP:(0):Old State = IKE_I_MM1  New State = IKE_DEST_SA


*Feb 28 17:10:13.895: CRYPTO_PKI(Cert Lookup) issuer="cn=CA-server,ou=Lab,
  o=Cisco,o=Com" serial number= 08
```

```
*Feb 28 17:10:13.895: CRYPTO_PKI: looking for cert in handle=59496E4, digest=
  A2 C5 9E 34 31 71 F1 65 F9 90 DD BC FD 15 26 EB


*Feb 28 17:10:13.895: ISAKMP:(1061):My ID configured as IPv4 Addr, but Addr not in
  Cert!
*Feb 28 17:10:13.895: ISAKMP:(1061):Using FQDN as My ID
*Feb 28 17:10:13.895: ISAKMP:(1061):SA is doing RSA signature authentication using
  id type ID_FQDN
*Feb 28 17:10:13.895: ISAKMP (1061): ID payload
      next-payload : 6
      type         : 2
      FQDN name    : router-B.cisco.com
      protocol     : 17
      port         : 500
      length       : 26
*Feb 28 17:10:13.895: ISAKMP:(1061):Total payload length: 26
*Feb 28 17:10:13.895: CRYPTO_PKI(Cert Lookup) issuer="cn=CA-
  server,ou=Lab,o=Cisco,o=Com" serial number= 08
*Feb 28 17:10:13.895: CRYPTO_PKI: looking for cert in handle=59496E4, digest=
```

It is now your turn to present your certificate to your peer (router-A) so that through the same process, you can be authenticated, as shown in Example 4-48.

Example 4-48 *Presenting Our Certificate to Peer*

```
router-B#
*Feb 28 17:10:13.895: ISAKMP (1061): constructing CERT payload for
  hostname=router-B.cisco.com,cn=router-B,ou=Lab,o=Cisco,o=Com
*Feb 28 17:10:13.895: ISAKMP:(1061): using the CA-server trustpoint's keypair to
  sign
```

Note   Looking at the debug output on router-A would show the exact same steps.

For reference only, Example 4-49 shows the remaining ISAKMP and IPSec debug output. As it does not contain any PKI related message, it is not analyzed here.

Example 4-49 *Final ISAKMP Negotiations (Not Analyzed Here)*

```
router-B#
*Feb 28 17:10:13.903: ISAKMP:(1061): sending packet to 10.3.1.11 my_port 500
  peer_port 500 (R) MM_KEY_EXCH
*Feb 28 17:10:13.903: ISAKMP:(1061):Sending an IKE IPv4 Packet.
*Feb 28 17:10:13.903: ISAKMP:(1061):Input = IKE_MESG_INTERNAL, IKE_PROCESS_COMPLETE
*Feb 28 17:10:13.903: ISAKMP:(1061):Old State = IKE_R_MM5  New State =
  IKE_P1_COMPLETE
```

```
*Feb 28 17:10:13.931: CRYPTO_PKI: unlocked trustpoint CA-server, refcount is 0
*Feb 28 17:10:13.931: ISAKMP:(1061):Input = IKE_MESG_INTERNAL, IKE_PHASE1_COMPLETE
*Feb 28 17:10:13.931: ISAKMP:(1061):Old State = IKE_P1_COMPLETE  New State =
  IKE_P1_COMPLETE


*Feb 28 17:10:13.947: ISAKMP (1061): received packet from 10.3.1.11
  dport 500 sport 500 Global (R) QM_IDLE
*Feb 28 17:10:13.947: ISAKMP: set new node -807768439 to QM_IDLE
*Feb 28 17:10:13.947: ISAKMP:(1061): processing HASH payload. message ID = -
  807768439
*Feb 28 17:10:13.947: ISAKMP:(1061): processing SA payload. message ID = -807768439
*Feb 28 17:10:13.947: ISAKMP:(1061):Checking IPSec proposal 1
*Feb 28 17:10:13.947: ISAKMP: transform 1, ESP_AES
*Feb 28 17:10:13.947: ISAKMP:    attributes in transform:
*Feb 28 17:10:13.947: ISAKMP:       encaps is 1 (Tunnel)
*Feb 28 17:10:13.947: ISAKMP:       SA life type in seconds
*Feb 28 17:10:13.947: ISAKMP:       SA life duration (basic) of 3600
*Feb 28 17:10:13.947: ISAKMP:       SA life type in kilobytes
*Feb 28 17:10:13.947: ISAKMP:       SA life duration (VPI) of  0x0 0x46 0x50 0x0
*Feb 28 17:10:13.947: ISAKMP:       authenticator is HMAC-SHA
*Feb 28 17:10:13.947: ISAKMP:       key length is 128
*Feb 28 17:10:13.947: ISAKMP:(1061):atts are acceptable.
*Feb 28 17:10:13.947: ISAKMP:(1061): processing NONCE payload. message ID = -
  807768439
*Feb 28 17:10:13.947: ISAKMP:(1061): processing ID payload. message ID = -807768439
*Feb 28 17:10:13.947: ISAKMP:(1061): processing ID payload. message ID = -807768439
*Feb 28 17:10:13.947: ISAKMP:(1061):QM Responder gets spi
*Feb 28 17:10:13.947: ISAKMP:(1061):Node -807768439, Input = IKE_MESG_FROM_PEER,
  IKE_QM_EXCH
*Feb 28 17:10:13.947: ISAKMP:(1061):Old State = IKE_QM_READY  New State =
  IKE_QM_SPI_STARVE
*Feb 28 17:10:13.947: ISAKMP:(1061): Creating IPSec SAs
*Feb 28 17:10:13.947:             inbound SA from 10.3.1.11 to 10.3.1.12 (f/i)  0/ 0
        (proxy 0.0.0.0 to 0.0.0.0)
*Feb 28 17:10:13.947:             has spi 0xB51A36C2 and conn_id 0
*Feb 28 17:10:13.947:             lifetime of 3600 seconds
*Feb 28 17:10:13.947:             lifetime of 4608000 kilobytes
*Feb 28 17:10:13.947:             outbound SA from 10.3.1.12 to 10.3.1.11 (f/i) 0/0
        (proxy 0.0.0.0 to 0.0.0.0)
*Feb 28 17:10:13.947:             has spi  0x5C0DEC34 and conn_id 0
*Feb 28 17:10:13.947:             lifetime of 3600 seconds
*Feb 28 17:10:13.947:             lifetime of 4608000 kilobytes
*Feb 28 17:10:13.947: ISAKMP:(1061): sending packet to 10.3.1.11 my_port 500
  peer_port 500 (R) QM_IDLE
*Feb 28 17:10:13.947: ISAKMP:(1061):Sending an IKE IPv4 Packet.
```

```
*Feb 28 17:10:13.947: ISAKMP:(1061):Node -807768439, Input = IKE_MESG_INTERNAL,
  IKE_GOT_SPI
*Feb 28 17:10:13.947: ISAKMP:(1061):Old State = IKE_QM_SPI_STARVE  New State =
  IKE_QM_R_QM2
*Feb 28 17:10:13.947: ISAKMP (1061): received packet from 10.3.1.11 dport 500
sport
  500 Global (R) QM_IDLE
*Feb 28 17:10:13.947: ISAKMP:(1061):deleting node -807768439 error FALSE reason
"QM
  done (await)"
*Feb 28 17:10:13.947: ISAKMP:(1061):Node -807768439, Input = IKE_MESG_FROM_PEER,
  IKE_QM_EXCH
*Feb 28 17:10:13.947: ISAKMP:(1061):Old State = IKE_QM_R_QM2  New State =
  IKE_QM_PHASE2_COMPLETE
router-B#
router-B#
router-B#no debug all
All possible debugging has been turned off
```

router-B#

At the end, the complete bidirectional authentication process was successful, leading to
an established IPsec tunnel between router-A and router-B, as shown in Example 4-50.

Example 4-50   *IPsec Tunnel Established*

```
*Feb 28 17:10:19.803: %LINEPROTO-5-UPDOWN: Line protocol on Interface Tunnel0,
  changed state to up
router-B#
```

The example analyzed earlier shows you all the steps performed during the use of certificate-based authentication. This is an IKE/ISAKMP-based example, but any authentication process would be similar.

Troubleshooting Flow Charts

The flow charts in Figures 4-2, 4-3, and 4-4 illustrate the troubleshooting processes for initial configuration and key generation, CA authentication and enrollment, and certificate-based authentication.

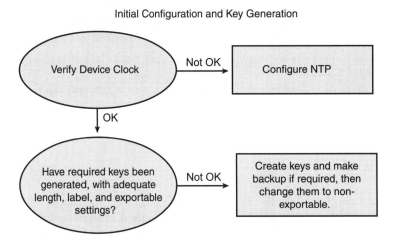

Figure 4-2 *Troubleshooting Initial Config and Key Generation*

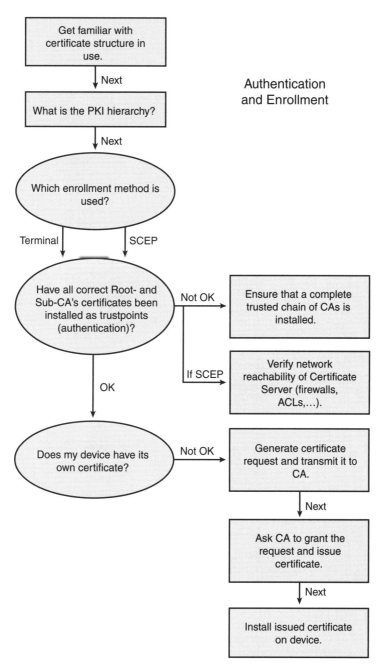

Figure 4-3 *Troubleshooting CA Authentication and Enrollment*

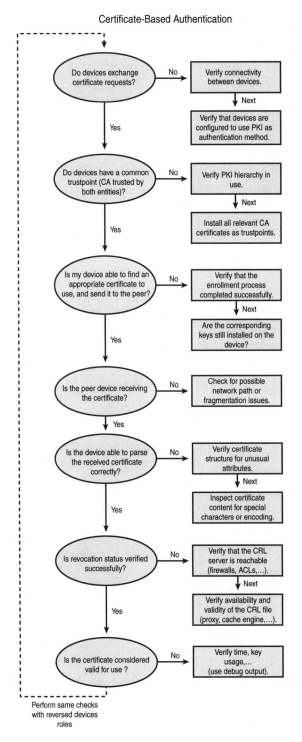

Figure 4-4 *Troubleshooting Certificate-Based Authentication*

Summary

This chapter analyzed some of the common issues that can affect you during the lifetime of your PKI deployment. Because it is impossible to list all possible failure scenarios, details about the expected successful workflow was shown. Based on that information, you can identify deviations that would potentially be the cause of the problems you observe.

For most troubleshooting processes, a good theoretical background can drastically help you understand the debug messages and the expected workflow. This is fully applicable to PKI technologies as well.

Chapter 5

Generic PKI Designs

This chapter covers the following topics:

- Basic Design with Flat CA Architecture

- Hierarchical Architecture

- Hierarchical Architecture Without Chaining

- Hierarchical Architecture with Chaining

Two baseline architectures are available for enterprises. A basic, flat architecture is best suited for small enterprises. Larger enterprises are best served with a hierarchical model, which offers two approaches: one based on certificate chaining, which helps define the flows of trust in the network, and the second based on standard certificate authentication.

Different deployments within enterprises have different requirements. The requirement drivers can be defined by organizational lines, regulatory lines, technical requirements, and scaling. A small-sized deployment where trust among hosts is shared in a simple, equal framework, a basic, flat CA architecture can be deployed. In an environment in which there are multiple business units, large numbers of hosts, and other lines along which separation of trust must occur within an enterprise, a hierarchical approach would be most appropriate.

Basic Design with Flat CA Architecture

The basic flat architecture, designed for small scale deployments, consists of a certificate authority (CA), which interacts directly with end spokes. In this architecture, end hosts request certificates from a central authority (see Figure 5-1).

This PKI provides a secure mechanism for distributing certificates on a small scale, which includes previously discussed components, such as external FTP servers and revocation methods.

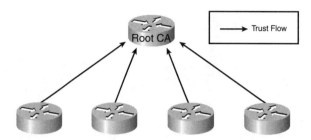

Figure 5-1 *Basic PKI Architecture*

Solution Elements

This PKI solution has a single root CA involved. Previously discussed best practices still apply. For example, an external FTP server should be used for storing the database. This ensures that if an outage occurs, the single root CA can be recovered, as covered in Chapter 3, "PKI Processes and Procedures." The individual spokes enroll directly into the root CA and obtain a certificate.

Example 5-1 *Basic CA and Spoke Configuration 3845-root-ca#* **show run**

```
...
crypto pki server root-ca
 database archive pkcs12 password 7 843595F
 grant auto rollover ca-cert
 grant auto
 lifetime crl 0 10
 cdp-url http://www.crl.cisco.com/ca.crl
 database url ftp://172.26.129.252

Spoke configuration
spoke# show run
....
crypto pki trustpoint root-ca
 enrollment url http://10.254.0.10:80
```

Hierarchical Architecture

A PKI for a network might need to support thousands of end devices from various organizations. A flat architecture would be problematic for this type of environment. Many end spokes would have direct access to the infrastructure's root certificate server, and that type of access would constitute a significant security risk. Secondarily, the flow of trust would be unilateral; all spokes would trust all spokes because they all trust the same root. For example, devices in the accounting department would successfully authenticate with devices in marketing. Clearly, the need for hierarchy exists.

Chapter 2, "Understanding PKI Building Blocks," introduced the concept of a CA, which can act on behalf of a root CA. This concept is termed a *subordinate CA* and is one of the critical building blocks for a hierarchical design. The subordinate CA (sub-CA) acts as an authority for its domain and distribute certificates.

The hierarchical design has two key variations. In one variation, the concept of certificate chaining is used to enable a degree of bottom-up validation. In the other variation, certificate chaining is not permitted for validation purposes. This chapter discusses the dynamics of both approaches.

To have a hierarchy, you need to properly set up a new subordinate CA. A subordinate CA enrolls in the root and hands out certificates on behalf of the root. To set up a subordinate CA, follow these steps:

Step 1.   Set up the subordinate CA.

```
S-3825-du-subca# conf t


Enter configuration commands, one per line. End with Cntl-Z.
S-3825-du-subca(config)# crypto pki server du-subca
S-3825-du-subca(cs-server)# database level complete
S-3825-du-subca(cs-server)# database archive pkcs12 password 7
   13061E010803557878
S-3825-du-subca(cs-server)# database url [ftp://1010.26.185.99]
S-3825-du-subca(cs-server)# grant auto rollover ca-cert
S-3825-du-subca(cs-server)# grant auto
S-3825-du-subca(cs-server)# lifetime crl 0 5
S-3825-du-subca(cs-server)# lifetime certificate 1000 0 30
S-3825-du-subca(cs-server)# cdp-url [http://10.26.185.99/du-subca.crl]
S-3825-du-subca(cs-server)# mode sub-cs
S-3825-du-subca(cs-server)# auto-rollover
S-3825-du-subca(cs-server)#
```

Step 2.   Set up the subordinate CA trust point.

```
S-3825-du-subca(cs-server)# crypto pki trustpoint du-subca
S-3825-du-subca(ca-trustpoint)# enrollment url http://10.254.0.14:80
S-3825-du-subca(ca-trustpoint)# revocation-check crl none
S-3825-du-subca(ca-trustpoint)# rsakeypair du-subca
S-3825-du-subca(ca-trustpoint)# exit
S-3825-du-subca(config)# end
```

Step 3.   Verify the communication to the FTP server.

```
S-3825-du-subca# ping 10.26.185.99


Type escape sequence to abort.
Sending 5, 100-byte ICMP Echos to 10.26.185.99, timeout is 2 seconds:
.!!!!
```

Step 4.   Apply the **no shutdown** command to the subordinate CA server.

This makes the subordinate CA enroll with the root CA. To enroll with the root CA, the subordinate CA must accept the root CA certificate. As soon as no shutdown is applied, the subordinate CA starts the enrollment process.

```
S-3825-du-subca(config)# crypto pki server du-subca
S-3825-du-subca(cs-server)# no shut
% Some server settings cannot be changed after CA certificate
  generation.
% Generating 1024 bit RSA keys, keys will be non-exportable...[OK]

Writing du-subca.ser !
The certificate has the following attributes:
Fingerprint MD5: 7F626D1E 07C1C3AC 30220222 25F76AE2
Fingerprint SHA1: 8CFD5BB1 60ECBF8B 10BB4188 9CB11BDC E8829B6E
```

Step 5.   Accept the root CA certificate.

```
% Do you accept this certificate? [yes/no]: yes
Trustpoint CA certificate accepted.%
% Create a challenge password. You will need to verbally provide this
    password to the CA Administrator in order to revoke your
      certificate.
    For security reasons your password will not be saved in the
      configuration.
    Please make a note of it.

Password: x
Re-enter password: xx

% Certificate request sent to Certificate Authority

% Enrollment in progress...
```

Step 6.   Go to the root CA and manually grant the subordinate CA enrollment request.

```
S-3825-root-ca# crypto pki server root-ca grant all
Writing 1D0.crt !
Writing 1D0.cnm !
Writing root-ca.ser !
S-3825-root-ca#
```

Step 7.   Go to the subordinate CA and verify that it receives the certificate.

```
S-3825-du-subca#
Writing du-subca.crl !
% Exporting Certificate Server signing certificate and keys...
```

```
Writing du-subca_00002.p12 !

storing the serial number to ftp server
Loading du-subca.ser
[OK - 32/4096 bytes]
storing the crl file to the ftp server
Loading du-subca.crl
[OK - 218/4096 bytes]

S-3825-du-subca# show crypto pki server
Certificate Server du-subca:
    Status: enabled
    State: enabled
    Server's configuration is locked   (enter "shut" to unlock it)
    Issuer name: CN=du-subca
    CA cert fingerprint: 42A3E048 6CFE2607 2D6E47B8 83A14556
    Server configured in subordinate server mode
    Upper CA cert fingerprint: 7F626D1E 07C1C3AC 30220222 25F76AE2
    Granting mode is: auto
    Last certificate issued serial number: 0x1
    CA certificate expiration timer: 16:03:07 EST May 3 2008
    CRL NextUpdate timer: 15:04:17 EST May 3 2008
    Current primary storage dir: ftp://10.26.185.99
    Database Level: Complete - all issued certs written as
      <serialnum>.cer
    Auto-Rollover configured, overlap period 30 days
```

Step 8.   Verify that certificates are on the subordinate CA.

```
S-3825-du-subca# show crypto pki certificates
Certificate (subordinate CA certificate)
  Status: Available
  Certificate Serial Number: 0x1D0
  Certificate Usage: Signature
  Issuer:
    cn=root-ca
  Subject:
    cn=du-subca
  CRL Distribution Points:
    http://10.26.185.99/root-ca.crl
  Validity Date:
    start date: 14:58:59 EST May 3 2008
    end   date: 16:03:07 EST May 3 2008
  Associated Trustpoints: du-subca
```

```
CA Certificate
  Status: Available
  Certificate Serial Number: 0x1CE
  Certificate Usage: Signature
  Issuer:
    cn=root-ca
  Subject:
    cn=root-ca
  Validity Date:
    start date: 12:03:07 EST May 3 2008
    end   date: 16:03:07 EST May 3 2008
  Associated Trustpoints: du-subca
```

Hierarchical Architecture Without Chaining

A hierarchical model has several common goals. These goals include regionalization of sub-CAs based on either function or geography and a layer of separation between the root CA for the organization and end hosts. In IKE, certificate chaining is enabled by default as part of the protocol suite; however, IKE cannot tolerate gaps. In SSL, certificate chaining must be enabled explicitly for any type chaining awareness to exist.

The following example is a hierarchical solution that does not use certificate chaining. For any two hosts to communicate, they need to be enrolled in at least one shared certificate authority. Figure 5-2 has three host communities: Marketing, ACCOUNTING Accounts Payable, and ACCOUNTING Accounts Receivable.

In this hierarchy, marketing's subordinate CA will be enrolled with the corporate CA. The h/w (Accounts Payable) and s/w (Accounts receivable) subordinate CAs will be enrolled only with the ACCOUNTING subordinate CA. The ACCOUNTING subordinate CA will be enrolled in the corporate root CA. In keeping with the example, you have the hypothetical departments: Accounts Payable, Accounts receivable, and marketing as part of a device manufacturing enterprise. The marketing end hosts will be enrolled only in the marketing subordinate CA. Marketing hosts know only of the existence of the marketing CA, and consequently, can authenticate only other marketing hosts. Accounts Payable ACCOUNTING enrolls in the Accounts Payable subordinate CA. Consequently, Accounts Payable hosts know of the existence of only the Accounts Payable CA and can authenticate only other Accounts Payable hosts. The same scenario plays out with Accounts receivable hosts, respectively. In this scenario, Accounts Payable hosts cannot authenticate Accounts receivable hosts or marketing hosts.

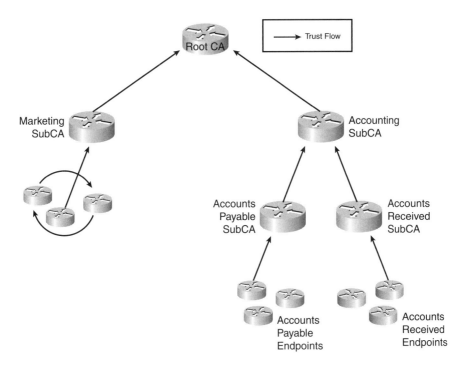

Figure 5-2   *Hierarchical PKI Architecture*

Example 5-2   *Basic Hierarchical Deployment Example ROOT CA Configuration*

```
3845-root-ca# show run
...

crypto pki server root-ca
 database archive pkcs12 password 7 104D000A061843595F
 grant auto rollover ca-cert
 lifetime crl 0 10
 lifetime certificate 1000 2
 lifetime ca-certificate 480 4
 cdp-url http://171.70.65.136/stenneti/root-ca.crl
 auto-rollover 0 1
 database url ftp://172.26.129.252
 database url crl ftp://172.26.129.252
!
crypto pki trustpoint root-ca
 revocation-check crl
 rsakeypair root-ca
!
```

```
Example Subordinate CA configuration
!
crypto pki server ra-subca
 database level complete
 database archive pkcs12 password 7 13061E010803557878
 grant auto rollover ca-cert
 grant auto
 lifetime crl 0 5
 lifetime certificate 480 0 30
 cdp-url http://171.70.65.136/stenneti/ra-subca.crl
 mode sub-cs
 auto-rollover
 database url crl ftp://172.26.129.252
 database url p12 ftp://172.26.129.252
!
crypto pki trustpoint ra-subca
 enrollment url http://10.254.0.10:80
 revocation-check crl none
 rsakeypair ra-subca
 regenerate
!
```

Figure 5-3 illustrates the flow of trust in this network. Marketing users enroll in marketing and can successfully authenticate other marketing clients. When marketing attempts to communicate with Accounts Payable ACCOUNTING, this fails because Accounts Payable ACCOUNTING and marketing do not know about each others' certificate authorities. This model enables containment of trust flow. In this case, Accounts Payable accountants have no need to access any marketing systems, and if certificates are used for authentication, those connections will not be authenticated.

Hierarchical Architecture with Chaining

In a hierarchical model, the use of certificate chaining provides for an extra tool in establishing flows of trust. Trust flow is defined as relationships that permit the exchange of information. Trust must exist among any grouping of hosts that want an authenticated exchange of information.

Certificate Chaining

Certificate chaining is the process of performing a recursive authentication until a trusted authority is reached. Upon receiving a certificate to authenticate, the end device attempts to authenticate up the chain until a trusted certificate is found. When that certificate is discovered, the certificates, which have issuers subordinate to the trusted certificate discovered during chaining, are vouched for. In Example 5-2, as long as the device has simply authenticated and retrieved the certificate from the root CA using the **crypto pki authenticate** command, the device can recursively trust the certificates up to the root CA.

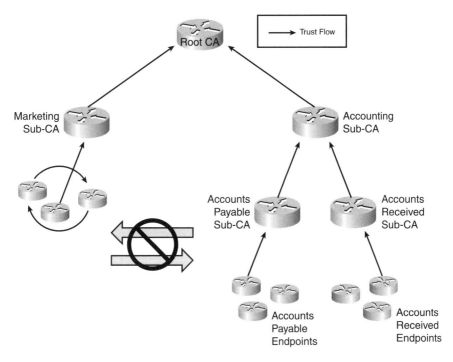

Figure 5-3 *Hierarchical PKI Trust Flow*

Note   Certificate chaining is enabled by default as part of IKE. There can be no gaps in the chain of trust.

Example 5-3 *Certificate Chaining Configuration*

```
crypto pki trustpoint ra
 enrollment url http://192.168.159.243:12345
 chain-validation continue root-ca
 serial-number
 ip-address 192.168.134.146
 revocation-check none
 rsakeypair r35-1-keys
 auto-enroll 80 regenerate
```

Example 5-4   *Certificate Chaining with IKE and Spoke Authenticating with an Externally Stored Root CA certificate. The Storage Location Is Defined by the Database* **url** *Command.*

```
root-ca
=======

crypto pki server root-ca
 database level complete
 database archive pkcs12 password 7 104D000A061843595F
 grant auto
 lifetime certificate 480
 lifetime ca-certificate 1000
 cdp-url http://172.26.185.99/root-ca.crl
 database url ftp://172.26.185.99
 !
crypto pki trustpoint root-ca
 revocation-check crl
 rsakeypair root-ca




Sub-ca server
=============

crypto pki server ra-subca
 database level complete
 database archive pkcs12 password 7 060506324F41584B56
 grant auto rollover ca-cert
 grant auto
 lifetime certificate 480
 lifetime ca-certificate 700
 mode sub-cs
 auto-rollover 90
 database url ftp://172.26.185.99
 !
crypto pki trustpoint ra-subca
 enrollment url http://10.254.0.10:80
 revocation-check crl
 rsakeypair ra-subca
 !
crypto pki trustpoint ra
 enrollment url http://192.168.159.243:12345
 serial-number
 ip-address 192.168.159.243
```

```
 revocation-check none
 rsakeypair ra
 auto-enroll 80 regenerate

spoke
==========

crypto pki trustpoint root-ca
 enrollment url http://172.26.185.128:80
 revocation-check none
!
crypto pki trustpoint ra
 enrollment url http://192.168.159.243:12345
 serial-number
 ip-address 192.168.134.146
 revocation-check none
 rsakeypair r35-1-keys
 auto-enroll 80 regenerate
```

In Example 5-3, the spoke has enrolled only in the sub-CA "ra". The root CA's certificate is stored on an external server that is not the root CA itself. The spoke obtains the root CA's certificate by authenticating to the trustpoint root using the command **crypto PKI authenticate.** This obtains the root CA's certificate but does not enroll the spoke in the root. The spoke obtains the spoke certificate from the subordinate CA. If the spoke is presented with a certificate from another issued directly from the root CA, this certificate will be accepted and this host will be trusted.

Example 5-5   *Sample Output of Crypto PKI Authenticate*

```
(config)# crypto pki authenticate root-ca

Certificate has the following attributes:
Fingerprint: 0123 4567 89AB CDEF 0123
Do you accept this certificate? [yes/no] y#
```

Summary

Different deployments within enterprises have different requirements. The requirement drivers can be defined by organizational lines, regulatory lines, technical requirements, and scaling. A small-sized deployment where trust among hosts is shared in a simple, equal framework, a basic, flat CA architecture can be deployed. In an environment where there are multiple business units, large numbers of hosts, and other lines along which separation of trust must occur within an enterprise, a hierarchical approach would be most appropriate. In a scenario where SSL/TLS-based trust occurs and trust flows are complicated, or where generically trust flows are more involved between organizational units, a hierarchy with chaining may be more appropriate. The basic tenants and leading practices within each of these architectures are generally the same. External FTP servers are still recommended, for example, and other leading practices as described in previous chapters.

Chapter 6

Integration in Large-Scale Site-to-Site VPN Solutions

This chapter covers the following topics:

■ How Do VPN Technologies Use PKI as Service?

■ IKE Using Digital Certificates

■ PKI Design and Leading Practices

■ GETVPN PKI Design and Leading Practices

You can use PKI in large-scale VPN solutions—mainly the DMVPN and GETVPN. These two technologies are popular VPN solutions, especially for large enterprise customers. Integrating PKI into these VPN technologies involves IKE negotiation, digital certificates, hierarchical design for CA servers, and enrollment methods for obtaining certificates. Deployment of these concepts enables you to build large-scale VPN solutions using PKI.

How Do VPN Technologies Use PKI as a Service?

Current Cisco VPN technologies, such as point-to-point IPsec, IPsec/GRE, DMVPN, GETVPN, and EzVPN, use IKE as underlying protocol for authenticated key exchange. The IKE protocol is a hybrid of the Oakley and SKEME protocols and operates inside a framework defined by Internet Security Association and Key Management Protocol (ISAKMP), which defines packet formats, retransmission timers, and message construction requirements. Oakley and SKEME define the steps two peers must take to establish a shared, authenticated key. IKE uses the ISAKMP language to express these and other exchanges. It is a generic protocol and the specification is defined in RFC2407, which defines how IKE negotiates IPSec SA.

IKE uses the concept of Security Association (SA), but it is different from IPsec SA. The purpose of IKE SA is to define how peers communicate, which is to state what encryption algorithm the peers use to encrypt IKE traffic, and so on.

The primary purpose of IKE is to establish an authenticated key exchange between two peers, using the IKE SA process to derive the keys. While doing the IKE authentication, the two peers need to authenticate each other, which can be done by either using pre-shared keys or PKI.

IKE Using Digital Certificates

As explained in Chapter 1, "Crypto Refresh," IKE needs a mechanism to authenticate two VPN peers, and digital certificates are one of the options available to authenticate the VPN peers. Figure 6-1 shows how IKE uses PKI for authentication.

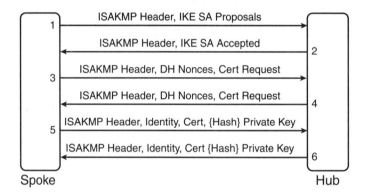

Figure 6-1   *IKE Exchange Steps*

The key difference between IKE using the preshared and the public key lies in Steps 5 and 6. IKE using preshared authentication uses hash as the method to authenticate both the peers. When using PKI, the peers encrypt the hash with their respective private keys. The hash is then decrypted using the respective public key of the peers. Each peer would need to know the public key of the other peer by looking into the certificate, which is exchanged in Step 5 and Step 6.

PKI Design and Leading Practices

Following are some of the best practices for deploying PKI design:

- **WAN connectivity:** Because customers deploy delay-sensitive applications, you need to have multiple connections to reach from branch to main office, which means having redundant service providers at the main office and at the branches. If it is cost-prohibitive to have redundant providers at the branches, you need to have dual service providers at the main office, which is WAN edge, and have branches divided between the service providers, for example, if company X has 500 branches. Then one design alternative could be to have dual private WAN providers so that WAN edge connects to both providers, and the branches from 1–250 connected to SP1, and the branches from 251–500 connect to SP2. The design in this chapter has each branch having dual connections, that is, one connection to each service provider. Figure 6-2 illustrates how a large-scale DMVPN design with high availability might appear.

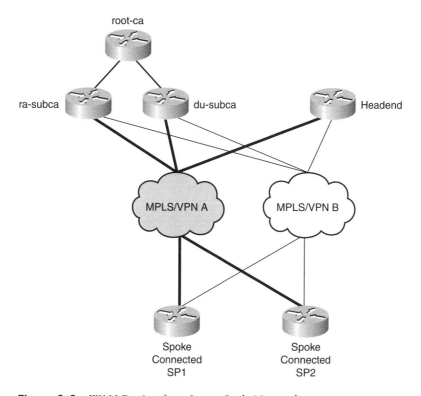

Figure 6-2   *WAN Design for a Large-Scale Network*

■ **PKI Architecture:** For a large-scale VPN deployment, you need a root CA with dual subordinate CAs. Figure 6-3 illustrates hierarchical architecture.

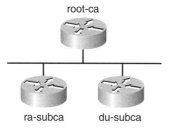

Figure 6-3   *PKI Hierarchical Architecture*

Following are some of the best practices for deploying PKI hierarchical architecture:

- **Grant mode of the subordinate CAs:** By default, the granting mode of the subordinate CAs is auto, which means the subordinate CA would automatically grant a certificate to spoke/hub to whoever requests it. This is easier to deploy but provides no administrative control. The other alternative is to grant certificates manually. This option provides better control but does not scale well; therefore, the administrator needs to decide which option is suitable for the deployment.

- **Enrollment method for spoke and hub:** Although there are multiple methods to enroll with the CA server, the most preferred method is SCEP, which uses HTTP protocol.

- **HTTP port on CA server:** By default, the HTTP server listens on port 80, but for better security the CA server needs to be configured to listen on any nonstandard port, for example 12345.

DMVPN Deployment Models

A Dynamic Multipoint virtual private network (DMVPN) is a Cisco IOS solution to build VPNs in an easy and scalable manner. DMVPN is built upon two technologies: Next Hop Resolution Protocol (NHRP) and multipoint GRE interface. DMVPN architecture consists mainly of a DMVPN hub router that terminates or facilitates connections to various remotely located DMVPN spoke routers.

Note   To obtain more information about DMVPN architecture, go to the following URL: http://www.cisco.com/en/US/docs/solutions/Enterprise/WAN_and_MAN/DMVPDG.html.

- **DMVPN models:** The most common deployments models are hub-and-spoke or spoke-to-spoke. Regardless of the method chosen, both hub and spoke need to enroll with the CA server. The key consideration is whether spokes need to enroll with both subordinate CAs or to their regional subordinate CA only. As discussed in Chapter 5, "Generic PKI Designs," there are two options to consider. The first option is for spokes to enroll with all the respective subordinate CAs, and the second option is for spokes to enroll with only one subordinate CA and use the root CA certificate to validate the other spoke. The second option is for spokes to obtain a root CA certificate to validate the subordinate CA certificate does not add significant delay to build the VPN tunnel because the spokes would need to perform only a quick check on the validity of the subordinate CA.

■ **DMVPN deployment model for hub and spoke:** This deployment model is illustrated in Figure 6-4.

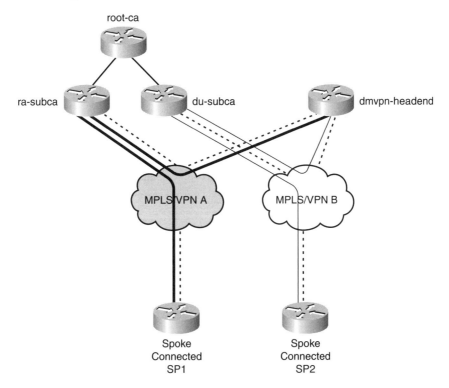

Figure 6-4 *DMVPN PKI Enrollment for Hub-and-Spoke Model*

In the preceding topology, the dmvpn-headend needs to enroll with both subordinate CAs; however, the spoke router can enroll with only the corresponding subordinate CA, which is attached to the respective provider. With the previous design, the dmvpn-headend can authenticate either of the spokes because the spoke will never initiate communication directly to another spoke, and it would always establish communication with headend only.

■ **DMVPN deployment with spoke-to-spoke connectivity:** This requires that each spoke can authenticate any other spoke. The hub is not involved in authentication. The topology, as shown in Figure 6-5, illustrates the spoke-to-spoke connectivity.

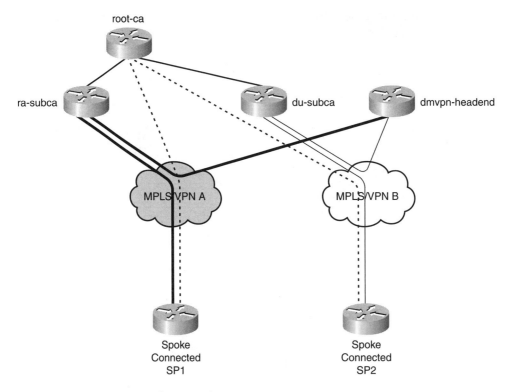

Figure 6-5 *DMVPN Spoke-to-Spoke Connectivity*

■ As shown in Figure 6-5, Spoke 1 connects to MPLS/VPN A (SP1), and Spoke 2 connects to MPLS/VPN B (SP2). Because the requirement is for spoke-to-spoke connectivity, spoke- 1 can talk to Spoke 2 without going through the hub router; this means
  that Spoke 1 should establish a DMVPN tunnel directly with Spoke 2. To provide
  that connectivity, the following two conditions should be met:

  ■ ra-subca and du-subca, which are the subordinate CA servers, should connect to
    both SP1 and SP2.

  ■ Spoke 1 and Spoke 2 should enroll with their regional service providers, in this
    case ra-subca, and du-subca.

  ■ Spoke 1 and Spoke 2 (as shown with dotted lines) must obtain root-CA certifi-
    cate for doing certificate chaining. The need for doing certificate chaining is
    provided next.

The obvious question is how does Spoke 1 authenticate to Spoke 2, considering that both
are enrolled with different subordinate CAs? The answer is in Chapter 5 where it is mentioned that in the preceding scenario, the spokes should either enroll with both subordinate CAs or should use certificate chaining.

DMVPN Integration with PKI

DMVPN deployed with PKI brings not only stronger authentication but also makes it a better security solution than using a preshared key model. In a traditional preshared key model, spokes are removed from the network by removing the pair-wise key on both the hub and the spoke router. This might create a security hole because this operation needs to be done on all the hubs. Deploying PKI simplifies this process by supporting revocation of certificates, which makes certain certificates invalid because they have expired or are not needed. This feature helps remove spokes when they are not needed. Figure 6-6 illustrates how different VPN technologies use PKI to authenticate each other.

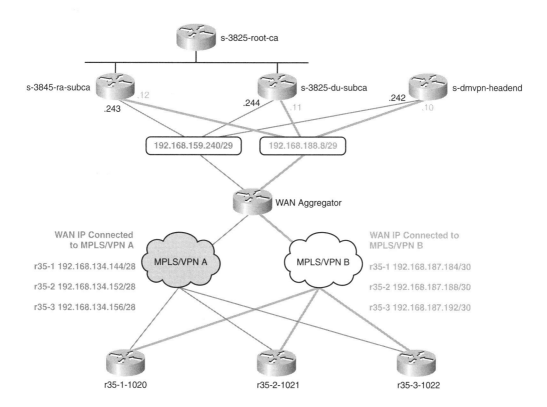

Figure 6-6 *PKI for Different VPN Technologies*

The previous topology has two service providers for the private WAN network. The figure illustrates dual service providers, which are becoming more common among enterprise customers. Table 6-1 describes the devices used in this topology.

Before you dive into the DMVPN deployment using PKI as a service, look first at the network topology. The details of the DMVPN connections are shown in Figure 6-7.

Table 6-1   *Description of Devices in the Lab Topology*

Hostname	Role	Description
r35-1-1020	Spoke	Connected to MPLS/VPN A
r35-2-1021	Spoke	Connected to MPLS/VPN B
r35-3-1022	Spoke	Connected to MPLS/VPN B
s-3845-ra-subca	Subordinate CA server	Connected to MPLS/VPN A
s-3825-root-ca	Root CA server	Located at inside secure network
s-3825-du-subca	Subordinate CA server	Connected to MPLS/VPN B
s-dmvpn-headend	DMVPN headend	Connected to both MPLS/VPN A and MPLS/VPN B

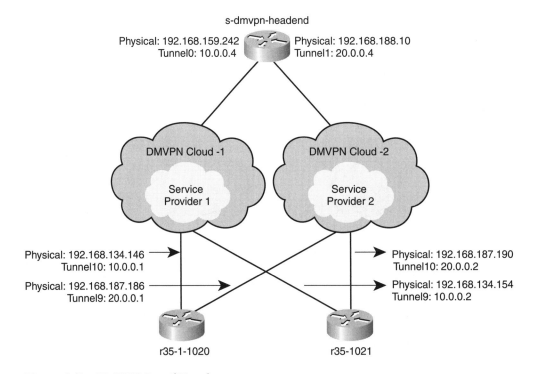

Figure 6-7   *DMVPN Detail Topology*

As you can see from Figure 6-7, the spokes have two physical and logical interfaces (tunnels) connected to the headend using different service providers. The headend is also connected to both service providers and also terminates both dmvpn clouds. This information should help you to navigate the details in the next few sections.

DMVPN with Hub-and-Spoke Model

Figure 6-8 illustrates the deployment of DMVPM for a hub-and-spoke model.

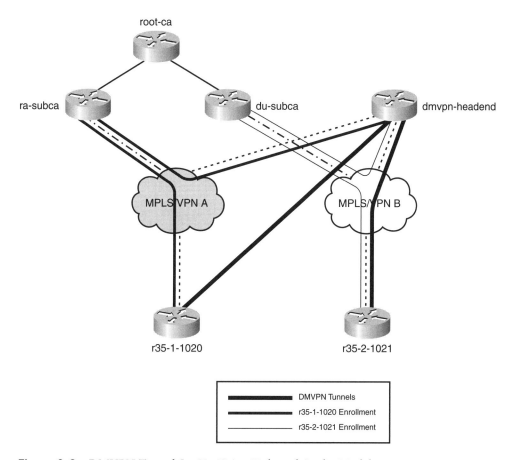

Figure 6-8 *DMVPN Tunnel Set Up Using Hub-and-Spoke Model*

Each subordinate CA (Sub-ca1 and Sub-ca2) connects to its respective service providers: MPLS/VPN A and MPLS/VPN B. In addition, the dmvpn-headend connects to both MPLS/VPN A and MPLS/VPN B (dual-homed). Example 6-1 illustrates how spokes enroll with both subordinate CAs and how dmvpn-headend can authenticate them using digital certificates. Table 6-2 lists the devices used for this example.

Step 1. The subordinate CA server should be up and running; the **show crypto pki server** following command verifies the status of subordinate CA server.

Example 6-1   *Verifying the Subordinate CA Server Status*

```
ra-subca# show crypto pki server
Certificate Server ra-subca:
    Status: enabled
    State: enabled
    Server's configuration is locked  (enter "shut" to unlock it)
    Issuer name: CN=ra-subca
    CA cert fingerprint: ECE8BE9E 9C5179A5 ABD983A2 6E5F5DE8
    Server configured in subordinate server mode
    Upper CA cert fingerprint: ECE8BE9E 9C5179A5 ABD983A2 6E5F5DE8
    Granting mode is: manual
    Last certificate issued serial number (hex): C
    CA certificate expiration timer: 12:21:19 EST Jan 28 2011
    CRL NextUpdate timer: 22:52:07 EST Jun 16 2009
    Current primary storage dir: ftp://172.26.185.99
    Database Level: Complete - all issued certs written as <serialnum>.cer
    Auto-Rollover configured, overlap period 90 days
    Autorollover timer: 12:21:19 EST Oct 30 2010
ra-subca#
```

Table 6-2   *Devices Used for Illustrating DMVPN with Dual Service Providers*

Description	Device Name
Spoke-1	r35-1-1020
Spoke-2	r35-2-1021
Headend	s-dmvpn-headend
Sub-ca1	ra-subca
Sub-ca2	du-subca

Step 2.   After verifying that subordinate CA server is in active state, configure the enrollment on the spoke devices, as shown in Example 6-2.

Example 6-2   *Configuring Enrollment for Spoke r35-1-1020*

```
crypto pki trustpoint ra
 enrollment url http://192.168.159.243:12345  ! pointing to ra-subca server
 serial-number
 ip-address 192.168.159.243
 revocation-check none
 rsakeypair ra
 auto-enroll 80 regenerate
```

Step 3.   With the enrollment configured, refer to the steps in Chapter 3, "PKI Processes and Procedures," to complete the enrollment.

Step 4.   After the enrollment is complete on the spoke, configure the hub router for enrollment, as shown in Example 6-3.

Example 6-3   *Configuring Enrollment for Hub s-dmvpn-headend*

```
crypto pki trustpoint ra
 enrollment url http://192.168.159.243:12345 ! pointing to ra-subca server
 revocation-check none
 rsakeypair hub-keys
 auto-enroll 70 regenerate
```

Step 5.   After both the hub and spokes have obtained the certificates, configure DMVPN on the hub and spoke to use digital certificates for authentication.

For the hub and spoke to use digital certificates, the ISAKMP policy must be configured, which should use rsa-signature for authentication. The configuration in Example 6-4 on the spoke router illustrates the configuration needed for a spoke to use digital certificates for DMVPN.

Example 6-4   *Configuring ISAKMP Policy, ISAKMP Profile, and DMVPN Tunnel on Spoke Router*

```
crypto isakmp policy 1
 encr 3des
 hash md5
 group 2

crypto isakmp profile r35-profile
      match identity host domain cisco.com
   match identity address 192.168.159.242 255.255.255.255

crypto ipsec transform-set 3DES_MD5 esp-3des esp-md5-hmac
 mode transport
!
crypto ipsec profile ESE_DMVPN
 set transform-set 3DES_MD5
 set isakmp-profile r35-profile
!
interface Tunnel10
 ip address 10.0.0.1 255.255.255.0
 no ip redirects
 ip mtu 1400
 ip nhrp authentication DMVPNGET
 ip nhrp map multicast dynamic
 ip nhrp map 10.0.0.4 192.168.159.242
 ip nhrp map multicast 192.168.159.242
```

```
    ip nhrp network-id 1234
    ip nhrp holdtime 90
    ip nhrp nhs 10.0.0.4
    ip nhrp registration timeout 30
    ip ospf network broadcast
    tunnel source 192.168.134.146
    tunnel mode gre multipoint
    tunnel key 1234
    tunnel protection ipsec profile ESE_DMVPN
!
interface FastEthernet0/0.3410
 description link to Internet
 encapsulation dot1Q 3410
 ip address 192.168.187.186 255.255.255.252
!
```

Step 6.   With the preceding configuration, the spoke is ready to communicate with the Hub router. Next, configure the DMVPN configuration on Hub router, as shown in Example 6-5.

Example 6-5   *Configuring DMVPN on Hub Router*

```
crypto isakmp policy 2
 encr 3des
 hash md5
 group 2
crypto isakmp profile dmvpn-profile
    keyring zebra
    match identity host domain cisco.com
    match identity address 192.168.134.146 255.255.255.255
!
crypto ipsec transform-set 3DES_MD5 esp-3des esp-md5-hmac
 mode transport
!
crypto ipsec profile ESE_DMVPN
 set transform-set 3DES_MD5
 set isakmp-profile dmvpn-profile

!
interface Tunnel0
 ip address 10.0.0.4 255.255.255.0
 no ip redirects
 ip mtu 1400
 ip nhrp authentication DMVPNGET
```

```
ip nhrp map multicast dynamic
ip nhrp network-id 1234
ip nhrp holdtime 90
ip nhrp registration timeout 120
ip nhrp redirect
ip tcp adjust-mss 1360
ip ospf network broadcast
tunnel source 192.168.159.242
tunnel mode gre multipoint
tunnel key 1234
tunnel protection ipsec profile ESE_DMVPN
end
!
!
interface GigabitEthernet0/1.240
encapsulation dot1Q 240
 ip address 192.168.159.242 255.255.255.248
```

With the preceding configuration, the DMVPN tunnel is established between the hub-and-spoke router.

Step 7. Verify the DMVPM tunnel has been established, as shown in Example 6-6.

Example 6-6 *Verifying the DMVPN Tunnel Establishment*

```
s-dmvpn-headend# show crypto isakmp sa
IPv4 Crypto ISAKMP SA
dst               src               state       conn-id slot status
192.168.188.6    192.168.187.190 QM_IDLE          15632    0 ACTIVE
192.168.188.6    192.168.187.194 QM_IDLE          15633    0 ACTIVE
192.168.134.146 192.168.159.242 QM_IDLE          15631    0 ACTIVE
192.168.159.242 192.168.167.250 QM_IDLE          15634    0 ACTIVE


IPv6 Crypto ISAKMP SA


s-dmvpn-headend#
```

Now that you have enrolled Hub s-dmvpn-headend and spoke r35-1-1020 with their regional subordinate CA (ra-subca), enroll the other spoke r35-2-1021 with its regional service provider du-subca.

Step 8. Verify that the *du-subca* server is active and can grant certificates to the branches. As noted in the best practices description, the grant mode should be set to manual. The default behavior is auto, as shown in Example 6-7.

Example 6-7   *Verifying the Subordinate CA Server Status*

```
S-3825-du-subca# show crypto pki server
Certificate Server du-subca:
    Status: enabled
    State: enabled
    Server's configuration is locked  (enter "shut" to unlock it)
    Issuer name: CN=du-subca
    CA cert fingerprint: A6298B11 A50948FF C170D745 CD7DFABC
    Server configured in subordinate server mode
    Upper CA cert fingerprint: ABD85DC7 C152AE90 4949A459 B91F0A39
    Granting mode is: manual
    Last certificate issued serial number (hex): 1
    CA certificate expiration timer: 16:06:24 EST Feb 12 2011
    CRL NextUpdate timer: 16:18:57 EST Mar 27 2009
    Current primary storage dir: ftp://xxx.26.185.99
    Database Level: Complete - all issued certs written as <serialnum>.cer
    Auto-Rollover configured, overlap period 90 days
    Autorollover timer: 16:06:24 EST Nov 14 2010
```

Step 9.   Configure the trust point on the dmvpn-headend router pointing to du-subca, by using trust point du, as shown in Example 6-8.

Example 6-8   *Configuring the Trust Point on dmvpn-headend*

```
crypto pki trustpoint du
 enrollment url http://192.168.188.10:12345
 revocation-check crl
 rsakeypair hub-keys
 auto-enroll 70 regenerate
```

Step 10.   As explained in Chapter 3, complete the enrollment of the headend to the second subordinate CA server du-subca.

Step 11.   Configure the trust point on another spoke r35-2-1021, as shown in Example 6-9.

Example 6-9   *Configuring the Trust Point on spoke r35-2-1021*

```
crypto pki trustpoint du
 enrollment url http://192.168.188.10:12345
 revocation-check none
 rsakeypair r35-2-keys
 auto-enroll 70 regenerate
```

Step 12.   Enroll this spoke r35-2-1021 to the du-subca. After the spoke is enrolled, configure DMVPN tunnel using digital certificates as the authentication method, as shown in Example 6-10.

Example 6-10   *Configuring DMVPN Configuration on Spoke r35-2-1021*

```
crypto isakmp policy 1
 encr 3des
 hash md5
 group 2
crypto isakmp identity hostname
crypto isakmp profile r35-profile
   match identity host domain cisco.com
  match identity address 192.168.134.146 255.255.255.255
!
!
crypto ipsec transform-set 3DES_MD5 esp-3des esp-md5-hmac
 mode transport
!
crypto ipsec profile ESE_DMVPN
 set transform-set 3DES_MD5
 set isakmp-profile r35-profile
!
interface Tunnel10
 ip address 20.0.0.2 255.255.255.0
 ip mtu 1400
 ip nhrp authentication DMVPNGET
 ip nhrp map 20.0.0.4 192.168.188.6
 ip nhrp map multicast 192.168.188.6
 ip nhrp network-id 2345
 ip nhrp holdtime 90
 ip nhrp nhs 20.0.0.4
 ip nhrp registration timeout 30
 tunnel source 192.168.187.190
 tunnel destination 192.168.188.6
 tunnel key 1234
 tunnel protection ipsec profile ESE_DMVPN
end
```

With the preceding configuration, the DMVPN tunnel should come up between r35-2-1021 and s-dmvpn-headend.

Step 13.   Use the following **show crypto** commands on either end of the tunnel to verify that the DMVPN tunnel with PKI is enabled.

Example 6-11 *Verifying* crypto isakmp *on the dmvpn-headend Router*

```
s-dmvpn-headend# show crypto isakmp sa
IPv4 Crypto ISAKMP SA
dst              src              state           conn-id slot status
192.168.188.6    192.168.187.186 QM_IDLE          13060    0 ACTIVE
192.168.159.242 192.168.167.250 QM_IDLE          13063    0 ACTIVE
192.168.188.6    192.168.187.190 QM_IDLE          13064    0 ACTIVE
```

DMVPN Integration with PKI Using a Spoke-to-Spoke Model

The following example illustrates how DMVPN integrates with PKI using a spoke-to-spoke model. Table 6-3 lists the devices used for this example.

Table 6-3 *Device for Illustrating DMVPN with a Spoke-to-Spoke Model*

Description	Device Name
Spoke-1	r35-1-1020
Spoke-2	r35-2-1021
Headend	dmvpn-headend
Subordinate CA1	ra-subca
Subordinate CA2	du-subca
root	S-3825-root CA

Deploying the architecture model shown in Figure 6-5 requires obtaining a root CA certificate. The root CA is needed because spokes are enrolled with different subordinate CAs, and for every spoke to talk to every other spoke, every spoke would need to enroll with all the subordinate CAs. For example, if there are 1000 spokes and four subordinate CAs, each spoke would need to have four enrollments so that it could authenticate all the spokes. This would mean lot of enrollments; the alternative is certificate chaining explained in Chapter 5. Figure 6-9 illustrates this process.

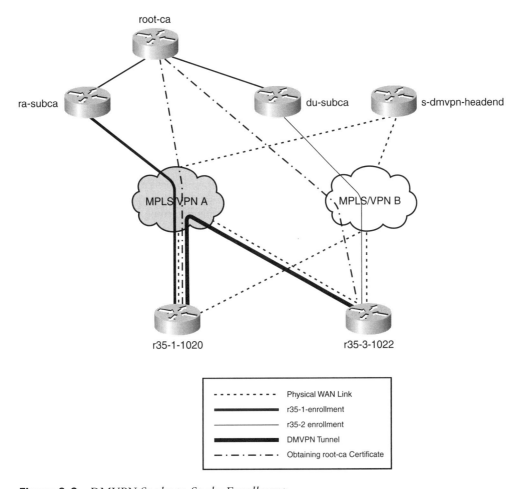

Figure 6-9 *DMVPN Spoke-to-Spoke Enrollment*

Step 1.   To implement certificate chaining, define two trust points on each spoke.

In this example, spoke-1 (r35-1-1020) needs two trust points. The first trust point enrolls with ra-subca, and the second trust point obtains the root CA certificate, as illustrated in Example 6-12.

Example 6-12 *Configuration of Trust Points on the Spoke*

```
crypto pki trustpoint ra
 enrollment url http://192.168.159.243:12345
 serial-number
 ip-address 192.168.159.243
 chain-validation continue root-ca
 revocation-check none
```

```
  rsakeypair ra
  auto-enroll 80 regenerate
!
crypto pki trustpoint root-ca
  enrollment url http://172.26.185.128:12345
  revocation-check none
!
```

The first trust point is used to enroll with sub-ca, and second one is only meant to obtain the root CA certificate, not to enroll with the root CA. To obtain the root CA certificate, authenticate the spoke router with the root CA, as described in Chapter 3. The example preceding shows how to obtain the root CA certificate using SCEP, which means that the root CA certificate must be online and should be reachable to spoke routers. Allowing the root CA to be online may cause security impacts. The other choice could be to retrieve the root CA certificate using a TFTP server or by using a cut-and-paste method.

Step 2.   After authenticating the root CA server, the spoke r35-1 will have the root CA certificate in its nvram. Enroll the spoke with its regional subordinate CA (ra-subca). After enrollment, the spoke will also have its certificate in the nvram. Example 6-13 shows the certificates obtained by the spoke.

Example 6-13   *Displaying the Certificates on the Spoke Router*

```
r35-1-1020# show crypto pki certificates
Certificate
  Status: Available
  Certificate Serial Number (hex): 06
  Certificate Usage: General Purpose
  Issuer:
    cn=ra-subca
  Subject:
    Name: r35-1-1020.cisco.com
    IP Address: 192.168.159.243
    Serial Number: FTX1048A6QA
    serialNumber=FTX1048A6QA+ipaddress=192.168.159.243+hostname=
      r35-1-1020.cisco.com
  CRL Distribution Points:
    http://172.26.185.99/ra-subca.crl
  Validity Date:
    start date: 17:53:25 EST Aug 5 2009
    end   date: 16:53:25 EST Feb 1 2010
    renew date: 16:53:25 EST Dec 27 2009
  Associated Trustpoints: ra
  Storage: nvram:ra-subca#6.cer
```

```
CA Certificate
  Status: Available
  Certificate Serial Number (hex): 01
  Certificate Usage: Signature
  Issuer:
    cn=root-ca
  Subject:
    cn=root-ca
  Validity Date:
    start date: 17:34:05 EST Nov 15 2008
    end   date: 17:34:05 EST Nov 14 2013
  Associated Trustpoints: root-ca
  Storage: nvram:root-ca#1CA.cer

CA Certificate
  Status: Available
  Certificate Serial Number (hex): 08
  Certificate Usage: Signature
  Issuer:
    cn=root-ca
  Subject:
    cn=ra-subca
  CRL Distribution Points:
    http://172.26.185.99/root-ca.crl
  Validity Date:
    start date: 11:21:19 EST Jan 28 2009
    end   date: 11:21:19 EST Jan 28 2011
  Associated Trustpoints: ra
  Storage: nvram:root-ca#8CA.cer


r35-1-1020#
```

Step 3.   Configure the DMVPN configuration on the spoke. The key difference between a hub-and-spoke and spoke-to-spoke model is the capability to establish tunnels without going to the hub router, and this is made possible by configuring the tunnel mode as multipoint on the spokes. Example 6-14 shows the tunnel configuration with the remaining configuration parameters similar to those in the hub-and-spoke model.

Example 6-14 *Configuring DMVPN Tunnel Configuration on the Spoke*

```
interface Tunnel10
 ip address 10.0.0.1 255.255.255.0
 no ip redirects
 ip mtu 1400
 ip nhrp authentication DMVPNGET
 ip nhrp map multicast dynamic
 ip nhrp map 10.0.0.4 192.168.159.242
 ip nhrp map multicast 192.168.159.242
 ip nhrp network-id 1234
 ip nhrp holdtime 90
 ip nhrp nhs 10.0.0.4
 ip nhrp registration timeout 30
 ip nhrp shortcut
 ip ospf network broadcast
 tunnel source 192.168.134.146
 tunnel mode gre multipoint
 tunnel key 1234
 tunnel protection ipsec profile ESE_DMVPN
```

Step 4. Next, configure the trust point on the other spoke, which is connected to different service provider and is enrolled with a different sub-ca (r35-2-1021 enrolling with du-subca).

Example 6-15 *Configuring Trust Point on the Spoke r35-2-1021*

```
!
crypto pki trustpoint root
 enrollment url http://172.26.185.128:80
 revocation-check none
!
crypto pki trustpoint du
 enrollment url http://192.168.188.10:12345
 serial-number
 ip-address 192.168.187.190
 revocation-check none
 rsakeypair r35-2
!
```

Step 5. Repeat the previous step to enroll r35-2-1021 with trust point du and authenticate with trust point root. Verify the certificates in spoke r35-2, as shown in Example 6-16.

Example 6-16 *Displaying the Certificates in the r35-2-1021*

```
r35-2-1021# show crypto pki certificates
Certificate
```

```
   Status: Available
   Certificate Serial Number (hex): 03
   Certificate Usage: General Purpose
   Issuer:
     cn=du-subca
   Subject:
     Name: r35-2-1021.cisco.com
     IP Address: 192.168.187.190
     Serial Number: FTX1048A6Q0
     serialNumber=FTX1048A6Q0+ipaddress=192.168.187.190+hostname=
       r35-2-1021.cisco.com
   CRL Distribution Points:
     http://172.26.185.99/du-subca.crl
   Validity Date:
     start date: 18:07:53 EST Aug 6 2009
     end   date: 17:07:53 EST Feb 2 2010
   Associated Trustpoints: du

CA Certificate
   Status: Available
   Certificate Serial Number (hex): 09
   Certificate Usage: Signature
   Issuer:
     cn=root-ca
   Subject:
     cn=du-subca
   CRL Distribution Points:
     http://172.26.185.99/root-ca.crl
   Validity Date:
     start date: 16:06:24 EST Feb 12 2009
     end   date: 16:06:24 EST Feb 12 2011
   Associated Trustpoints: du

CA Certificate
   Status: Available
   Certificate Serial Number (hex): 01
   Certificate Usage: Signature
   Issuer:
     cn=root-ca
   Subject:
     cn=root-ca
   Validity Date:
     start date: 17:34:05 EST Nov 15 2008
     end   date: 17:34:05 EST Nov 14 2013
```

```
Associated Trustpoints: root
Storage: nvram:root-ca#1CA.cer
```

Step 6.   Define the DMVPN configuration on both spoke routers, which should be configured with a tunnel as multipoint, as shown in Example 6-17.

Example 6-17   *Configuring DMVPN Tunnel on r35-2-1021*

```
!
interface Tunnel10
 ip address 20.0.0.2 255.255.255.0
 ip mtu 1400
 ip nhrp authentication DMVPNGET
 ip nhrp map 20.0.0.4 192.168.188.10
 ip nhrp map multicast 192.168.188.10
 ip nhrp network-id 2345
 ip nhrp holdtime 90
 ip nhrp nhs 20.0.0.4
 ip nhrp registration timeout 30
ip nhrp shortcut
 tunnel source 192.168.187.190
 tunnel destination 192.168.188.10
 tunnel key 1234
 tunnel protection ipsec profile ESE_DMVPN
```

DMVPN Migration from Preshared Authentication to Digital Certificates

Example 6-18 illustrates how to migrate a spoke router that has a DMVPN tunnel to the hub (using a preshared key) to a DMVPM tunnel that uses digital certificates for authentication. Table 6-4 lists the devices used for this example.

Table 6-4   *Devices for Illustrating Migration of Spoke Router*

Description	Device Name
Spoke 1	r35-1-1020
Headend	s-dmvpn-headend
Sub-ca1	ra-subca

The example shows the initial configuration for *r35-1-1020.*

Example 6-18 *Configuring DMVPN on the Spoke, Using Preshared Key*

```
crypto keyring giraffe
  pre-shared-key address 192.168.159.242 key CISCO
!
crypto isakmp policy 1
 encr 3des
 hash md5

 authentication pre-share
 group 2
crypto isakmp profile r35-profile
   keyring giraffe
   match identity host domain cisco.com
   match identity address 192.168.159.242 255.255.255.255
!
!
crypto ipsec transform-set 3DES_MD5 esp-3des esp-md5-hmac
 mode transport
!
crypto ipsec profile ESE_DMVPN
 set transform-set 3DES_MD5
 set isakmp-profile r35-profile
!
interface Tunnel10
 ip address 10.0.0.1 255.255.255.0
 no ip redirects
 ip mtu 1400
 ip nhrp authentication DMVPNGET
 ip nhrp map multicast dynamic
 ip nhrp map 10.0.0.4 192.168.159.242
 ip nhrp map multicast 192.168.159.242
 ip nhrp network-id 1234
 ip nhrp holdtime 90
 ip nhrp nhs 10.0.0.4
 ip nhrp registration timeout 30
 ip nhrp shortcut
 ip ospf network broadcast
 tunnel source 192.168.134.146
 tunnel mode gre multipoint
 tunnel key 1234
 tunnel protection ipsec profile ESE_DMVPN
```

The s-dmvpn-headend configuration has two ISAKMP policies: The first is used to match the spokes with preshared keys, and the second is used to match the digital certificates. By having both policies, the dmvpn-headend can establish tunnels with spokes having either preshared keys or digital certificates. This policy is used until all the spokes are migrated to digital certificates. When the migration finishes, the dmvpn-headend can have only the ISAKMP policy, as shown in Example 6-17.

Note The ISAKMP profile provides a template for matching identities. In Example 6-19, the ISAKMP profile matches either domain name or preshared secret.

Example 6-19 *Illustration of the Relevant DMVPN Hub Configuration*

```
crypto keyring zebra
  pre-shared-key address 192.168.187.190 key CISCO
  pre-shared-key address 192.168.187.194 key CISCO
  pre-shared-key address 192.168.134.146 key CISCO
!

crypto isakmp policy 1 ! The first policy is meant for pre-shared authentication.
 encr 3des
 hash md5
 authentication pre-share
 group 2
!
crypto isakmp policy 2 ! The second policy for rsa-signature authentication
 encr 3des
 hash md5
 group 2
!
crypto keyring giraffe
  pre-shared-key address 192.168.159.242 key CISCO
!
crypto isakmp profile dmvpn-profile
! The isakmp profile will match either pre-shared key or keyring zebra configured
  on the hub.
   keyring giraffe
   match identity host domain cisco.com
   match identity address 192.168.134.146 255.255.255.255
!
crypto ipsec transform-set 3DES_MD5 esp-3des esp-md5-hmac
 mode transport
!
crypto ipsec profile ESE_DMVPN
 set transform-set 3DES_MD5
 set isakmp-profile dmvpn-profile
```

With the preceding configuration of the hub router, the spoke can establish the DMVPN tunnel with the hub router. The **show** commands verify the following:

■ The DMVPN tunnel is up.

■ The tunnel uses preshared key for authentication.

Example 6-20   *Verifying the DMVPN Status*

```
r35-1-1020# show crypto isakmp sa
IPv4 Crypto ISAKMP SA
dst             src              state          conn-id slot status
192.168.159.242 192.168.134.146 QM_IDLE          4001    0 ACTIVE


r35-1-1020# show crypto isakmp sa detail
Codes: C - IKE configuration mode, D - Dead Peer Detection
       K - Keepalives, N - NAT-traversal
       X - IKE Extended Authentication
       psk - Preshared key, rsig - RSA signature
       renc - RSA encryption
IPv4 Crypto ISAKMP SA


C-id  Local             Remote          I-VRF     Status Encr Hash Auth DH
Lifetime Cap.

4001  192.168.134.146 192.168.159.242           ACTIVE 3des md5  psk  2  23:51:08
        Engine-id:Conn-id =  AIM-VPN/EPII-PLUS:1


IPv6 Crypto ISAKMP SA


r35-1-1020#
```

The following steps illustrate the process of migrating from the preshared key implementation to a certificate-based authentication environment.

Step 1.   As shown in previous examples, configure the spoke to obtain a certificate by enrolling with a subordinate CA server. To accomplish this task, r35-1-1020 should enroll with ra-subca.

Example 6-21   *Configuring the Trust Point on the spoke r35-1-1020*

```
crypto pki trustpoint ra
 enrollment url http://192.168.159.243:12345
 serial-number
 ip-address 192.168.134.146
 revocation-check none
```

```
rsakeypair ra
auto-enroll 80 regenerate
!
```

Step 2.   Change the ISAKMP policy on the spoke to use RSA signatures.

Example 6-22   *Configuring ISAKMP Policy on the Spoke*

```
crypto isakmp policy 1
 encr 3des
 hash md5
 group 2
```

Step 3.   Flap the tunnel so that the DMVPM tunnel tries to establish with the new
authentication method, which is digital signatures.

Example 6-23   *Flapping the Tunnel*

```
r35-1-1020(config)# interface tunnel 1
shut
no shut
```

Step 4.   Verify that the DMVPN tunnel is established and also if it has used digital
signatures for authentication.

Example 6-24   *Verifying the DMVPN Tunnel*

```
r35-1-1020# show crypto isakmp sa
IPv4 Crypto ISAKMP SA
dst              src              state         conn-id slot status


192.168.159.242 192.168.134.146 QM_IDLE          4003     0 ACTIVE r35-profile


IPv6 Crypto ISAKMP SA


r35-1-1020# show crypto isakmp sa detail
Codes: C - IKE configuration mode, D - Dead Peer Detection
       K - Keepalives, N - NAT-traversal
       X - IKE Extended Authentication
       psk - Preshared key, rsig - RSA signature
       renc - RSA encryption
IPv4 Crypto ISAKMP SA


C-id  Local            Remote          I-VRF    Status Encr Hash Auth DH Lifetime
   Cap.
```

```
4003   192.168.134.146 192.168.159.242           ACTIVE 3des md5  rsig 2  23:53:33
       Engine-id:Conn-id =  AIM-VPN/EPII-PLUS:3


IPv6 Crypto ISAKMP SA


r35-1-1020#
```

The spoke has successfully established a DMVPN tunnel to the headend router using digital certificates.

GETVPN PKI Design and Leading Practices

PKI can also be deployed in a GETVPN solution.

GETVPN Overview

GETVPN is an innovative Cisco technology based on GDOI (RFC 3547).GETVPN provides secure VPN connectivity to customers. In traditional IPsec deployments to establish a secure connectivity between peers, there needs to be a tunnel established. However, this would need a tunnel to be established at every node, which makes it harder to scale. GETVPN solves this problem because the nature of GETVPN is any-to-any connectivity without having a definitive tunnel relationship with the peer.

Note   For detailed information on GETVPN, go to http://www.cisco.com/en/US/prod/collateral/vpndevc/ps6525/ps9370/ps7180/GETVPN_DIG_version_1_0_External.pdf.

The key architecture components of GETVPN are the group member (GM) and key server (KS). All the routers who participate in GETVPN need to register with the KS. After registration, the KS pushes the keys to all the group members, which they use to communicate with each other. Because of this, the group members don't need to establish a security association before communication. This provides a significant advantage over other VPN technologies, namely the availability of keys before communication that reduces the call set up time. Figure 6-10 shows the GETVPN behavior.

GET VPN Deployment Models

To deploy GETVPN with PKI as its authentication mechanism, first ensure the PKI infrastructure is properly built (refer to Chapter 5). Example 6-25 details the steps required for this deployment. The configuration examples used use the common topology, which was shown in Figure 6-6.

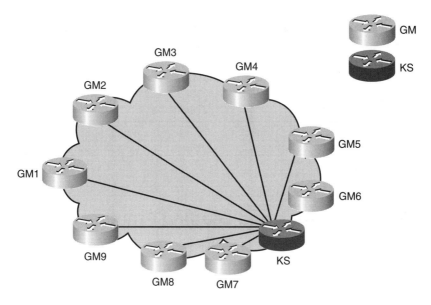

Figure 6-10   *GETVPN Overview Diagram*

During the registration of GM with the KS, the IKE is used to authenticate the session, which can be done by using preshared keys or by using digital certificates. In this deployment model, you look at a solution that provides both redundancy and scalability. To achieve that option in GETVPN, you need multiple key servers so that the group members can register with any of them.

GETVPN Deployment with Dual Key Servers and Dual Subordinate CAs

Example 6-25 and Figure 6-11 illustrate the deployment model with dual key servers, along with hierarchical PKI design.

Spoke 1 enrolls with ra-subca, and spoke 2 enrolls with du-subca. Because this design includes that hierarchical concept for both PKI and redundancy for the key servers in GETVPN, two subordinate CAs can provide redundancy for PKI, and two key servers can provide redundancy for GETVPN architecture. For redundancy you need a combination of two key servers and two subordinate CAs, which would mean four different devices. In this current solution, to reduce the number of devices used to implement this solution, consolidate both functions (key server and subordinate CA) in a single device. The following are the reasons for this consolidation:

■ Key servers are involved only in control traffic; they are not involved in data traffic. Therefore, they can be colocated with the PKI service, which is also mostly control plane traffic.

■ By colocating the key server and subordinate CA server, consolidation of services means both functions can operate on a single device. However, deploying the key server and subordinate CA server should be considered if high scalability is desired. The option suggested in this design is only one of the methods.

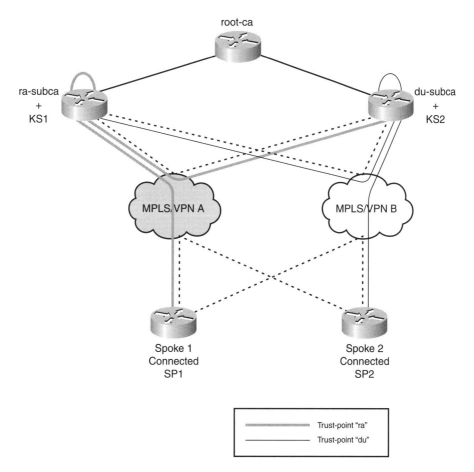

Figure 6-11   *GETVN Deployment with Dual Key Servers and Hierarchical Design*

The following key steps are required to implement the previous solution:

1. Enroll spoke 1 with ra-subca.

2. Enroll spoke 2 with du-subca.

3. Enroll key server 1 locally using trust-point ra.

4. Enroll key server 2 locally using trust-point du.

5. Enroll key server 1 with du-subca, using trust point du, which ensures that in case KS2 fails, the spokes previously enrolled with du-subca, using trust point du, will authenticate with ra-subca using trust point du.

6. Enroll key server 2 with ra-subca, using trust point ra, which ensures that in case KS1 fails, the spokes previously authenticated with KS1 using trust point ra, will use the same trust point ra to authenticate with KS2.

7. Configure the key server 1 for GETVPN functionality in co-op mode.

8. Configure the key server 2 for GETVPN functionality in co-op mode.

9. After the enrollment is done, the Key server can have two certificates:

   A. Certificate obtained after enrolling with subordinate CA server defined on the same device

   B. Certificate obtained after enrolling with subordinate CA server defined on remote device

10. Configure co-op between the key servers.

11. Configure GETVPN between the GM and the KS.

PKI Integration with GETVPN

Example 6-25 illustrates how to integrate PKI with GETVPN, as illustrated in Figure 6-10. Table 6-5 lists the devices used for this example.

Table 6-5 *PKI Integration Example Devices*

Description	Device Name
Spoke -1	r35-1-1020
Spoke -2	r35-2-1021
Sub-ca-server 1+ Key server 1	ra-subca
Sub-ca-server 2 + Key server 2	du-subca

There is some commonality between this example and the DMVPN example: primarily, the enrollment of the spoke device. In this case, r35-1-1020 is enrolled with the sub-ca server ra-subca.

Step 1. Configure r35-1-1020 to obtain the certificate.

Example 6-25 *Configuring Enrollment for Spoke r35-1-1020*

```
crypto pki trustpoint ra
 enrollment url http://192.168.159.243:12345
 serial-number
 ip-address 192.168.134.146
 revocation-check none
```

```
 rsakeypair r35-1-keys
 auto-enroll 80 regenerate
!
```

Step 2.   Configure spoke-2 (r35-2-1021) to obtain the certificate.

Example 6-26   *Configuring Enrollment for Spoke r35-2-1021*

```
crypto pki trustpoint du
 enrollment url http://192.168.188.10:12345
 serial-number
 ip-address 192.168.187.190
 revocation-check none
 rsakeypair r35-2
```

Step 3.   With the trust points configured, refer to the steps mentioned in Chapter 3 to complete the enrollment.

Step 4.   After the enrollment is complete on the spoke, configure the key server for enrollment.

As previously mentioned, in this design, you would have both key server and subordinate CA functions integrated on the same router. Therefore, the key server component will be configured on the sub-ca server ra-subca, which means that you need to configure enrollment on the same router ra-subca to enroll with the other component sub-ca server situated in the same box.

Example 6-27   *Configuring Enrollment for Key Server Located in the sub-ca*

```
crypto pki trustpoint ra
 enrollment url http://192.168.159.243:12345
 serial-number
 ip-address 192.168.159.243
 revocation-check crl
 rsakeypair ra
 auto-enroll 80 regenerate
```

Step 5.   Configure other key server, du-subca, to enroll locally to obtain a certificate.

Example 6-28   *Configuring Enrollment for Key Server Located in the sub-ca*

```
crypto pki trustpoint du
 enrollment url http://192.168.159.244:12345
 serial-number
 ip-address 192.168.159.244
 revocation-check none
 rsakeypair du
```

After completing the enrollments, both group member routers can now register with their respective key-servers: r35-1-1020 can register with ra-subca, and r35-2-1021 can register with du-subca. However, here comes the tricky part. How does the group member, say r35-2-1021 (which is enrolled with key server S-3825-du-subca), authenticate with the key server S-3845-ra-subca? This authentication would fail because each one is enrolled with different trust point. There are two solutions to solve this problem:

A. Enroll the key server with both trust points ra and du.

B. Obtain the root certificate on the group members.

Depending upon the ease-of-use for your deployment, you might pick either of the options. In the current example, follow solution number A.

Step 6.   Configure key server 1 (s-3845-ra-subca) to enroll with trust point du so that it can authenticate spokes such as r35-2-1022, which are enrolled with trust point du.

Example 6-29 *Configuring Enrollment for du on key-server1, Which Is s-3845-ra-subca*

```
crypto pki trustpoint du
 enrollment url http://192.168.188.11:12345
 serial-number
 ip-address 192.168.188.12
 revocation-check crl
 rsakeypair ra
 auto-enroll 80 regenerate
```

After this configuring, enroll with du trust point.

Step 7.   Configure enrollment for second key-server (S-3825-du-subca). This key server must enroll with trust point, ra.

Example 6-30 *Configuring Enrollment for Trust Point ra, on KEY server 2, Which is S-3825-du-subca*

```
crypto pki trustpoint ra
 enrollment url http://192.168.188.12:12345
 serial-number
 ip-address 192.168.188.11
 revocation-check crl
 rsakeypair du
 auto-enroll 80 regenerate
```

Both key servers are now enrolled with both trust points, ensuring that both key servers can authenticate any spoke.

After both the key server and spoke have obtained certificates, configure GETVPN on spoke and the key server.

Step 8.   Enable the co-op key server feature.

Example 6-31   *Configuring co-op on the Key Server ra-subca*

```
crypto gdoi group GETVPN
 identity number 552587
 server local
  rekey lifetime seconds 300
  rekey retransmit 10 number 3
  rekey authentication mypubkey rsa ra-coop.cisco.com
  rekey transport unicast
  sa ipsec 1
   profile getvpn
   match address ipv4 gm-encrypt
   replay time window-size 5
  address ipv4 192.168.159.243
  redundancy        ! this configures co-op key server option
   local priority 75 ! indicates the priority of the key server
   peer address ipv4 192.168.159.244  ! indicates the peer IP address of Co-op
key server
```

Step 9.   With the preceding configuration, the key server ra-subca is ready to be operational in co-op key server mode. Configure the other co-op key server, du-subca.

Example 6-32   *Configuring co-op on the Key Server du-subca*

```
crypto gdoi group GETVPN
 identity number 552587
 server local
  rekey lifetime seconds 300
  rekey retransmit 10 number 3
  rekey authentication mypubkey rsa ra-coop.cisco.com
  rekey transport unicast
  sa ipsec 1
   profile getvpn
   match address ipv4 sa-acl
   replay time window-size 5
  address ipv4 192.168.159.244
  redundancy        ! configures co-op key server option
   local priority 100 ! configures redundancy
   peer address ipv4 192.168.159.243 ! peer IP address
```

Step 10. Verify that key servers are now in co-op key server mode.

Example 6-33   *Verifying the co-op Key Server Status*

```
S-3825-du-subca# show crypto gdoi ks coop
Crypto Gdoi Group Name :GETVPN
        Group handle: 2147483650, Local Key Server handle: 2147483650

        Local Address: 192.168.159.244
        Local Priority: 100
        Local KS Role: Primary    , Local KS Status: Alive
        Primary Timers:
                Primary Refresh Policy Time: 20
                Remaining Time: 11
                Antireplay Sequence Number: 51168

        Peer Sessions:
        Session 1:
                Server handle: 2147483651
                Peer Address: 192.168.159.243
                Peer Priority: 75
                Peer KS Role: Secondary , Peer KS Status: Alive
                Antireplay Sequence Number: 2

          IKE status: Established
          Counters:
            Ann msgs sent: 51154
            Ann msgs sent with reply request: 2
                Ann msgs recv: 0
            Ann msgs recv with reply request: 3
            Packet sent drops: 12
            Packet Recv drops: 0
            Total bytes sent: 11118883
            Total bytes recv: 470


S-3825-du-subca#
```

Step 11. Configure the GETVPN on the spokes.

For the key server and spoke to use digital certificates for IKE authentication, the ISAKMP policy must be configured, which should use rsa-signature for authentication. Moreover, configuring crypto isakmp profile assists in matching the identities. This is more useful when there is a hybrid scenario, with some spokes using preshared keys and some using certificates.

Example 6-34   *Configuring GETVPN on the Spoke Device*

```
crypto isakmp policy 1
 encr 3des
 hash md5
 group 2
!
crypto isakmp profile r35-getvpn-profile
   match identity host domain cisco.com
!
crypto gdoi group r35-getvpn
 identity number 552587
 server address ipv4 192.168.159.243
!
crypto map r35-getvpn isakmp-profile r35-getvpn-profile
crypto map r35-getvpn 10 gdoi
 set group r35-getvpn
 match address no-encryption-acl
 qos pre-classify
!
interface FastEthernet0/0.3220
 description private mpls network
 encapsulation dot1Q 3220
 ip address 192.168.134.146 255.255.255.248
 crypto map r35-getvpn
```

Step 12.   Configure the key server (ra-subca) so that it can accept the GETVPN connections.

Example 6-35   *Configuring GETVPN on the Key Server*

```
crypto pki trustpoint ra
 enrollment url http://192.168.159.243:12345
 serial-number
 ip-address 192.168.159.243
 revocation-check crl
 rsakeypair ra
 auto-enroll 80 regenerate
!
crypto isakmp policy 2
 encr 3des
 hash md5
 group 2
```

```
!
crypto isakmp profile ra-profile
   keyring zebra
   match identity user-fqdn domain cisco.com
!
!
crypto ipsec transform-set 3DES_MD5 esp-3des esp-md5-hmac
!
crypto ipsec profile getvpn
 set transform-set 3DES_MD5
 set isakmp-profile ra-profile
!
crypto gdoi group GETVPN
 identity number 552587
 server local
  rekey lifetime seconds 300
  rekey retransmit 10 number 3
  rekey authentication mypubkey rsa ra-coop.cisco.com
  rekey transport unicast
  sa ipsec 1
   profile getvpn
   match address ipv4 gm-encrypt
   replay time window-size 5
  address ipv4 192.168.159.243
!
ip access-list extended sa-acl
 deny    esp any any
 deny    tcp any any eq bgp
 deny    tcp any eq bgp any
 deny    tcp any any eq 22
 deny    tcp any eq 22 any
 deny    tcp any any eq tacacs
 deny    tcp any eq tacacs any
 deny    udp any any eq ntp
 deny    udp any any eq 1645
 deny    udp any any eq 1646
 deny    udp any any eq 1812
 deny    udp any any eq 1813
 deny    udp any any eq syslog
 deny    ip any host 239.192.1.190
 permit udp host 192.168.159.243 any
 permit ip host 192.168.159.243 any
 permit ip any any
!
!
```

Step 13. After completing the configuration on both the key server and Group member, verify that the GETVPN session is established.

Example 6-36 *Verifying the GETVPN Session on the GM*

```
r35-1-1020# show crypto gdoi gm
Group Member Information For Group r35-getvpn:
    IPSec SA Direction       : Both
    ACL Received From KS      : gdoi_group_r35-getvpn_temp_acl
    Re-register
        Remaining time       : 2846 secs
r35-1-1020#show crypto isakmp sa
IPv4 Crypto ISAKMP SA
dst               src               state           conn-id slot status
192.168.134.146 192.168.159.244 GDOI_REKEY        5095      0 ACTIVE
192.168.134.146 192.168.159.244 GDOI_REKEY        5094      0 ACTIVE
192.168.159.243 192.168.134.146 GDOI_IDLE         7007      0 ACTIVE


IPv6 Crypto ISAKMP SA


r35-1-1020#
```

Step 14. Finally, verify the GETVPN session on the key server.

Example 6-37 *Verifying the GETVPN Session on the Key Server*

```
S-3845-ra-subca# show crypto gdoi ks
Total group members registered to this box: 1


Key Server Information For Group GETVPN:
    Group Name               : GETVPN
    Group Identity           : 552587
    Group Members            : 1
    IPSec SA Direction       : Both
    ACL Configured:
      access-list gm-encrypt
    Redundancy               : Configured
        Local Address        : 192.168.159.243
        Local Priority       : 75
        Local KS Status      : Alive
        Local KS Role        : Secondary
```

PKI Troubleshooting with VPN Examples

Although it is impossible to figure out all the issues that might occur, what follows are some ways to deal with common problems during deployment.

NTP Issues

NTP issues are one of the most common reasons for failing authentication using digital certificates. Because certificates are valid only for certain duration, they all carry an expiration date that has to be validated by the router; thus, the router requires a properly functioning clock. In situations in which a router loses connectivity to the NTP source, or when there is a misconfiguration of proper clock time on the router, it cannot validate the digital certificates, which prevent the VPN tunnels from being established. Example 6-38 includes the messages you see on the router log when it is unable to validate the certificate.

Example 6-38   *Output of the Console Message When the Certificate Is Invalid*

```
*Feb  1 06:20:00.095: CRYPTO_PKI: New CRL Not Yet Valid (router time not synched
  to CA?)
*Feb  1 06:20:00.095:     CRL published: 10:46:41 EST Apr 2 2009
*Feb  1 06:20:00.095:       Router time: 01:20:00 EST Feb 1 2002
*Feb  1 06:20:00.095: %PKI-4-CRLINSERTFAIL: Trustpoint "ra" unknown
(error 1804:E_VALIDITY : validity period start later than end)
*Feb  1 06:20:00.095: %PKI-3-CERTIFICATE_INVALID_NOT_YET_VALID:
Certificate chain validation has failed.
```

To fix this problem, make sure that the router can synchronize with the clocks. Example 6-39 illustrates the ntp configuration on the group member and how to verify the ntp association.

Example 6-39   *Configuring ntp on the Group Member*

```
r35-1-1020# show running-config | include ntp
ntp server 172.26.129.252
r35-1-1020# show ntp associations

  address         ref clock       st    when   poll reach  delay  offset    disp
*~172.26.129.252  10.81.254.131    2     992    1024   377  0.000  -1.291  18.693
 * sys.peer, # selected, + candidate, - outlyer, x falseticker, ~ configured
r35-1-1020#
```

CRL Checking

It is common for the VPN router to not reach the location of the CRL server during the authentication phase. When this connection fails, it prevents bringing up the tunnels.

Note   To understand how CRL verification is performed on routers, refer to Chapter 3.

Following are some of the useful **debug** commands that can assist in troubleshooting certificate problems:

- **debug crypto isakmp:** Turns on the **isakmp debug** process

- **debug crypto pki transactions:** Debugs messages between the client and the PKI server

- **debug crypto pki callbacks:** Turns on **debug** for pki callbacks

- **debug crypto pki validations:** Turns on **debug** for validation messages

Follow these steps to troubleshoot certificate problems:

Step 1.   Examine the r35-1 certificate.

Example 6-40   *r35-1-certificate*

```
r35-1-1020# show crypto pki cer
r35-1-1020# show crypto pki certificates
Certificate
  Status: Available
  Certificate Serial Number (hex): 06
  Certificate Usage: General Purpose
  Issuer:
    cn=ra-subca
  Subject:
    Name: r35-1-1020.cisco.com
    IP Address: 192.168.159.243
    Serial Number: FTX1048A6QA
    serialNumber=FTX1048A6QA+ipaddress=192.168.159.243+hostname=r35-1-
1020.cisco.com
  CRL Distribution Points:
    http://172.26.185.99/ra-subca.crl
  Validity Date:
    start date: 17:53:25 EST Aug 5 2009
    end   date: 16:53:25 EST Feb 1 2010
    renew date: 16:53:25 EST Dec 27 2009
  Associated Trustpoints: ra
  Storage: nvram:ra-subca#6.cer
```

Step 2.   To simulate the problem of s-dmvpn-headend losing connectivity to crl location (172.26.185.99/ra-subca.crl), shut down the interface connecting to the crl location.

Example 6-41 *Simulating the Problem*

```
s-dmvpn-headend# show ip int brief
Interface              IP-Address      OK? Method Status                  Protocol
GigabitEthernet0/1     unassigned      YES NVRAM  up                      up
GigabitEthernet0/1.240 192.168.159.242 YES NVRAM  up                      up
GigabitEthernet0/1.241 192.168.188.10  YES manual up                      up
FastEthernet0/2        unassigned      YES NVRAM  administratively down    down
GigabitEthernet0/2     10.254.1.13     YES NVRAM  up                      up
GigabitEthernet0/3     172.26.185.246  YES NVRAM  up                      up
SSLVPN-VIF0            unassigned      NO  unset  up                      up
Loopback0              192.168.197.133 YES NVRAM  up                      up
Tunnel0                10.0.0.4        YES NVRAM  up                      up
Tunnel1                20.0.0.4        YES NVRAM  up                      up
s-dmvpn-headend# conf t
Enter configuration commands, one per line.  End with CNTL/Z.
s-dmvpn-headend(config)# interface gigabitEthernet 0/3
s-dmvpn-headend(config-if)# shut
s-dmvpn-headend(config-if)# end
```

Step 3. Flap the tunnel at the spoke r35-1-1020 to initiate a fresh DMVPN tunnel setup. The current **debug** shows why the authentication is failing; in this case, the s-dmvpn-headend cannot open http connection to 172.26.185.99. See this same line in the following **debug** output.

Example 6-42 illustrates the output of a debug.

Example 6-42 *Debug Output*

```
s-dmvpn-headend#
.Aug 25 13:55:33.796: ISAKMP (0:0): received packet from 192.168.134.146 dport
  500 sport 500 Global (N) NEW SA
.Aug 25 13:55:33.796: ISAKMP: Created a peer struct for 192.168.134.146, peer
  port 500
.Aug 25 13:55:33.796: ISAKMP: New peer created peer = 0x7184E84 peer_handle =
  0x8000001F
.Aug 25 13:55:33.796: ISAKMP: Locking peer struct 0x7184E84, refcount 1 for
  crypto_isakmp_process_block
.Aug 25 13:55:33.796: ISAKMP: local port 500, remote port 500
.Aug 25 13:55:33.796: ISAKMP: Find a dup sa in the avl tree during calling
  isadb_insert sa = 85B1AA4
.Aug 25 13:55:33.796: ISAKMP:(0):Input = IKE_MESG_FROM_PEER, IKE_MM_EXCH
.Aug 25 13:55:33.796: ISAKMP:(0):Old State = IKE_READY  New State = IKE_R_MM1

.Aug 25 13:55:33.796: ISAKMP:(0): processing SA payload. message ID = 0
.Aug 25 13:55:33.796: ISAKMP:(0): processing vendor id payload
```

```
.Aug 25 13:55:33.796: ISAKMP:(0): vendor ID seems Unity/DPD but major 69 mismatch
.Aug 25 13:55:33.796: ISAKMP (0:0): vendor ID is NAT-T RFC 3947
.Aug 25 13:55:33.796: ISAKMP:(0): processing vendor id payload
.Aug 25 13:55:33.796: ISAKMP:(0): vendor ID seems Unity/DPD but major 245 mismatch
.Aug 25 13:55:33.796: ISAKMP (0:0): vendor ID is NAT-T v7
.Aug 25 13:55:33.796: ISAKMP:(0): processing vendor id payload
.Aug 25 13:55:33.796: ISAKMP:(0): vendor ID seems Unity/DPD but major 157 mismatch
.Aug 25 13:55:33.796: ISAKMP:(0): vendor ID is NAT-T v3
.Aug 25 13:55:33.796: ISAKMP:(0): processing vendor id payload
.Aug 25 13:55:33.796: ISAKMP:(0): vendor ID seems Unity/DPD but major 123 mismatch
.Aug 25 13:55:33.796: ISAKMP:(0): vendor ID is NAT-T v2
.Aug 25 13:55:33.796: ISAKMP:(0):found peer pre-shared key matching
   192.168.134.146
.Aug 25 13:55:33.796: ISAKMP:(0): local preshared key found
.Aug 25 13:55:33.796: ISAKMP : Scanning profiles for xauth ... dmvpn-profile
```

The first step during any negotiation is ISAKMP policy negotiation. You can see here that r35-1-1020 has presented the following policies to the dmvpn-headend.

```
.Aug 25 13:55:33.796: ISAKMP:(0):Checking ISAKMP transform 1 against priority 1
   policy
.Aug 25 13:55:33.796: ISAKMP:       encryption 3DES-CBC
.Aug 25 13:55:33.796: ISAKMP:       hash MD5
.Aug 25 13:55:33.796: ISAKMP:       default group 2
.Aug 25 13:55:33.796: ISAKMP:       auth RSA sig
.Aug 25 13:55:33.796: ISAKMP:       life type in seconds
.Aug 25 13:55:33.796: ISAKMP:       life duration (VPI) of  0x0 0x1 0x51 0x80
.Aug 25 13:55:33.796: ISAKMP:(0):Authentication method offered does not match
   policy!
.Aug 25 13:55:33.796: ISAKMP:(0):atts are not acceptable. Next payload is 0
.Aug 25 13:55:33.796: ISAKMP:(0):Checking ISAKMP transform 1 against priority 2
   policy
.Aug 25 13:55:33.796: ISAKMP:       encryption 3DES-CBC
.Aug 25 13:55:33.796: ISAKMP:       hash MD5
.Aug 25 13:55:33.796: ISAKMP:       default group 2
.Aug 25 13:55:33.796: ISAKMP:       auth RSA sig
.Aug 25 13:55:33.796: ISAKMP:       life type in seconds
.Aug 25 13:55:33.796: ISAKMP:       life duration (VPI) of  0x0 0x1 0x51 0x80
.Aug 25 13:55:33.796: ISAKMP:(0):atts are acceptable. Next payload is 0
```

This finishes the first basic ISAKMP policy negotiation.

```
.Aug 25 13:55:33.796: ISAKMP:(0):Acceptable atts:actual life: 0
.Aug 25 13:55:33.796: ISAKMP:(0):Acceptable atts:life: 0
.Aug 25 13:55:33.796: ISAKMP:(0):Fill atts in sa vpi_length:4
.Aug 25 13:55:33.796: ISAKMP:(0):Fill atts in sa life_in_seconds:86400
```

```
.Aug 25 13:55:33.796: ISAKMP:(0):Returning Actual lifetime: 86400
.Aug 25 13:55:33.796: ISAKMP:(0)::Started lifetime timer: 86400.


.Aug 25 13:55:33.796: ISAKMP:(0): processing vendor id payload
.Aug 25 13:55:33.796: ISAKMP:(0): vendor ID seems Unity/DPD but major 69 mismatch
.Aug 25 13:55:33.796: ISAKMP (0:0): vendor ID is NAT-T RFC 3947
.Aug 25 13:55:33.796: ISAKMP:(0): processing vendor id payload
.Aug 25 13:55:33.796: ISAKMP:(0): vendor ID seems Unity/DPD but major 245 mismatch
.Aug 25 13:55:33.796: ISAKMP (0:0): vendor ID is NAT-T v7
.Aug 25 13:55:33.796: ISAKMP:(0): processing vendor id payload
.Aug 25 13:55:33.796: ISAKMP:(0): vendor ID seems Unity/DPD but major 157 mismatch
.Aug 25 13:55:33.796: ISAKMP:(0): vendor ID is NAT-T v3
.Aug 25 13:55:33.796: ISAKMP:(0): processing vendor id payload
.Aug 25 13:55:33.796: ISAKMP:(0): vendor ID seems Unity/DPD but major 123 mismatch
.Aug 25 13:55:33.796: ISAKMP:(0): vendor ID is NAT-T v2
.Aug 25 13:55:33.796: ISAKMP:(0):Input = IKE_MESG_INTERNAL, IKE_PROCESS_MAIN_MODE
.Aug 25 13:55:33.796: ISAKMP:(0):Old State = IKE_R_MM1  New State = IKE_R_MM1


.Aug 25 13:55:33.796: ISAKMP:(0): constructed NAT-T vendor-rfc3947 ID
.Aug 25 13:55:33.796: ISAKMP:(0): sending packet to 192.168.134.146 my_port 500
  peer_port 500 (R) MM_SA_SETUP
.Aug 25 13:55:33.796: ISAKMP:(0):Sending an IKE IPv4 Packet.
.Aug 25 13:55:33.796: ISAKMP:(0):Input = IKE_MESG_INTERNAL, IKE_PROCESS_COMPLETE
.Aug 25 13:55:33.796: ISAKMP:(0):Old State = IKE_R_MM1  New State = IKE_R_MM2
```

The IKE second step negotiation also succeeds. In the next phase, peers send certificate requests.

```
.Aug 25 13:55:33.800: ISAKMP (0:0): received packet from 192.168.134.146 dport
  500 sport 500 Global (R) MM_SA_SETUP
.Aug 25 13:55:33.800: ISAKMP:(0):Input = IKE_MESG_FROM_PEER, IKE_MM_EXCH
.Aug 25 13:55:33.800: ISAKMP:(0):Old State = IKE_R_MM2  New State = IKE_R_MM3


.Aug 25 13:55:33.800: ISAKMP:(0): processing KE payload. message ID = 0
.Aug 25 13:55:33.804: ISAKMP:(0): processing NONCE payload. message ID = 0
.Aug 25 13:55:33.808: ISAKMP:(13478): processing CERT_REQ payload. message ID = 0
```

The certificate request payload indicates which certificates are requested by sender. You can see from this certificate request that the peer wants certificates issued by cn=ra-subca.

```
.Aug 25 13:55:33.808: ISAKMP:(13478): peer wants cert issued by cn=ra-subca
.Aug 25 13:55:33.808: ISAKMP:(13478): processing vendor id payload
.Aug 25 13:55:33.808: ISAKMP:(13478): vendor ID is DPD
.Aug 25 13:55:33.808: ISAKMP:(13478): processing vendor id payload
.Aug 25 13:55:33.808: ISAKMP:(13478): speaking to another IOS box!
.Aug 25 13:55:33.808: ISAKMP:(13478): processing vendor id payload
.Aug 25 13:55:33.808: ISAKMP:(13478): vendor ID seems Unity/DPD but major 2
  mismatch
```

```
.Aug 25 13:55:33.808: ISAKMP:(13478): vendor ID is XAUTH
.Aug 25 13:55:33.808: ISAKMP:received payload type 20
.Aug 25 13:55:33.808: ISAKMP (13478): His hash no match - this node outside NAT
.Aug 25 13:55:33.808: ISAKMP:received payload type 20
.Aug 25 13:55:33.808: ISAKMP (13478): No NAT Found for self or peer
.Aug 25 13:55:33.808: ISAKMP:(13478):Input = IKE_MESG_INTERNAL,
  IKE_PROCESS_MAIN_MODE
.Aug 25 13:55:33.808: ISAKMP:(13478):Old State = IKE_R_MM3  New State = IKE_R_MM3
```

The DMVPN headend is now sending the CERT_REQ to the remote peer r35-1-1020 by asking it to present the certificate issued by cn=ra-subca.

```
.Aug 25 13:55:33.808: ISAKMP (0:13478): constructing CERT_REQ for issuer cn=
  ra-subca
.Aug 25 13:55:33.808: ISAKMP:(13478): sending packet to 192.168.134.146 my_port
  500 peer_port 500 (R) MM_KEY_EXCH
.Aug 25 13:55:33.808: ISAKMP:(13478):Sending an IKE IPv4 Packet.
.Aug 25 13:55:33.808: ISAKMP:(13478):Input = IKE_MESG_INTERNAL,
  IKE_PROCESS_COMPLETE
.Aug 25 13:55:33.808: ISAKMP:(13478):Old State = IKE_R_MM3  New State = IKE_R_MM4
```

In this phase, the peers would send their identities, this example is between r35-1-1020, and s-dmvpn-headend. You can see from the following debugs the headend is checking the validity of the certificate presented by the remote peer.

```
.Aug 25 13:55:33.840: ISAKMP (0:13478): received packet from 192.168.134.146
  dport 500 sport 500 Global (R) MM_KEY_EXCH
.Aug 25 13:55:33.840: ISAKMP:(13478):Input = IKE_MESG_FROM_PEER, IKE_MM_EXCH
.Aug 25 13:55:33.840: ISAKMP:(13478):Old State = IKE_R_MM4  New State =
  IKE_R_MM5

.Aug 25 13:55:33.840: ISAKMP:(13478): processing ID payload. message ID = 0
.Aug 25 13:55:33.840: ISAKMP (0:13478): ID payload
     next-payload : 6
     type         : 2
     FQDN name    : r35-1-1020.cisco.com
     protocol     : 17
     port         : 500
     length       : 28
.Aug 25 13:55:33.840: ISAKMP:(0):: peer matches dmvpn-profile profile
```

The remote peer has the domain name cisco.com, which matches the dmvpn-profile.

```
.Aug 25 13:55:33.840: ISAKMP:(13478): processing CERT payload. message ID = 0
```

Now it is trying to verify the signature of the certificate.

```
.Aug 25 13:55:33.840: ISAKMP:(13478): processing a CT_X509_SIGNATURE cert
.Aug 25 13:55:33.840: CRYPTO_PKI: Adding peer certificate
.Aug 25 13:55:33.840: CRYPTO_PKI: Added x509 peer certificate - (549) bytes
```

```
.Aug 25 13:55:33.840: ISAKMP:(13478): peer's pubkey isn't cached
.Aug 25 13:55:33.840: CRYPTO_PKI: crypto_pki_get_cert_record_by_subject()
.Aug 25 13:55:33.840: CRYPTO_PKI: Found a subject match
.Aug 25 13:55:33.840: CRYPTO_PKI: validation path has 1 certs

.Aug 25 13:55:33.840: CRYPTO_PKI: Check for identical certs
.Aug 25 13:55:33.840: CRYPTO_PKI(Cert Lookup) issuer="cn=ra-subca" serial
  number= 06

.Aug 25 13:55:33.840: CRYPTO_PKI: looking for cert in handle=7F4176C, digest=
  52 68 4A 2F E8 79 BC 11 20 26 2E 29 0B 73 05 DE

.Aug 25 13:55:33.840: CRYPTO_PKI: Cert record not found, returning E_NOT_FOUND
.Aug 25 13:55:33.840: CRYPTO_PKI: Create a list of suitable trustpoints
.Aug 25 13:55:33.840: CRYPTO_PKI: crypto_pki_get_cert_record_by_issuer()
```

The dmvpn-headend has found the issuer match, which is ra. Now the headend will try to validate the certificate using the trust point.

```
.Aug 25 13:55:33.840: CRYPTO_PKI: Found a issuer match
.Aug 25 13:55:33.840: CRYPTO_PKI: Suitable trustpoints are: ra,
.Aug 25 13:55:33.840: CRYPTO_PKI: Attempting to validate certificate using ra
.Aug 25 13:55:33.840: CRYPTO_PKI: Using ra to validate certificate
.Aug 25 13:55:33.840: CRYPTO_PKI(make trusted certs chain)
.Aug 25 13:55:33.840: P11:C_CreateObject:
.Aug 25 13:55:33.844:   CKA_CLASS: PUBLIC KEY
.Aug 25 13:55:33.844:   CKA_KEY_TYPE: RSA
.Aug 25 13:55:33.844:   CKA_MODULUS:
      FA 17 48 60 C5 19 1A 8F 89 54 2D 71 1B 1C 37 AB
      86 1B E9 D8 D5 EC 43 4F 36 35 F0 05 1A 3F CD E5
      69 2E B2 95 B1 DE 93 53 FD 9F 3C 0A 35 9C AC 3B
      D6 1A F3 E3 9B 84 6F 52 10 70 A1 5D 42 5D E1 8D
      83 A2 FC 16 9F 1C C5 12 1A AF 58 8E E1 54 FF 2F
      91 69 91 15 9C 7B 12 8A 22 5A 55 BF 95 3C 60 AA
      B9 E3 76 0E 3F 37 D3 93 7A 3D 04 A6 61 31 6D 07
      CB DD 33 7E 64 07 24 1E B5 5B 5A 5F 30 EC E1 FB

.Aug 25 13:55:33.844:   CKA_PUBLIC_EXPONENT:  01 00 01

.Aug 25 13:55:33.844:   CKA_VERIFY_RECOVER:  01

.Aug 25 13:55:33.844: P11:C_CreateObject: 140575960
.Aug 25 13:55:33.844: P11:C_GetMechanismInfo slot 1 type 3 (invalid mechanism)
.Aug 25 13:55:33.844: P11:C_GetMechanismInfo slot 1 type 1
.Aug 25 13:55:33.844: P11:C_VerifyRecoverInit - 341
.Aug 25 13:55:33.844: P11:C_VerifyRecover - 341
```

```
.Aug 25 13:55:33.844: P11:found pubkey in cache using index = 341
.Aug 25 13:55:33.844: P11:public key found is :
     30 81 9F 30 0D 06 09 2A 86 48 86 F7 0D 01 01 01
     05 00 03 81 8D 00 30 81 89 02 81 81 00 FA 17 48
     60 C5 19 1A 8F 89 54 2D 71 1B 1C 37 AB 86 1B E9
     D8 D5 EC 43 4F 36 35 F0 05 1A 3F CD E5 69 2E B2
     95 B1 DE 93 53 FD 9F 3C 0A 35 9C AC 3B D6 1A F3
     E3 9B 84 6F 52 10 70 A1 5D 42 5D E1 8D 83 A2 FC
     16 9F 1C C5 12 1A AF 58 8E E1 54 FF 2F 91 69 91
     15 9C 7B 12 8A 22 5A 55 BF 95 3C 60 AA B9 E3 76
     0E 3F 37 D3 93 7A 3D 04 A6 61 31 6D 07 CB DD 33
     7E 64 07 24 1E B5 5B 5A 5F 30 EC E1 FB 02 03 01
     00 01


.Aug 25 13:55:33.844: P11:CEAL:CRYPTO_NO_ERR
.Aug 25 13:55:33.844: P11:C_DestroyObject 8495908:155
.Aug 25 13:55:33.844: CRYPTO_PKI: Certificate is verified
```

The certificate is verified. The next step is to verify the revocation status of the certificate.

```
.Aug 25 13:55:33.844: CRYPTO_PKI: Checking certificate revocation
.Aug 25 13:55:33.844: CRYPTO_PKI: Starting CRL revocation
```

The dmvpn-headend is trying to retrieve the crl using the http protocol.

```
.Aug 25 13:55:33.848: CRYPTO_PKI: locked trustpoint ra, refcount is 1
.Aug 25 13:55:33.848: CRYPTO_PKI: can not resolve server name/IP address
.Aug 25 13:55:33.848: CRYPTO_PKI: Using unresolved IP Address 172.26.185.99
.Aug 25 13:55:33.848: CRYPTO_PKI: socket connect error.
.Aug 25 13:55:33.848: CRYPTO_PKI: status = 0: failed to open http connection
.Aug 25 13:55:33.848: CRYPTO_PKI: unlocked trustpoint ra, refcount is 0
.Aug 25 13:55:33.848: CRYPTO_PKI: Send HTTP header:
GET /ra-subca.crl HTTP/1.0
Host: 172.26.185.99
```

The http connection failed because the http server at 172.26.185.99 is not responding.

```
.Aug 25 13:55:33.848: CRYPTO_PKI: status = 65535: failed to send out the pki
  message
.Aug 25 13:55:33.848: CRYPTO_PKI: transaction Unknown completed
.Aug 25 13:55:33.848: CRYPTO_PKI: Poll CRL callback
.Aug 25 13:55:33.848: CRYPTO_PKI: status = 106: Blocking chain verification
  callback received status
.Aug 25 13:55:33.848: CRYPTO_PKI: Certificate validation failed
.Aug 25 13:55:33.848: %CRYPTO-5-IKMP_INVAL_CERT: Certificate received from
  192.168.134.146 is bad: CA request failed!
```

Because the crl revocation check has failed, the dmvpn-headend has rejected the certificate it has received from the spoke r35-1-1020.

Summary

In this chapter, you learned how to use PKI as a service for the two most popular VPN technologies: DMVPN and GETVPN. These two technologies need a way to authenticate their peers during the key negotiation phase, which can be done by either using pre-shared keys or by using digital certificates. Using digital certificates, which can be enabled using PKI as service, can help the scalability of large-scale deployment and management.

DMVPN has two popular deployment models: hub-and-spoke and spoke-to-spoke. Although deploying the hub-and-spoke model, the spokes need to enroll with any of their regional subordinate CAs, whereas the Hub enrolls with both the subordinate CAs. For the spoke-to-spoke model to validate a spoke enrolled with a different sub-ca, the receiver of the tunnel needs to obtain the root CA certificate so that it can go up the chain to validate the spoke.

GETVPN is another Cisco innovative technology, which does not use a central hub device for establishing tunnels but needs a key server to distribute the group keys to its members. All the group members need to register with the key server, and during the registration process they need to authenticate each other, which can be done using pre-shared keys or digital certificates using PKI service. To obtain the certificates, the group members and key servers must enroll with the same subordinate CA so that the key server can issue the keys to the GMs. The key servers take a dual role of being the key server and also being the subordinate CA server.

Chapter 7

Integration in Remote Access VPN Solutions

This chapter covers the following topics:

- How Remote Access Solutions Use PKI as a Service
- Cisco ASA IPsec VPN Remote Access
- Cisco VPN Client Using Digital Certificates
- Cisco ASA SSL VPN Remote Access

Remote access to central office resources is highly critical for remote workers' productivity, and there is an increasing demand to provide the remote workers with the same user experience as if they were located at the main office. There is also a major shift in corporate deployment of centralized resources and services. All these factors drive the need to provide highly secure, available remote access for telecommuters, "road warriors," and mobile workers.

The Cisco remote access solution provides highly secure and available remote access for remote workers. The Cisco Easy VPN and SSL VPN address the remote access solution, but the strength of these solutions is dependent on having a strong authentication mechanism between the clients and the servers. Digital certificates provide a highly reliable service for remote access VPN solutions. This chapter discusses how these remote access solutions use PKI as a service for authentication.

Cisco IPsec VPN Remote Access

The Cisco IPsec VPN remote access solution leverages IKE protocol for key negotiation between the clients and the gateways. As previously discussed, there are two methods in which both client and gateway authenticate with each other before deriving the keys: preshared keys or digital certificates. For remote access, you cannot have a preshared key for every user because the headend does not know the identity of the user (the IP address in most situations). Therefore, the remote users use a group-based preshared key for authentication.

However, the disadvantage of using group-based authentication is that whenever an individual needs to be removed from the group, the key can't be changed because there are other members in the group who are still using the same key. Therefore, having PKI would solve the problem because each individual has a certificate, and when revoked that particular individual is removed from the group without affecting the other members. To make remote access solution more secure, gateways must enable x-auth. This feature would also provide additional authentication of the users in addition to PKI. Therefore, to enhance better authentication, the remote users should use digital certificates and x-auth for per-user authentication. The discussion on using PKI as a service for remote access solutions begins with an overview of Easy VPN.

Easy VPN Overview

The Easy VPN is a Cisco Solution to provide VPN access for remote devices. The two components of this solution are Easy VPN Server and Easy VPN client.

The Easy VPN Server feature enables Cisco IOS routers and Cisco Adaptive Security Appliances (ASA) to act as headend devices in site-to-site or remote-access VPNs. The feature pushes security policies defined at the central site to the remote device so that it has up-to-date policies in place before a connection is established. It can also terminate VPN tunnels initiated by remote workers running the Cisco VPN Client software on PCs. This flexibility enables mobile and remote workers to access critical data and applications on their corporate intranet.

Deploying IPsec VPN Remote Access on the ASA

Deployment of a remote access solution using ASA as a VPN gateway for remote clients is described next. Figure 7-1 illustrates the topology used for the example.

Following are some of the design considerations for the topology in Figure 7-1:

■ The subordinate CAs should be reachable by a WAN, which is the Internet in the current example. This enables the remote clients to obtain their certificates.

■ The subordinate CAs and ASAs can be reachable via an internal network or through the Internet. This design assumes that they would reach through the Internet.

■ The ASAs are used as VPN gateways and are configured in active/standby mode.

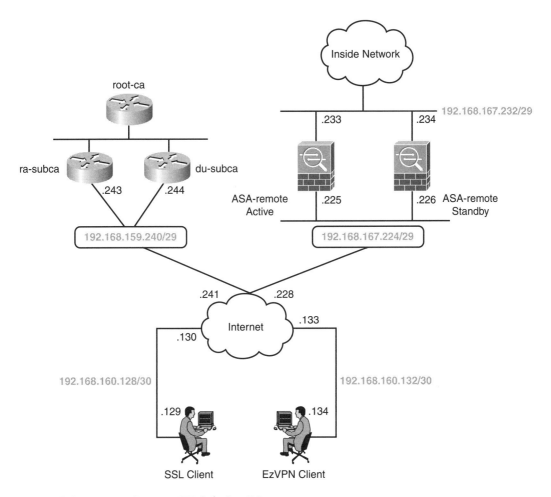

Figure 7-1 *Remote Access VPN Solution Diagram*

Certificate Chaining

As explained in Chapter 5, "Generic PKI Designs," a layer of separation is between the actual clients, the root CA, and the layer of separation (sub-ca). Therefore, root CA signs the certificate of subordinate CA (ra-subca in this example), and the sub-ca signs the certificates of the actual users (ASA-remote, SSL Client, and Cisco VPN client). Figure 7-2 illustrates this chain.

The end clients such as Cisco VPN client, SSL client, and ASA VPN gateway use certificates for authentication. As mentioned in the previous chapter, we also use hierarchical design for remote access integration. However, there is a key difference between the behavior of ASA and the IOS routers. The hierarchical design does not enforce that all the devices should have both the root CA and subordinate CA certificates. If the clients require a root CA certificate, the hierarchical design provides it to them, but it is not mandatory. However, ASA requires certificate chaining to be operational. Hence, we need to obtain a root CA certificate in addition to the subordinate CA certificate.

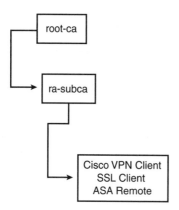

Figure 7-2 *Certificate Chaining*

The root CA certificate can be obtained through several methods such as SCEP, manual enrollment, and TFTP. Obtaining the root CA certificate using SECP is easiest, but it means that the root CA certificate must be online and reachable, and that can raise security concerns. Therefore, obtaining the root CA certificate using manual enrollment is the best method to alleviate security concerns. Example 7-1 illustrates how to obtain root CA certificate:

To obtain a root CA certificate using manual enrollment, follow these steps:

Step 1. Configure the trust point on the ASA, and specify that the enrollment method is by a terminal:

```
ASA-remote1(config)# crypto ca trustpoint root
ASA-remote1(config-ca-trustpoint)# enrollment terminal
```

Step 2. Obtain the root CA certificate from the root CA server by cutting it from the root CA server and pasting it to the ASA. The root CA certificate is then displayed on the server:

```
S-3825-root-ca(config)# crypto pki export root-ca pem terminal
% The specified trustpoint is not enrolled (root-ca).
% Only export the CA certificate in PEM format.
% CA certificate:
-----BEGIN CERTIFICATE-----
MIIB/TCCAWagAwIBAgIBATANBgkqhkiG9w0BAQQFADASMRAwDgYDVQQDEwdyb290
LWNhMB4XDTA4MTExNTIyMzQwNVoXDTEzMTExNDIyMzQwNVowEjEQMA4GA1UEAxMH
```

```
cm9vdC1jYTCBnzANBgkqhkiG9w0BAQEFAAOBjQAwgYkCgYEA7WzVwWQR/F4MF4CK
5Fb2KhO5vcdDClbEcx9sLHjVqFe4wafqJo9rUILWIbjdbNBxGiAJjMYO8ymils32
HVtWlloLDh8bd5QXoNP1B0CcJbpT0yrCCKZaOp6zJBWkdezp1ZXj0iRJO7PWZ69U
bcEQlPcDkLWZDNSPNIpeVYieZZ0CAwEAAaNjMGEwDwYDVR0TAQH/BAUwAwEB/zAO
BgNVHQ8BAf8EBAMCAYYwHwYDVR0jBBgwFoAUDkMCSiWkFtEXEC4a0UrEnEV/QdAw
HQYDVR0OBBYEFA5DAkolpBbRFxAuGtFKxJxFf0HQMA0GCSqGSIb3DQEBBAUAA4GB
AN8UfdApFWFGmlOuU2PkAsA8RMUVhKrfmWvkFFofkpxgwmbNqmpz1JuPujTLfexQ
Q7ukqebalUkxo0oVW5RpiEbbdllNqBsGvcOupXFJ8BrY4E2QWlVPKJvdDVOb+30I
yzace7FKYm6uy7V36gzM+5vtHDZLQS2IJd+R1Uhg5DJ0
-----END CERTIFICATE-----
Paste this output on ASA.
ASA-remote1(config)# crypto ca authenticate root
Enter the base 64 encoded CA certificate.
End with the word "quit" on a line by itself
-----BEGIN CERTIFICATE-----
MIIB/TCCAWagAwIBAgIBATANBgkqhkiG9w0BAQQFADASMRAwDgYDVQQDEwdyb290
LWNhMB4XDTA4MTExNTIyMzQwNVoXDTEzMTExNDIyMzQwNVowEjEQMA4GA1UEAxMH
cm9vdC1jYTCBnzANBgkqhkiG9w0BAQEFAAOBjQAwgYkCgYEA7WzVwWQR/F4MF4CK
5Fb2KhO5vcdDClbEcx9sLHjVqFe4wafqJo9rUILWIbjdbNBxGiAJjMYO8ymils32
HVtWlloLDh8bd5QXoNP1B0CcJbpT0yrCCKZaOp6zJBWkdezp1ZXj0iRJO7PWZ69U
bcEQlPcDkLWZDNSPNIpeVYieZZ0CAwEAAaNjMGEwDwYDVR0TAQH/BAUwAwEB/zAO
BgNVHQ8BAf8EBAMCAYYwHwYDVR0jBBgwFoAUDkMCSiWkFtEXEC4a0UrEnEV/QdAw
HQYDVR0OBBYEFA5DAkolpBbRFxAuGtFKxJxFf0HQMA0GCSqGSIb3DQEBBAUAA4GB
AN8UfdApFWFGmlOuU2PkAsA8RMUVhKrfmWvkFFofkpxgwmbNqmpz1JuPujTLfexQ
Q7ukqebalUkxo0oVW5RpiEbbdllNqBsGvcOupXFJ8BrY4E2QWlVPKJvdDVOb+30I
yzace7FKYm6uy7V36gzM+5vtHDZLQS2IJd+R1Uhg5DJ0
-----END CERTIFICATE-----


quit

INFO: Certificate has the following attributes:
Fingerprint:     abd85dc7 c152ae90 4949a459 b91f0a39
Do you accept this certificate? [yes/no]: yes

Trustpoint CA certificate accepted.

% Certificate successfully imported
ASA-remote1(config)#
```

Table 7-1 illustrates the difference in the configuration for IOS devices and the ASA.

Table 7-1 *Differences in Enrollment Between IOS Devices and ASA*

s-dmvpn-headend	ASA-remote1
crypto pki trustpoint ra	crypto ca trustpoint ra
enrollment url http://192.168.159.243:12345	enrollment retry count 10
serial-number none	enrollment url http://192.168.159.243:12345
fqdn s-dmvpn-headend.cisco.com	fqdn ASA-remote1.cisco.com
ip-address none	subject-name OU=Solutions,O=Cisco sys-tems,CN=r35-5,L=Morrisville,ST=NC,C=US
password	crl configure
subject-name OU=Solutions,O=Cisco systems,CN=ASA-remote1.cisco.com, L=Morrisvill	
	!
e,ST=NC,C=US	crypto ca trustpoint root
revocation-check none	enrollment terminal
auto-enroll!	crl configure

Figure 7-3 shows how the certificate hierarchy displays on a Windows machine.

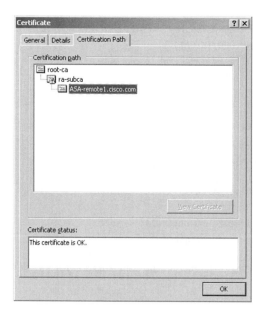

Figure 7-3 *Certificate Hierarchy*

As illustrated in Figure 7-3, the root CA signs the subordinate CA, and the subordinate CA signs the VPN gateway.

The ASA enrolls with the sub-CAs and obtains the root CA certificate.

After the enrollment, the remote clients establish the VPN session using the certificates obtained earlier as the source of Identity.

As a reminder, you need three key steps enrollment:

1. Verify NTP is present, which ensures the device has the right clock.

2. Generate rsa keys.

3. Configure, authenticate, and enroll with the trustpoint.

Enrollment can be accomplished using different methods, such as SCEP and manual enrollment. Example 7-1 illustrates how to perform this enrollment using SCEP; however, if you do want to use manual enrollment, refer to Chapter 3, "PKI Processes and Procedures."

The following configurations show these enrollment steps on ASA.

Example 7-1 *Configuration of Enrollment on the ASA*

```
crypto ca trustpoint ra
 enrollment url http://192.168.159.243:12345
 fqdn ASA-remote1.cisco.com
 subject-name C=US, ST=NC, L=Morrisville, O=Cisco Systems, OU=solutions,
  CN=ASA-remote1.cisco.com
 id-usage ssl-ipsec code-signer
 crl configure


ASA-remote1(config)# crypto ca authenticate ra

INFO: Certificate has the following attributes:
Fingerprint:     ece8be9e 9c5179a5 abd983a2 6e5f5de8
Do you accept this certificate? [yes/no]: yes

Trustpoint 'ra' is a subordinate CA and holds a non self-signed certificate.

Trustpoint CA certificate accepted.
ASA-remote1(config)# crypto ca enroll ra
%
% Start certificate enrollment ..
% Create a challenge password. You will need to verbally provide this
   password to the CA Administrator in order to revoke your certificate.
   For security reasons your password will not be saved in the configuration.
```

```
    Please make a note of it.
Password: *****
Re-enter password: *****


% The fully-qualified domain name in the certificate will be: ASA-remote1

% Include the device serial number in the subject name? [yes/no]: yes

% The serial number in the certificate will be: JMX1311L1C8

Request certificate from CA? [yes/no]: yes
% Certificate request sent to Certificate Authority
ASA-remote1(config)# The certificate has been granted by CA!

ASA-remote1(config)# end
ASA-remote1#
```

Because the scope of this book is primarily on PKI, the relevant configuration of the EzVPN server is shown in Example 7-2 only as a description of how EzVPN uses PKI as service for authentication.

Example 7-2   *Configuration of the ASA*

```
crypto isakmp enable outside
crypto isakmp policy 1
 authentication rsa-sig
 encryption 3des
 hash sha
 group 2
 lifetime 43200
crypto isakmp disconnect-notify
!
crypto ca certificate map REMOTE_VPN_MAP 10
 issuer-name co ra-subca


tunnel-group testgroup type remote-access
tunnel-group testgroup general-attributes
 address-pool testpool
tunnel-group testgroup ipsec-attributes
 trust-point ra
tunnel-group-map enable rules
tunnel-group-map REMOTE_VPN_MAP 10 testgroup
```

```
!
crypto ipsec transform-set 3DES_SHA esp-3des esp-sha-hmac
crypto ipsec security-association lifetime seconds 28800
crypto ipsec security-association lifetime kilobytes 4608000
crypto dynamic-map dyn1 1 set transform-set 3DES_SHA
crypto dynamic-map dyn1 1 set reverse-route
crypto map VPN_REMOTE_MAP 1 ipsec-isakmp dynamic dyn1
crypto map VPN_REMOTE_MAP 10 match address 101
crypto map VPN_REMOTE_MAP interface outside
```

Note Descriptions of the various components of remote access configuration, including tunnel groups, are beyond the scope of this book. For more information on tunnel groups, visit http://www.cisco.com/en/US/docs/security/asa/asa80/configuration/guide/vpnrmote.html.

Most of the previous configuration is straightforward. The creation of a certificate map, which is one of the keys in a remote access solution, is where a VPN gateway server maps the incoming user to the right tunnel interface. The previous configuration created a certificate map called REMOTE_VPN_MAP, which looks at the issuer id of the certificate (ra-subca in the example) and maps it to the tunnel group **testgroup**. The second consideration is a configuration of the trustpoint with the tunnel group, which can provide with ASA the right trustpoint to be used for authentication. With this configuration, the ASA is in a position to accept the remote access sessions initiated by the remote clients.

Note To obtain more information about certificate maps, go to

http://www.cisco.com/en/US/docs/security/asa/asa80/configuration/guide/cert_cfg.html#wp1046987.

Cisco VPN Client Using Digital Certificates

Cisco VPN client is software that enables customers to establish secure, end-to-end encrypted tunnels to any Cisco Easy VPN server. Following are the main benefits of the Cisco VPN client:

- Support for multiple operating systems

- Intelligent peer availability detection (DPD)

- Simple certificate enrollment protocol (SCEP)

The following steps are required to configure the Cisco VPN client to enroll with the subordinate CA and obtain its certificate:

Step 1.   Configure the VP client for enrolling a certificate, as shown in Figure 7-4.

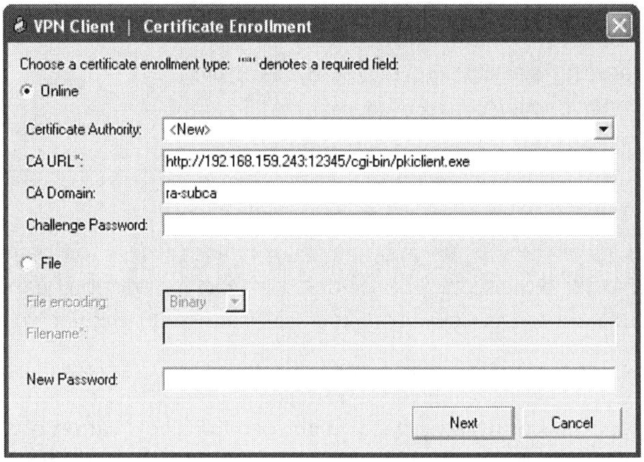

Figure 7-4   *Configuring VPN Enrollment*

Step 2.   Enter the remote client details, as shown in Figure 7-5.

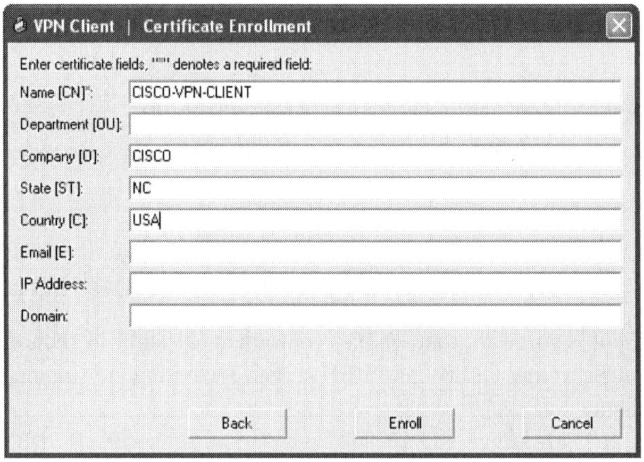

Figure 7-5   *Configuring Certificate Fields*

Step 3.   Select enroll; the Cisco-VPN client enrolls with ra-subca. Figure 7-6 shows a successful enrollment with ra-subca.

The preceding steps enable the remote VPN client to obtain its certificate and also the subordinate CA certificate. However, to validate the certificate of the subordinate CA, it

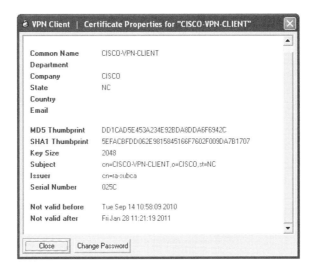

Figure 7-6   *Cisco VPN Client Certificate Details*

also needs the root CA certificate. To obtain the root CA certificate for validation purposes, follow these steps:

Step 1.   Export the root CA certificate to a place in which the clients can access them. In Example 7-3, the root CA exports the certificate using the PEM format.

Example 7-3   *Exporting the root-ca Certificate to an ftp Server*

```
S-3825-root-ca(config)# crypto pki export root-ca pem url
  ftp://172.26.129.252 3des cisco
% The specified trustpoint is not enrolled (root-ca).
% Only export the CA certificate in PEM format.
% Exporting CA certificate...
Address or name of remote host [172.26.129.252]?
Destination filename [root-ca.ca]?
Writing file to ftp://172.26.129.252/root-ca.ca
Writing root-ca.ca !
S-3825-root-ca(config)#
```

Step 2.   Import the root CA certificate, as shown in Figure 7-7.

Step 3.   Specify the location of the certificate, as shown in Figure 7-8.

Step 4.   Import the certificate, as shown in Figure 7-9.

Step 5.   Validate the ra-subca certificate using the root certificate present, as shown in Figure 7-10.

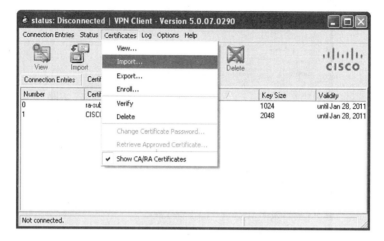

Figure 7-7 *Importing the root-ca certificate*

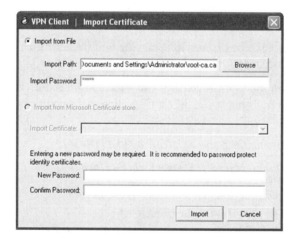

Figure 7-8 *Specify the Location of Certificate*

Figure 7-9 *Import the Certificate*

Both the remote VPN client and the VPN gateway have now obtained their certificates. Next, use these certificates as a means of digital authentication to establish the EzVPN session.

Figure 7-10 *Validate the Certificate*

Example 7-4 shows the right output when a remote client initiates a session to the VPN gateway.

Example 7-4 *Debug Output on the ASA Firewall*

```
%ASA-6-302015: Built inbound UDP connection 5127 for
outside:192.168.160.134/3362 (192.168.160.134/3362) to
identity:192.168.167.225/500 (192.168.167.225/500)
%ASA-7-713236: IP = 192.168.160.134, IKE_DECODE RECEIVED Message
(msgid=0) with payloads : HDR + SA (1) + VENDOR (13) +
VENDOR (13) + VENDOR (13) + VENDOR (13) + VENDOR (13) + NONE (0) total length :
  1144
%ASA-7-715047: IP = 192.168.160.134, processing SA payload
Rcv'd: Group 5  Cfg'd: Group 2
%ASA-7-713906: IP = 192.168.160.134, Oakley proposal is acceptable
%ASA-7-715047: IP = 192.168.160.134, processing VID payload
%ASA-7-715049: IP = 192.168.160.134, Received xauth V6 VID
%ASA-7-715047: IP = 192.168.160.134, processing VID payload
%ASA-7-715049: IP = 192.168.160.134, Received DPD VID
%ASA-7-715047: IP = 192.168.160.134, processing VID payload
%ASA-7-715049: IP = 192.168.160.134, Received Fragmentation VID
%ASA-7-715064: IP = 192.168.160.134, IKE Peer included IKE
fragmentation capability flags:  Main Mode:       True   Aggressive
Mode:   False
```

This is a major difference between the preshared key method and digital certificate method. The Aggressive mode is used in the preshared method, whereas the Main mode is used in digital certificates:

```
%ASA-7-715047: IP = 192.168.160.134, processing VID payload
%ASA-7-715049: IP = 192.168.160.134, Received NAT-Traversal ver 02 VID
%ASA-7-715047: IP = 192.168.160.134, processing VID payload
%ASA-7-715049: IP = 192.168.160.134, Received Cisco Unity client VID
%ASA-7-715047: IP = 192.168.160.134, processing IKE SA payload
%ASA-7-715028: IP = 192.168.160.134, IKE SA Proposal # 1, Transform
  # 21 acceptable  Matches global IKE entry # 1
```

The IKE SA proposal is acceptable to both client and server. Phase I is over, and Phase II begins. In this phase, the Diffie Hellman key exchange takes place:

```
%ASA-7-715046: IP = 192.168.160.134, constructing ISAKMP SA payload
%ASA-7-715046: IP = 192.168.160.134, constructing NAT-Traversal VID ver 02 payload
%ASA-7-715046: IP = 192.168.160.134, constructing Fragmentation VID
  + extended capabilities payload
%ASA-7-713236: IP = 192.168.160.134, IKE_DECODE SENDING Message
  (msgid=0) with payloads : HDR + SA (1) + VENDOR (13) + VENDOR (13)
  + NONE (0) total length : 128
%ASA-7-713236: IP = 192.168.160.134, IKE_DECODE RECEIVED Message
  (msgid=0) with payloads : HDR + KE (4) + NONCE (10) + NAT-D (130) +
NAT-D (130) + VENDOR (13) + VENDOR (13) + NONE (0) total length : 272
%ASA-7-715047: IP = 192.168.160.134, processing ke payload
%ASA-7-715047: IP = 192.168.160.134, processing ISA_KE payload
%ASA-7-715047: IP = 192.168.160.134, processing nonce payload
%ASA-7-715047: IP = 192.168.160.134, processing NAT-Discovery payload
%ASA-7-713906: IP = 192.168.160.134, computing NAT Discovery hash
%ASA-7-715047: IP = 192.168.160.134, processing NAT-Discovery payload
%ASA-7-713906: IP = 192.168.160.134, computing NAT Discovery hash
%ASA-7-715047: IP = 192.168.160.134, processing VID payload
%ASA-7-715038: IP = 192.168.160.134, Processing IOS/PIX Vendor ID
  payload (version: 1.0.0, capabilities: 00000408)
%ASA-7-715047: IP = 192.168.160.134, processing VID payload
%ASA-7-715049: IP = 192.168.160.134, Received Cisco Unity client VID
%ASA-7-715046: IP = 192.168.160.134, constructing ke payload
%ASA-7-715046: IP = 192.168.160.134, constructing nonce payload
%ASA-7-715046: IP = 192.168.160.134, constructing certreq payload
%ASA-7-715046: IP = 192.168.160.134, constructing Cisco Unity VID payload
%ASA-7-715046: IP = 192.168.160.134, constructing xauth V6 VID payload
%ASA-7-715048: IP = 192.168.160.134, Send IOS VID
%ASA-7-715038: IP = 192.168.160.134, Constructing ASA spoofing IOS
Vendor ID payload (version: 1.0.0, capabilities: 20000409)
%ASA-7-715046: IP = 192.168.160.134, constructing VID payload
%ASA-7-715048: IP = 192.168.160.134, Send Altiga/Cisco VPN3000/Cisco ASA GW VID
%ASA-7-715046: IP = 192.168.160.134, constructing NAT-Discovery payload
%ASA-7-713906: IP = 192.168.160.134, computing NAT Discovery hash
%ASA-7-715046: IP = 192.168.160.134, constructing NAT-Discovery payload
%ASA-7-713906: IP = 192.168.160.134, computing NAT Discovery hash
%ASA-7-713906: IP = 192.168.160.134, Generating keys for Responder...
```

The Easy VPN server asks the client to send its certificate:

```
%ASA-7-713236: IP = 192.168.160.134, IKE_DECODE SENDING Message
  (msgid=0) with payloads : HDR + KE (4) + NONCE (10) + CERT_REQ (7)
  + VENDOR (13) + VENDOR (13) + VENDOR (13) + VENDOR (13) + NAT-D
```

```
   (130) + NAT-D (130) + NONE (0) total length : 330
%ASA-7-715061: IP = 192.168.160.134, Rcv'd fragment from a new fragmentation
   set. Deleting any old fragments.
%ASA-7-715063: IP = 192.168.160.134, Successfully assembled an encrypted pkt
   from rcv'd fragments!
%ASA-7-713236: IP = 192.168.160.134, IKE_DECODE RECEIVED Message
   (msgid=0) with payloads : HDR + ID (5) + CERT (6) + CERT_REQ (7) +
   SIG (9) + NOTIFY (11) + NONE (0) total length : 1064
```

The Easy VPN server parses the certificate details of the client. It looks at the identity of the certificate details of the subject names, which are username, organization, group, state, and country.

```
%ASA-7-715047: IP = 192.168.160.134, processing ID payload
%ASA-7-713906: IP = 192.168.160.134, DER_ASN1_DN ID received, len 58
0000: 3038310B 30090603 55040813 024E4331    081.0...U....NC1
0010: 0E300C06 0355040A 13054349 53434F31    .0...U....CISCO1
0020: 19301706 03550403 13104349 53434F2D    .0...U....CISCO-
0030: 56504E2D 434C4945 4E54                 VPN-CLIENT


%ASA-7-715047: IP = 192.168.160.134, processing cert payload
%ASA-7-715047: IP = 192.168.160.134, processing cert request payload
```

The Easy VPN server also processes the signature of the certificate:

```
%ASA-7-715001: IP = 192.168.160.134, processing RSA signature
%ASA-7-715076: IP = 192.168.160.134, Computing hash for ISAKMP
%ASA-7-713906: Dump of received Signature, len 256:
0000: 813E6E86 E9648EC5 6CC5CA2F D35EA106    .>n..d..l../.^..
0010: E710AA33 7BEB7BFC E2DBDA8A 9CD58103    ...3{.{.........
0020: 713F423F 84DE4628 8F3053F1 7EFEF4C8    q?B?..F(.0S.~...
0030: 5AA413F8 DECB6C5E 80C7CEFA F00E5251    Z.....l^......RQ
0040: 8A38DE5C 71FF4B86 43C496AB A909FF74    .8.\q.K.C......t
0050: A2B55BC5 E3B5B007 27C4E168 024362AB    ..[.....'..h.Cb.
0060: 8246BB41 1E27EA99 F25D258B 9913EE76    .F.A.'...]%....v
0070: 94DC7F94 34E%ASA-7-715047: IP = 192.168.160.134, processing notify payload
%ASA-6-713172: IP = 192.168.160.134, Automatic NAT Detection
   Status:     Remote end is NOT behind a NAT device     This   end is
   NOT behind a NAT device
```

The NAT-ID payloads detect that the client is not behind a NAT device:

```
%ASA-7-713906: IP = 192.168.160.134, Trying to find group via cert rules...
%ASA-7-717036: Looking for a tunnel group match based on
   certificate maps for peer certificate with serial number: 01AF,
   subject name: cn=CISCO-VPN-CLIENT,o=CISCO,st=NC, issuer_name:
   cn=ra-subca.
```

The Easy VPN server tries to match the tunnel based on the subject name details of the client:

```
%ASA-7-717038: Tunnel group match found. Tunnel Group: testgroup,
   Peer certificate: serial number: 01AF, subject name: cn=CISCO-VPN-
   CLIENT,o=CISCO,st=NC, issuer_name: cn=ra-subca.
%ASA-7-713906: IP = 192.168.160.134, Connection landed on tunnel_group testgroup
```

The Easy VPN server successfully finds the tunnel **testgroup**:

```
%ASA-7-717025: Validating certificate chain containing 1 certificate(s).
%ASA-7-717029: Identified client certificate within certificate
   chain. serial number: 01AF, subject name: cn=CISCO-VPN-CLIENT,o=CISCO,st=NC.
%ASA-7-717030: Found a suitable trustpoint ra to validate certificate.
%ASA-6-717022: Certificate was successfully validated. serial
   number: 01AF, subject name:  cn=CISCO-VPN-CLIENT,o=CISCO,st=NC.
```

The Client certificate is validated with the trust point **ra**:

```
%ASA-6-717028: Certificate chain was successfully validated with warning,
   evocation status was not checked.
%ASA-7-713906: Group = testgroup, IP = 192.168.160.134, peer ID type 9 received
   (DER_ASN1_DN)
%ASA-7-715046: Group = testgroup, IP = 192.168.160.134, constructing ID payload
%ASA-7-715046: Group = testgroup, IP = 192.168.160.134, constructing cert payload
%ASA-7-715001: Group = testgroup, IP = 192.168.160.134, constructing RSA signature
%ASA-7-715076: Group = testgroup, IP = 192.168.160.134, Computing hash for ISAKMP
%ASA-7-713906: Constructed Signature Len: 128
```

The server has validated the client's certificate. It is now the server's turn to send its certificate to the client:

```
%ASA-7-713906: Constructed Signature:
0000: 6CF229C1 9796060A 223E22CE 48D2C5AB    l.)....."">".H...
0010: 871FE675 7F90C661 0BEAF6B8 41BEDA75    ...u...a....A..u
0020: 7A94558B EF80D2AB C4C3363F C16FA725    z.U.......6?.o.%
0030: 200D3BA4 028E3A64 9BFC05BE 4B75D146     .;...:d....Ku.F
0040: 1754E6AB B9733080 5A0D85BB 1F57A325    .T...s0.Z....W.%
0050: 36FE86B1 82197C74 380EDAF3 5876280C    6.....|t8...Xv(.
0060: 3449B9FA 09DB7F3E 4EA974A8 56EF3028    4I.....>N.t.V.0(
0070: 6F8B0EEC AACA29FE B3FB0A18%ASA-7-715046: Group = testgroup,
   IP = 192.168.160.134, constructing dpd vid payload
%ASA-7-713236: IP = 192.168.160.134, IKE_DECODE SENDING Message
   (msgid=0) with payloads : HDR + ID (5) + CERT (6) + SIG (9) +
   VENDOR (13) + NONE (0) total length : 795
```

The server sends its certificate, identity, signature, and the rest of the fields to the client. With this, the main mode negotiation steps are finished. Because it is a remote access, you need to perform x-auth to have a second factor of authentication with the client:

```
%ASA-7-715046: Group = testgroup, IP = 192.168.160.134, constructing blank hash
  payload
%ASA-7-715046: Group = testgroup, IP = 192.168.160.134, constructing qm hash
  payload
%ASA-7-713236: IP = 192.168.160.134, IKE_DECODE SENDING Message
  (msgid=b18db8ad) with payloads : HDR + HASH (8) + ATTR (14) + NONE
  (0) total length : 72
%ASA-7-713236: IP = 192.168.160.134, IKE_DECODE RECEIVED Message
  (msgid=b18db8ad) with payloads : HDR + HASH (8) + ATTR (14) + NONE
  (0) total length : 81
%ASA-7-715001: Group = testgroup, IP = 192.168.160.134, process_attr(): Enter!
%ASA-7-715001: Group = testgroup, IP = 192.168.160.134, Processing MODE_CFG
  Reply attributes.
%ASA-6-113012: AAA user authentication Successful : local database : user = test
%ASA-6-113009: AAA retrieved default group policy (DfltGrpPolicy) for user = test
%ASA-6-113008: AAA transaction status ACCEPT : user = test
```

The server has authenticated the x-auth replies from the client (**username** and **password**).

```
%ASA-7-715019: Group = testgroup, Username = test, IP =
  192.168.160.134, IKEGetUserAttributes: primary DNS = cleared
%ASA-7-715019: Group = testgroup, Username = test, IP =
  192.168.160.134, IKEGetUserAttributes: secondary DNS = cleared
%ASA-7-715019: Group = testgroup, Username = test, IP =
  192.168.160.134, IKEGetUserAttributes: primary WINS = cleared
%ASA-7-715019: Group = testgroup, Username = test, IP =
  192.168.160.134, IKEGetUserAttributes: secondary WINS = cleared
%ASA-7-715019: Group = testgroup, Username = test, IP =
  192.168.160.134, IKEGetUserAttributes: IP Compression = disabled
%ASA-7-715019: Group = testgroup, Username = test, IP =
  192.168.160.134, IKEGetUserAttributes: Split Tunneling Policy = Disabled
%ASA-7-715019: Group = testgroup, Username = test, IP =
  192.168.160.134, IKEGetUserAttributes: Browser Proxy Setting = no-modify
%ASA-7-715019: Group = testgroup, Username = test, IP =
  192.168.160.134, IKEGetUserAttributes: Browser Proxy Bypass Local = disable
%ASA-7-734003: DAP: User test, Addr 192.168.160.134: Session
  Attribute aaa.cisco.grouppolicy = DfltGrpPolicy
```

The Default Group policy was used in this case because no specific group policy was created. The attributes for different values such as DNS, WINS, Split-tunneling policy, and Browser proxy-settings are constructed for these users:

```
%ASA-7-734003: DAP: User test, Addr 192.168.160.134: Session Attribute
  aaa.cisco.username = test
```

```
%ASA-7-734003: DAP: User test, Addr 192.168.160.134: Session Attribute
  aaa.cisco.tunnelgroup = testgroup
%ASA-6-734001: DAP: User test, Addr 192.168.160.134, Connection
  IPSec: The following DAP records were selected for this connection:
  DfltAccessPolicy
 %ASA-7-713052: Group = testgroup, Username = test, IP = 192.168.160.134, User
  (test) authenticated.
%ASA-7-715046: Group = testgroup, Username = test, IP = 192.168.160.134,
  constructing blank hash payload
%ASA-7-715046: Group = testgroup, Username = test, IP = 192.168.160.134,
  constructing qm hash payload
%ASA-7-713236: IP = 192.168.160.134, IKE_DECODE SENDING Message
  (msgid=9da681cd) with payloads : HDR + HASH (8) + ATTR (14) + NONE
  (0) total length : 64
%ASA-7-713236: IP = 192.168.160.134, IKE_DECODE RECEIVED Message
  (msgid=9da681cd) with payloads : HDR + HASH (8) + ATTR (14) + NONE
  (0) total length : 60
%ASA-7-715001: Group = testgroup, Username = test, IP = 192.168.160.134,
  process_attr(): Enter!
%ASA-7-715001: Group = testgroup, Username = test, IP = 192.168.160.134,
  Processing cfg ACK attributes
%ASA-7-713236: IP = 192.168.160.134, IKE_DECODE RECEIVED Message
  (msgid=48a500e2) with payloads : HDR + HASH (8) + ATTR (14) + NONE
  (0) total length : 196
```

In remote access solutions, it is most common to push configuration information such as the IP address, DNS server's IP address, split-tunnel list, and other pertinent information to the client. To enable this VPN gateway, use the Mode-Configuration (MODECFG) feature. The next few lines show what kind of information is passed by the VPN gateway to the client:

```
%ASA-7-715001: Group = testgroup, Username = test, IP =
  192.168.160.134, process_attr(): Enter!
%ASA-7-715001: Group = testgroup, Username = test, IP =
  192.168.160.134, Processing cfg Request attributes
%ASA-7-715053: Group = testgroup, Username = test, IP =
  192.168.160.134, MODE_CFG: Received request for IPV4 address!
%ASA-7-715053: Group = testgroup, Username = test, IP =
  192.168.160.134, MODE_CFG: Received request for IPV4 net mask!
%ASA-7-715053: Group = testgroup, Username = test, IP =
  192.168.160.134, MODE_CFG: Received request for DNS server address!
%ASA-7-715053: Group = testgroup, Username = test, IP =
  192.168.160.134, MODE_CFG: Received request for WINS server address!
%ASA-5-713130: Group = testgroup, Username = test, IP =
  192.168.160.134, Received unsupported transaction mode attribute: 5
%ASA-7-715053: Group = testgroup, Username = test, IP =
  192.168.160.134, MODE_CFG: Received request for Banner!
%ASA-7-715053: Group = testgroup, Username = test, IP =
```

```
  192.168.160.134, MODE_CFG: Received request for Save PW setting!
%ASA-7-715053: Group = testgroup, Username = test, IP =
  192.168.160.134, MODE_CFG: Received request for Default Domain Name!
%ASA-7-715053: Group = testgroup, Username = test, IP =
  192.168.160.134, MODE_CFG: Received request for Split Tunnel List!
%ASA-7-715053: Group = testgroup, Username = test, IP =
  192.168.160.134, MODE_CFG: Received request for Split DNS!
%ASA-7-715053: Group = testgroup, Username = test, IP =
  192.168.160.134, MODE_CFG: Received request for PFS setting!
%ASA-7-715053: Group = testgroup, Username = test, IP =
  192.168.160.134, MODE_CFG: Received request for Client Browser Proxy Setting!
%ASA-7-715053: Group = testgroup, Username = test, IP =
  192.168.160.134, MODE_CFG: Received request for backup ip-sec peer list!
%ASA-7-715053: Group = testgroup, Username = test, IP =
  192.168.160.134, MODE_CFG: Received request for Client Smartcard Removal
  Disconnect Setting!
%ASA-7-715053: Group = testgroup, Username = test, IP =
  192.168.160.134, MODE_CFG: Received request for Application Version!
%ASA-6-713184: Group = testgroup, Username = test, IP =
  192.168.160.134, Client Type: WinNT  Client Application Version: 5.0.06.0160
%ASA-7-715053: Group = testgroup, Username = test, IP =
  192.168.160.134, MODE_CFG: Received request for FWTYPE!
%ASA-7-715053: Group = testgroup, Username = test, IP =
  192.168.160.134, MODE_CFG: Received request for DHCP hostname for DDNS is:
  vpn-client!
%ASA-7-715053: Group = testgroup, Username = test, IP =
  192.168.160.134, MODE_CFG: Received request for UDP Port!
%ASA-7-737001: IPAA: Received message 'UTL_IP_[IKE_]ADDR_REQ'
%ASA-5-737003: IPAA: DHCP configured, no viable servers found for tunnel-group
  'testgroup'
```

The client requests several pieces of information such as the IPV4 address, mask, DNS, WINS, and other pieces of information.

```
%ASA-6-737026: IPAA: Client assigned 192.168.0.10 from local pool
%ASA-6-737006: IPAA: Local pool request succeeded for tunnel-group 'testgroup'
```

The client is assigned an IP address from the pool:

```
%ASA-7-713906: Group = testgroup, Username = test, IP =
  192.168.160.134, Obtained IP addr (192.168.0.10) prior to initiating Mode
  Cfg (XAuth enabled)
%ASA-6-713228: Group = testgroup, Username = test, IP =
  192.168.160.134, Assigned private IP address 192.168.0.10 to remote user
%ASA-7-715046: Group = testgroup, Username = test, IP =
  192.168.160.134, constructing blank hash payload
%ASA-7-715055: Group = testgroup, Username = test, IP =
  192.168.160.134, Send Client Browser Proxy Attributes!
```

```
%ASA-7-715001: Group = testgroup, Username = test, IP =
   192.168.160.134, Browser Proxy set to No-Modify. Browser Proxy data will NOT
   be included in the mode-cfg reply
%ASA-7-715055: Group = testgroup, Username = test, IP =
   192.168.160.134, Send Cisco Smartcard Removal Disconnect enable!!
%ASA-7-715046: Group = testgroup, Username = test, IP =
   192.168.160.134, constructing qm hash payload
%ASA-7-713236: IP = 192.168.160.134, IKE_DECODE SENDING Message
   (msgid=48a500e2) with payloads : HDR + HASH (8) + ATTR (14) + NONE (0)
   total length : 166
%ASA-7-714003: IP = 192.168.160.134, IKE Responder starting QM: msg id = 6b5fd332
%ASA-7-715021: Group = testgroup, Username = test, IP =
   192.168.160.134, Delay Quick Mode processing, Cert/Trans Exch/RM DSID in progress
%ASA-7-715022: Group = testgroup, Username = test, IP =
   192.168.160.134, Resume Quick Mode processing, Cert/Trans Exch/RM DSID completed
%ASA-7-713906: Group = testgroup, Username = test, IP =
   192.168.160.134, Delete with reason code and text capabilities are negotiated
%ASA-5-713119: Group = testgroup, Username = test, IP =
   192.168.160.134, PHASE 1 COMPLETED
```

Phase I is completed, and Phase II begins:

```
%ASA-7-713121: IP = 192.168.160.134, Keep-alive type for this
   connection: DPD
%ASA-7-715080: Group = testgroup, Username = test, IP =
   192.168.160.134, Starting P1 rekey timer: 41040 seconds.
%ASA-7-713906: Group = testgroup, Username = test, IP =
   192.168.160.134, sending notify message
%ASA-7-715046: Group = testgroup, Username = test, IP =
   192.168.160.134, constructing blank hash payload
%ASA-7-715046: Group = testgroup, Username = test, IP =
   192.168.160.134, constructing qm hash payload
%ASA-7-713236: IP = 192.168.160.134, IKE_DECODE SENDING Message
   (msgid=e76d4a95) with payloads : HDR + HASH (8) + NOTIFY (11) +
   NONE (0) total length : 88
```

The primary unit initiates the first exchange in Phase II negotiation:

```
%ASA-7-720041: (VPN-Primary) Sending New Phase 1 SA message (type
   RA, remote addr 192.168.160.134, my cookie A8075915, his cookie
   AE641AB0) to standby unit
```

Because you have active-standby units, the active unit informs the stand-by unit about the current session:

```
%ASA-7-713236: IP = 192.168.160.134, IKE_DECODE RECEIVED Message
   (msgid=6b5fd332) with payloads : HDR + HASH (8) + SA (1) + NONCE
   (10) + ID (5) + ID (5) + NONE (0) total length : 1026
```

```
%ASA-7-715047: Group = testgroup, Username = test, IP =
  192.168.160.134, processing hash payload
%ASA-7-715047: Group = testgroup, Username = test, IP =
  192.168.160.134, processing SA payload
%ASA-7-715047: Group = testgroup, Username = test, IP =
  192.168.160.134, processing nonce payload
%ASA-7-715047: Group = testgroup, Username = test, IP = 192.168.160.134,
  processing ID payload
%ASA-7-714011: Group = testgroup, Username = test, IP = 192.168.160.134,
  ID_IPV4_ADDR ID received
192.168.0.10
```

The server processes the response to the first exchange it has sent to the client:

```
%ASA-7-713025: Group = testgroup, Username = test, IP =
  192.168.160.134, Received remote Proxy Host data in ID Payload:  Address
  192.168.0.10, Protocol 0, Port 0
%ASA-7-715047: Group = testgroup, Username = test, IP =
  192.168.160.134, processing ID payload
%ASA-7-714011: Group = testgroup, Username = test, IP =
  192.168.160.134, ID_IPV4_ADDR_SUBNET ID received—0.0.0.0—0.0.0.0
%ASA-7-713034: Group = testgroup, Username = test, IP =
  192.168.160.134, Received local IP Proxy Subnet data in ID Payload:
  Address 0.0.0.0, Mask 0.0.0.0, Protocol 0, Port 0
%ASA-7-713906: Group = testgroup, Username = test, IP =
  192.168.160.134, QM IsRekeyed old sa not found by addr
%ASA-7-713066: Group = testgroup, Username = test, IP =
  192.168.160.134, IKE Remote Peer configured for crypto map: dyn1
%ASA-7-715047: Group = testgroup, Username = test, IP =
  192.168.160.134, processing IPSec SA payload
%ASA-7-715027: Group = testgroup, Username = test, IP =
  192.168.160.134, IPSec SA Proposal # 12, Transform # 1 acceptable
  Matches global IPSec SA entry # 1
```

Both the server and client agree to the acceptable security association for Phase II
negotiation:

```
%ASA-7-713906: Group = testgroup, Username = test, IP =
  192.168.160.134, IKE: requesting SPI!
%ASA-7-715006: Group = testgroup, Username = test, IP =
  192.168.160.134, IKE got SPI from key engine: SPI = 0xe9619a1b
%ASA-7-713906: Group = testgroup, Username = test, IP =
  192.168.160.134, oakley constucting quick mode
%ASA-7-715046: Group = testgroup, Username = test, IP =
  192.168.160.134, constructing blank hash payload
%ASA-7-715046: Group = testgroup, Username = test, IP =
  192.168.160.134, constructing IPSec SA payload
```

```
%ASA-5-713075: Group = testgroup, Username = test, IP =
  192.168.160.134, Overriding Initiator's IPSec rekeying duration from 2147483
  to 28800 seconds
%ASA-7-715046: Group = testgroup, Username = test, IP =
  192.168.160.134, constructing IPSec nonce payload
%ASA-7-715001: Group = testgroup, Username = test, IP =
  192.168.160.134, constructing proxy ID
%ASA-7-713906: Group = testgroup, Username = test, IP =
  192.168.160.134, Transmitting Proxy Id:
  Remote host: 192.168.0.10  Protocol 0  Port 0
  Local subnet:  0.0.0.0  mask 0.0.0.0 Protocol 0  Port 0
%ASA-7-713906: Group = testgroup, Username = test, IP =
  192.168.160.134, Sending RESPONDER LIFETIME notification to Initiator
%ASA-7-715046: Group = testgroup, Username = test, IP =
  192.168.160.134, constructing qm hash payload
%ASA-7-714005: Group = testgroup, Username = test, IP =
  192.168.160.134, IKE Responder sending 2nd QM pkt: msg id = 6b5fd332
%ASA-7-713236: IP = 192.168.160.134, IKE_DECODE SENDING Message
  (msgid=6b5fd332) with payloads : HDR + HASH (8) + SA (1) + NONCE
  (10) + ID (5) + ID (5) + NOTIFY (11) + NONE (0) total length : 180
```

The server sends the important exchange, which has its ID along with Security
Association (SA):

```
%ASA-7-713236: IP = 192.168.160.134, IKE_DECODE RECEIVED Message
  (msgid=6b5fd332) with payloads : HDR + HASH (8) + NONE (0) total length : 52
%ASA-7-715047: Group = testgroup, Username = test, IP =
  192.168.160.134, processing hash payload
%ASA-7-713906: Group = testgroup, Username = test, IP =
  192.168.160.134, loading all IPSEC SAs
%ASA-7-715001: Group = testgroup, Username = test, IP =
  192.168.160.134, Generating Quick Mode Key!
%ASA-7-715001: Group = testgroup, Username = test, IP =
  192.168.160.134, Generating Quick Mode Key!
%ASA-6-602303: IPSEC: An outbound remote access SA (SPI=
  0x3521F351) between 192.168.167.225 and 192.168.160.134 (user= test) has been
  created.
%ASA-5-713049: Group = testgroup, Username = test, IP =
  192.168.160.134, Security negotiation complete for User (test)
  Responder, Inbound SPI = 0xe9619a1b, Outbound SPI = 0x3521f351
%ASA-7-715007: Group = testgroup, Username = test, IP =
  192.168.160.134, IKE got a KEY_ADD msg for SA: SPI = 0x3521f351
%ASA-6-602303: IPSEC: An inbound remote access SA (SPI=
  0xE9619A1B) between 192.168.167.225 and 192.168.160.134 (user= test) has been
  created.
%ASA-7-715077: Group = testgroup, Username = test, IP =
  192.168.160.134, Pitcher: received KEY_UPDATE, spi 0xe9619a1b
```

```
%ASA-7-715080: Group = testgroup, Username = test, IP =
   192.168.160.134, Starting P2 rekey timer: 27360 seconds.
%ASA-7-713204: Group = testgroup, Username = test, IP =
   192.168.160.134, Adding static route for client address: 192.168.0.10
%ASA-5-713120: Group = testgroup, Username = test, IP =
   192.168.160.134, PHASE 2 COMPLETED (msgid=6b5fd332)
```

The Phase II exchange is completed, and the SA is established:

```
%ASA-7-720041: (VPN-Primary) Sending Phase 2 Exchange message (my
   cookie A8075915, his cookie AE641AB0, old msg id 00000000, msg id 6B5FD332) to
   standby unit
%ASA-7-609001: Built local-host outside:192.168.0.255
%ASA-7-713236: IP = 192.168.160.134, IKE_DECODE RECEIVED Message
   (msgid=61bff7f1) with payloads : HDR + HASH (8) + NOTIFY (11) + NONE (0) total
   length : 84
%ASA-7-715047: Group = testgroup, Username = test, IP = 192.168.160.134,
   processing hash payload
%ASA-7-715047: Group = testgroup, Username = test, IP = 192.168.160.134,
   processing notify payload
%ASA-7-715075: Group = testgroup, Username = test, IP =
   192.168.160.134, Received keep-alive of type DPD R-U-THERE (seq number
   0xa101fba5)
%ASA-7-715036: Group = testgroup, Username = test, IP =
   192.168.160.134, Sending keep-alive of type DPD R-U-THERE-ACK (seq number
   0xa101fba5)
%ASA-7-715046: Group = testgroup, Username = test, IP =
   192.168.160.134, constructing blank hash payload
```

The Server sends the keep alive of type **R-U-There**, and the client responds to **R-U-THERE-ACK**, which confirms the establishment of IPSec connection.

SSL VPN Access

SSL VPN clients can also use digital certificates as an authentication mechanism. The process and configuration are detailed next.

SSL VPN Overview

The Secure Sockets Layer (SSL) Handshake Protocol was developed by Netscape Communications Corporation to provide security and privacy over the Internet using web browsers. This protocol runs over TCP and is treated as a user process for an operating system. It requires that all the applications talk directly to SSL rather than TCP. Applications willing to use SSL as a transport must be modified to talk to SSL; however,

TCP/IP does not require alteration. The current version for SSL is v3 and is the basis for the IETF standard TLS v1.0.

The SSL protocol helps protect application data through encryption and authentication. The protocol supports server and client authentication. The SSL protocol can negotiate encryption keys and authenticate the server before data is exchanged by the higher-level application. The SSL protocol maintains the confidentiality and integrity of the transmission channel by using encryption and authentication algorithms.

The Cisco SSL VPN solution comes in two flavors: Clientless VPN and AnyConnect. The Clientless solution is based on a Java/Active-x applet downloaded to the remote browser when the remote user connects to the SSL gateway. AnyConnect is a client dynamically installed on the remote desktop when the session is established.

Figure 7-11 and the following steps show the main steps to establish the AnyConnect solution:

1. The client initiates the session to the gateway using the browser.

2. The gateway sends its certificate chain, root CA, and certificate issued by the subordinate CA (ra-subca in the example). If the browser does not know the issuer of the certificate, it may report an error. This can happen when corporate deploys CAs, which is mainly used within a corporate set up. In those circumstances, the certificate needs to be imported to move forward with the session. Figure 7-12 shows an error that might be displayed on a client's browser.

3. The Client validates the certificate and might import the root CA and the ASA certificate. Figure 7-13 shows the browser when it accepts the root CA certificate.

4. The client and gateway perform negotiation for cipher suites and keys.

5. The gateway sends an initial login screen, as shown in Figure 7-14.

6. The user selects the group and enters credentials. The browser initiates the AnyConnect client installation on the user computer, as shown in Figure 7-15.

Figure 7-16 shows the AnyConnect client installed.

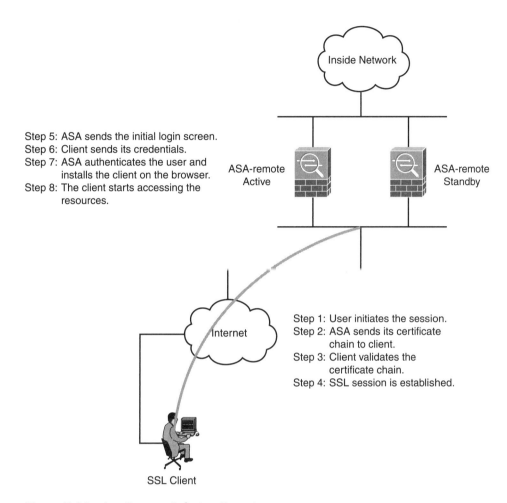

Step 5: ASA sends the initial login screen.
Step 6: Client sends its credentials.
Step 7: ASA authenticates the user and
        installs the client on the browser.
Step 8: The client starts accessing the
        resources.

Step 1: User initiates the session.
Step 2: ASA sends its certificate
        chain to client.
Step 3: Client validates the
        certificate chain.
Step 4: SSL session is established.

Figure 7-11   *AnyConnect Solution Overview*

Figure 7-12 *Error of the Certificate*

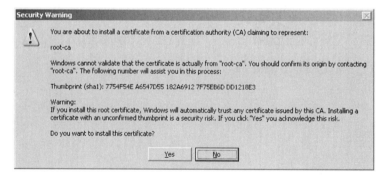

Figure 7-13 *Importing Root CA Certificate*

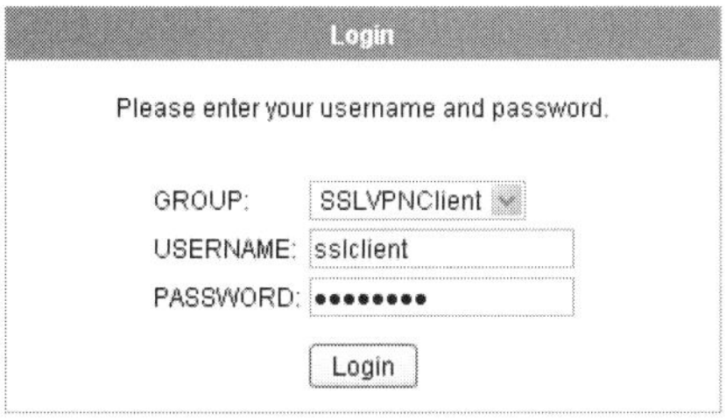

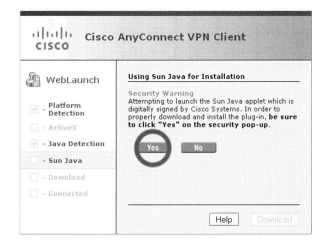

Figure 7-14   *Initial Screen*

Figure 7-15   *AnyConnect Client Installation*

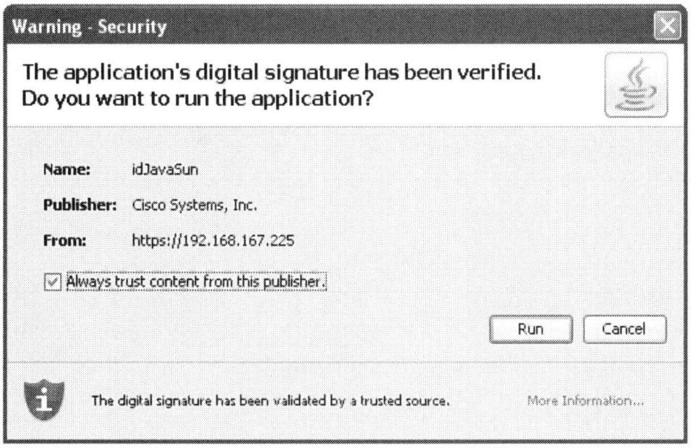

Figure 7-16   *AnyConnect Client Installed on the Computer*

Example 7-5 illustrates the configuration of the ASA gateway for accepting AnyConnect sessions.

Example 7-5   *Configuration of ASA Firewall*

```
group-policy SSLClientPolicy internal
group-policy SSLClientPolicy attributes
 vpn-tunnel-protocol svc
 default-domain value cisco.com
 address-pools value testpool
!
tunnel-group SSLClientProfile type remote-access
tunnel-group SSLClientProfile general-attributes
 default-group-policy SSLClientPolicy
tunnel-group SSLClientProfile webvpn-attributes
 group-alias SSLVPNClient enable
!
webvpn
  svc ask none default webvpn
  hidden-shares visible
  file-entry enable
  file-browsing enable
  url-entry enable
!
ip local pool testpool 192.168.0.10-192.168.0.15
```

After the AnyConnect session is established, you can use the following command to verify the session, as shown in Example 7-6.

Example 7-6   *Verifying the AnyConnect Session on the ASA*

```
ASA-remote1# show vpn-sessiondb svc

Session Type: SVC

Username     : sslclient            Index       : 12
Assigned IP  : 192.168.0.10         Public IP   : 192.168.160.130
Protocol     : Clientless SSL-Tunnel DTLS-Tunnel
License      : SSL VPN
Encryption   : RC4 AES128           Hashing     : SHA1
Bytes Tx     : 2402609              Bytes Rx    : 2381158
Group Policy : SSLClientPolicy      Tunnel Group : SSLClientProfile
Login Time   : 11:04:51 EST Wed Sep 15 2010
Duration     : 22h:15m:50s
Inactivity   : 0h:00m:00s
```

```
NAC Result    : Unknown
VLAN Mapping : N/A                      VLAN          : none

ASA-remote1#
```

Troubleshooting the AnyConnect Solution

Example 7-7 shows the debug output on ASA when the user does not accept the Gateway certificate.

Example 7-7 *Debugging Output on ASA*

```
ASA-remote1(config)# show debug
debug vpn-sessiondb  enabled at level 1
ASA-remote1(config)#
  (192.168.160.130/1236) to identity:192.168.167.225/443 (192.168.167.225/443)
%ASA-6-725001: Starting SSL handshake with client outside:192.168.160.130/1236 f
  or TLSv1 session.
%ASA-7-725010: Device supports the following 4 cipher(s).
%ASA-7-725011: Cipher[1] : RC4-SHA
%ASA-7-725011: Cipher[2] : AES128-SHA
%ASA-7-725011: Cipher[3] : AES256-SHA
%ASA-7-725011: Cipher[4] : DES-CBC3-SHA
%ASA-7-725008: SSL client outside:192.168.160.130/1236 proposes the following 11
 cipher(s).
%ASA-7-725011: Cipher[1] : DHE-RSA-AES256-SHA
%ASA-7-725011: Cipher[2] : DHE-DSS-AES256-SHA
%ASA-7-725011: Cipher[3] : AES256-SHA
%ASA-7-725011: Cipher[4] : DHE-RSA-AES128-SHA
%ASA-7-725011: Cipher[5] : DHE-DSS-AES128-SHA
%ASA-7-725011: Cipher[6] : RC4-MD5
%ASA-7-725011: Cipher[7] : RC4-SHA
%ASA-7-725011: Cipher[8] : AES128-SHA
%ASA-7-725011: Cipher[9] : EDH-RSA-DES-CBC3-SHA
%ASA-7-725011: Cipher[10] : EDH-DSS-DES-CBC3-SHA
%ASA-7-725011: Cipher[11] : DES-CBC3-SHA
%ASA-7-725012: Device chooses cipher : RC4-SHA for the SSL session with client
  outside:192.168.160.130/1236
%ASA-7-725014: SSL lib error. Function: SSL3_READ_BYTES Reason: sslv3 alert
  certificate unknown
%ASA-6-725006: Device failed SSL handshake with client outside:192.168.160.130/
  1236
```

Example 7-8 shows the debug for a session that is established correctly.

Example 7-8   *Debug Output for a Session That Is Established Correctly*

```
%ASA-6-725001: Starting SSL handshake with client outside:192.168.160.130/1248
  for TLSv1 session.
%ASA-6-725003: SSL client outside:192.168.160.130/1248 request to resume
  previous session.
%ASA-6-725002: Device completed SSL handshake with client outside:192.168.160.13
  0/1248
%ASA-6-302013: Built inbound TCP connection 28514 for outside:192.168.160.130/12
51 (192.168.160.130/1251) to identity:192.168.167.225/443 (192.168.167.225/443)
%ASA-6-725001: Starting SSL handshake with client outside:192.168.160.130/1251
for TLSv1 session.
%ASA-7-725010: Device supports the following 4 cipher(s).
%ASA-7-725011: Cipher[1] : RC4-SHA
%ASA-7-725011: Cipher[2] : AES128-SHA
%ASA-7-725011: Cipher[3] : AES256-SHA
%ASA-7-725011: Cipher[4] : DES-CBC3-SHA
%ASA-7-725008: SSL client outside:192.168.160.130/1251 proposes the following 6
  cipher(s).
%ASA-7-725011: Cipher[1] : AES256-SHA
%ASA-7-725011: Cipher[2] : AES128-SHA
%ASA-7-725011: Cipher[3] : DES-CBC3-SHA
%ASA-7-725011: Cipher[4] : RC4-SHA
%ASA-7-725011: Cipher[5] : RC4-MD5
%ASA-7-725011: Cipher[6] : DES-CBC-SHA
%ASA-7-725012: Device chooses cipher : RC4-SHA for the SSL session with client
  outside:192.168.160.130/1251
%ASA-6-725002: Device completed SSL handshake with client outside:
  192.168.160.130/1251
%ASA-7-737001: IPAA: Received message 'UTL_IP_[IKE_]ADDR_REQ'
%ASA-5-737003: IPAA: DHCP configured, no viable servers found for tunnel-group
  'SSLClientProfile'
%ASA-6-737026: IPAA: Client assigned 192.168.0.10 from local pool
%ASA-6-737006: IPAA: Local pool request succeeded for tunnel-group 'SSLClientPro
  file'
%ASA-7-720041: (VPN-Primary) Sending Update SVC Addr Data message Session Index
  81920 to standby unit
%ASA-5-722033: Group <SSLClientPolicy> User <sslclient> IP <192.168.160.130>
  First TCP SVC connection established for SVC session.
%ASA-6-722022: Group <SSLClientPolicy> User <sslclient> IP <192.168.160.130> TCP
  SVC connection established without compression
%ASA-7-720041: (VPN-Primary) Sending WebVPN Session Mgr Data message Session
  Index 81922 to standby unit
%ASA-4-722051: Group <SSLClientPolicy> User <sslclient> IP <192.168.160.130>
  Address <192.168.0.10> assigned to session
```

```
%ASA-6-734001: DAP: User sslclient, Addr 192.168.160.130, Connection AnyConnect:
 The following DAP records were selected for this connection: DfltAccessPolicy
```

Summary

In this chapter, you looked at how to use PKI as a service for the two most popular remote access solutions: IPsec VPN, and SSL VPN. You looked at practical examples on how to deploy and use certificates for these VPN technologies. ASA was mainly used as a VPN gateway, and the clients were Cisco VPN client, SSL clientless, and AnyConnect client.

For Cisco IPsec remote access solution, the VPN gateway looks at the client's certificate, selects the appropriate tunnel interface, and then uses that tunnel to establish the session. The Cisco VPN client enrolls with the subordinate CA and also obtains the root CA certificate so that it can authenticate the VPN gateway.

The Cisco SSL VPN solution is available as Clientless VPN and AnyConnect. The Clientless solution is based on Java/Active-x applet downloaded to the remote browser when the remote user connects to the SSL gateway. AnyConnect is a client dynamically installed on the remote desktop when the session is established. Both the clientless and AnyConnect client would validate the VPN gateway certificate, and then the session is established.

Chapter 8

Using 802.1X Certificates in Identity-Based Networking

This chapter covers the following topic:

■ EAP-TLS: Certificate-Based 802.1x

This chapter covers identity for end users using certificates. The technology covered in this chapter is EAP-TLS-based 802.1x using ACS 5.1. This chapter is not a deep dive into extensible authentication protocol (EAP), but rather illustrates a case study in which certificates can be used in this solution. It also covers Cisco Secure Access Control Server setup supporting basic certificate-based EAP.

In today's networks, there is a paradigm shift occurring, creating a dynamic and mobile environment. Consequently, this new dynamism presents the security space with an opportunity to change its paradigm, from one that was largely an afterthought to reduce availability to one essential to creating availability.

The most obvious of these shifts occurs in the end user space. For business to be more productive, end users need to have flexible accessibility. Also, end users need to collaborate together, which also fuels productivity.

This represents an opportunity for security to change and also *requires* security to change. The old static techniques can no longer scale to meet the needs of such a dynamic world. The new paradigm enables end users by identifying them dynamically at the edges and connecting them to the resources they need, transparently from anywhere, using any device they choose. This obviously requires a powerful approach to identity, and that approach must be integrated end-to-end in the infrastructure.

This section discusses how you can use PKI to drive this new paradigm when used with 802.1x, which for identity-based networking is used at the access layer of a network to provide (or deny) access to the network.

The glue between certificates, the CA, and the end user's 802.1x experience is Cisco Secure Access Control Server (ACS) running RADIUS. A common implementation using 802.1x and ACS integrates with a Microsoft domain controller and Microsoft CA. At a high level, ACS can get 802.1x authentication requests from network access points with users. Those requests can be checked against the CA and domain server to make an authentication decision. That decision then has an associated rule for authorization, which is enforced at the network access point.

EAP-TLS: Certificate-Based 802.1x

The purpose of this section is to provide information on how you can include certificates into the EAP. EAP-TLS is one such 802.1x mechanism for including certificates into this framework. EAP-TLS will not enable an end device onto the network infrastructure without undergoing certificate-based authentication. The use of a PKI to establish a cryptographically based, third-party authentication does not change in this deployment model. The root of checking certificates still relies on asymmetric encryption, where you verify that the CA has signed the end user's certificate.

When an ACS server and host obtain certificate credentials, EAP-TLS occurs via an intermediary network device. Figure 8-1 shows the EAP-TLS process.

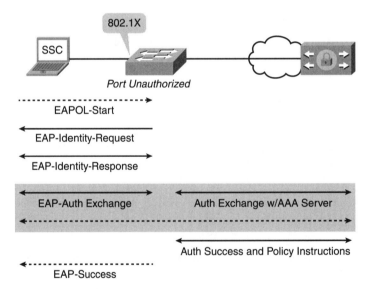

Figure 8-1 *802.1x Flow*

1. A host connects to the network. The network device sends an EAP request to the host.

2. The host sends an EAP response to the network device; the network device embeds the EAP packet that it received from the host into a RADIUS request and sends it to ACS.

3. ACS negotiates the EAP method for authentication. The server and client must reach agreement to use EAP-TLS (EAP request method 13) during EAP method negotiation to instantiate EAP-TLS authentication.

4. The client (host) and server (ACS) exchange certificates; this exchange involves several messages.

   EAP-TLS authentication is successful after the client and server have authenticated each other, and each side is aware that the other side has authenticated them.

5. ACS returns an EAP success message to the host and returns a RADIUS access-accept to the network device that includes session keys.

The initial configuration of ACS for a Microsoft-centric active directory (AD) deployment at a high level involves the following steps:

Step 1. Enroll ACS in the Certificate Authority.

Step 2. Add the CA in the identity store.

Step 3. Add AD as an external database.

Step 4. Configure a certificate authentication profile.

Step 5. Add an Access service for 802.1x.

Step 6. Configure the Access Service Identity policy.

Step 7. Configure Service Selection rule.

Note For questions about ACS terms and components, see the links found at http://www.cisco.com/en/US/partner/docs/net_mgmt/cisco_secure_access_control_system /5.1/user/guide/introd.html.

Step 1: Enroll ACS in the Certificate Authority

To obtain a certificate for the ACS server, log in to the CA server and generate a request from the ACS.

1. Log into ACS and go to **System administration > configuration > local server certificates > local certificates >add**.

2. Select the radio button for generating a signing request, as shown in Figure 8-2.

At this point, you will be asked to follow on-screen instructions and then export the request. After getting a certificate back from the CA for the ACS, the next step is to bind the certificate.

1. Log into ACS and go to **System administration > configuration > local server certificates > local certificates > add**.

2. Select the radio button to bind the certificate, and then browse and upload the certificate, as shown in Figure 8-3.

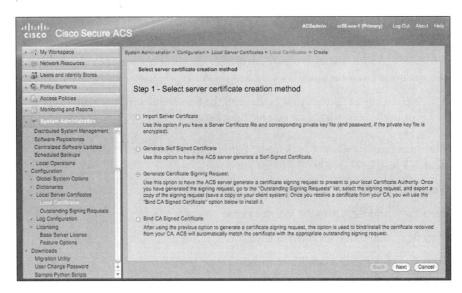

Figure 8-2   *Requesting a Certificate*

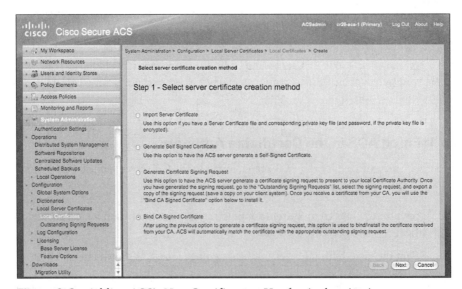

Figure 8-3   *Adding ACS's New Certificate to Use for Authentication*

Make sure to select the Used for EAP check box. You have now enrolled ACS into the CA used for EAP authentication. This is the certificate used by ACS for the mutual authentication.

Step 2: Add the CA in the Identity Store

Next, add to the certificate store the CA's certificate that will be issuing certificates. This allows ACS to recognize the certificate authority as valid. Figure 8-4 shows how to add the CA. Make sure to select **Trust for Client with EAP-TLS** check box, as shown in Figure 8-4.

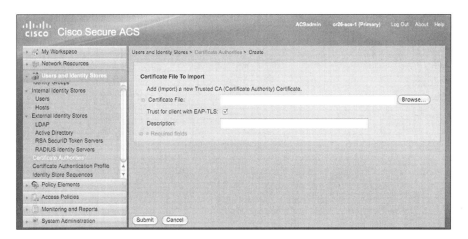

Figure 8-4   *Adding a CA's Certificate to the ACS External Identity Store*

It is also required that ACS becomes part of the active directory domain. This enables ACS to use the domain as an external identity store. Figure 8-5 illustrates how to add ACS into the domain.

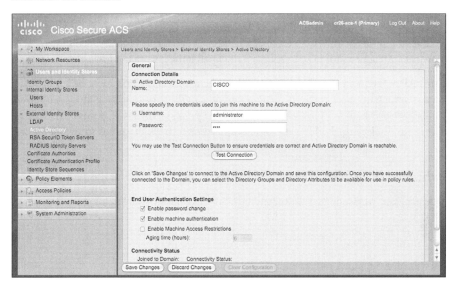

Figure 8-5   *Adding an Active Directory as an External Identity store*

Step 3: Add AD as an External Database

At this point, ACS is enrolled in the domain, the external identity store for the CA is defined, and ACS is enrolled in the CA. Next you must add the profile for the methods used by ACS to review certificate credentials, which is the *certificate authentication profile*. Figure 8-6 illustrates how to add a certificate authentication profile. The default profile using a common name often works for most deployments, and this step might not be required.

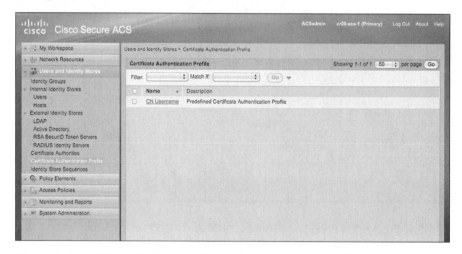

Figure 8-6 *Adding a Default Certificate Authentication Profile*

Step 4: Configure a Certificate Authentication Profile

At this point, you have enrolled the ACS server in the CA and AD. ACS also has the certificate required for the root CA server that hands out certificates for EAP-TLS. Also, ACS now has instructions for how to handle fields within the certificate for authentication.

For EAP authentication to occur, the EAP authentication method must be set up. The first step is setting up the service for EAP; then you can identify the associated identity and authorization handling. This is done by going to **Access Policies > Access Services > Create** and selecting the **Identity** and **Authorization** check boxes, as shown in Figure 8-7.

Step 5: Add an Access Service for 802.1x

The access type used must be selected. In our case, as illustrated in Figure 8-8, it is EAP-TLS.

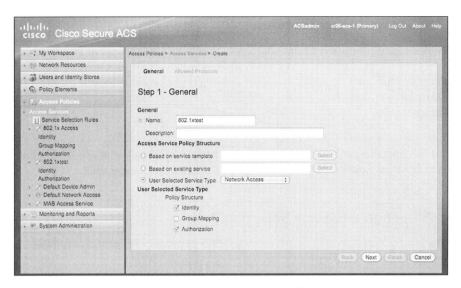

Figure 8-7 *Creating the Access Service to Support Identity and Authorization*

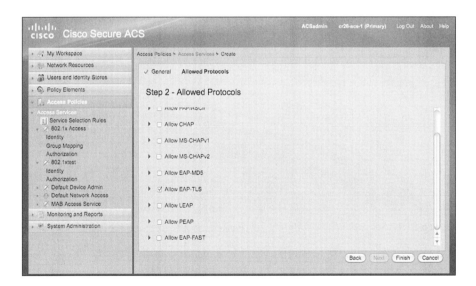

Figure 8-8 *Enabling EAP-TLS for the Access Service*

Step 6: Configure the Access Service Identity Policy

Now the access service for 802.1x has been created. Identity and authorization were selected to set up for the access service, and now you must set up the identity policy. As illustrated in Figure 8-9, you can use the default certificate authentication profile CN username, which instructs the service to use the common name as the identity validation parameter.

Next the authorization policy for that service will be identified. You can assume a simple condition for this network: If the certificate check succeeds, allow access. This is the default authorization policy illustrated, and no change needs to be made.

Step 7: Configure Service Selection Rule

The last configuration step on ACS is to tell ACS to use this new service that has just been created. This is done by the service selection policy, as illustrated in Figure 8-10.

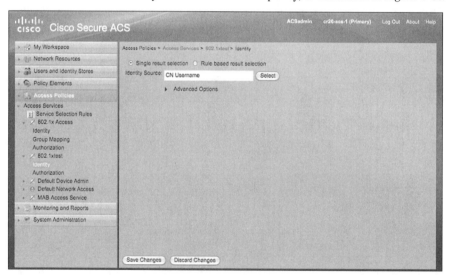

Figure 8-9   *Setting Up the Identity for the Access Service*

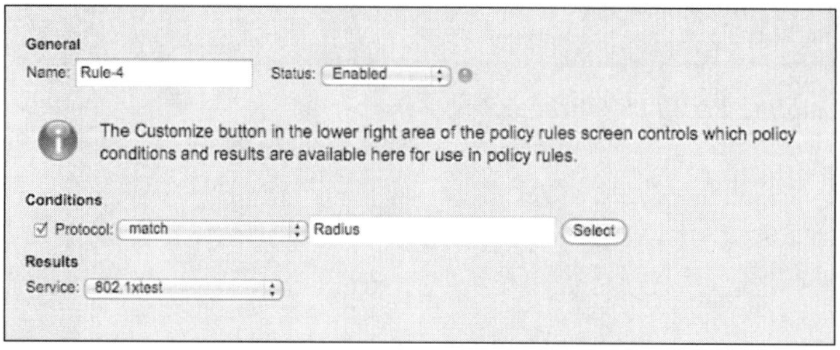

Figure 8-10   *Creating a Service Selection Policy*

Now ACS is set up to use certificates to authenticate requests from 802.1x-enabled switches.

Setting Up the Switch for EAP

To configure EAP-TLS on the router or switch, the device needs to connect to the radius server and have 802.1x authentication enabled on the port.

```
aaa new-model
aaa authentication dot1x default group radius
aaa authorization network default group radius
aaa accounting dot1x default start-stop group radius
!
dot1x system-auth-control
!
interface Gigabit 1/0/5
switchport mode access
switchport access vlan 30
authentication port-control auto
dot1x pae-authenticator
dot1x tx-period 5
!
radius-server host 10.100.10.117 1813 key cisco123
```

Additionally, the switch should exist in ACS.

It is recommended that a fallback mechanism be used. A variety of mechanisms are available, depending on the scenario. These mechanisms include MAC address Authentication Bypass (MAB), guest vlan access, and webauth proxy. Each mechanism can be used in combination with 802.1x EAP-TLS.

Summary

Identity represents a unique security opportunity in the end-user space. Security, which is often an afterthought or additional expense, can now be used as a network enabler. Users and devices can have certificates associated to them that enable access at the port level to the systems those users and devices specifically need. 802.1x, EAP-TLS, and ACS can work together to create a new approach to enable network access.

Chapter 9

PKI in Unified Communications

This chapter is dedicated to integrating PKI concepts into your Unified Communication infrastructure.

That is one important step in securing UC through the following:

- Authentication and encryption of calls

- Integration in your Network Admission Control (802.1x) solution

The Cisco Unified Communications infrastructure (mainly IP Phones and voice gateways) can benefit from integration into your PKI.

This chapter starts by setting the foundations of PKI implementation in Cisco UC solutions. Then you see how devices can be provisioned with certificates to build trusted chains. Finally, you review typical applications in which the availability of certificates can bring some interesting benefits: voice calls security, ASA Firewall TLS Proxy feature, and IP Phones 802.1x authentication.

PKI Concepts in Cisco UC

Although the main PKI foundations are still present in Cisco UC implementations, a few specific concepts have been developed or added, mainly with the aim to ease use and deployment.

You need to understand a few functions and acronyms that will be used later in this chapter because they will be integrated later on in the reviewed application examples.

Manufacturer Installed Certificate (MIC)

Every IP Phone (from the latest generations of products) has a public and private key pair, and a dedicated certificate installed when leaving the factory. That certificate, known as a

Manufacturer Installed Certificate (MIC), is issued by a common Cisco Manufacturing CA, which is a subordinate of the Cisco Root CA.

The Common Name (CN) in those certificates is created from the phone model and its MAC address; for example, CN=CP-7961G-GE-SEP00ABXXXXXXXX.

That's good because it means that each IP Phone can immediately participate into PKI processes. However, because all phone certificates have the same issuer (Cisco Manufacturing CA), any Cisco IP Phone (including the ones bought by your neighbor) will authenticate successfully. It is therefore required to also perform authorization based on the CN to get more granular control.

Another aspect is the lifetime of the certificates: MICs are valid for 10 years from the manufacturing date. Although ten years is already significant for the lifetime of IT equipment, some setups definitely survive longer. As MIC's cannot be renewed, relying solely on them can become a long term blocking point.

Local Certificates

To overcome those limitations, you need to use a local and more controlled PKI.

A Locally Significant Certificate (LSC) is one that you create (you see later how to do this) and is installed on the IP Phone. It is stored in parallel with the MIC and will not replace it. When an LSC is installed, it takes precedence over the MIC.

The Certificate Authority Proxy Function (CAPF) is the software entity, residing on the CUCM server, responsible for creation, distribution, and maintenance of the LSCs. The CAPF can be autonomous, with a self-signed certificate or be integrated into an existing (companywide, for example) PKI. Each Cisco Unified Communications Manager (CUCM) server will have its own certificate, by default self-signed or issued from an external certificate authority. There is no concept of MIC for CUCM servers.

Creating Trust

From the preceding, you can understand that you can end up with multiple disconnected PKI topologies, without any trust relationship in between. These topologies include the following:

■   MIC certificates, based on Cisco CA

■   Self-signed certificates for each components (CUCM servers, TFTP servers, and so on)

■   CAPF certificate and LSCs for phones

How do you get the different components to work together in a secure manner? The solution is to use a secure list of trusted certificates, known as Certificates Trusted List (CTL) file.

Such a list is created using a digital envelope in which all trusted certificates (and associated public keys) are packaged. The envelope is then signed by an administrator using a

USB security token. The token is provided by Cisco and contains a key pair (protected by password) and a certificate issued by Cisco Manufacturing CA, which is trusted in the default factory configuration of IP Phones.

For security and redundancy reasons, it is required to sign the CTL file using two administrator tokens, which are stored in the file. After a CTL file has been downloaded by the phones, it can only be replaced by a new CTL file signed by one of the tokens present in the current CTL file. That mechanism prevents the distribution of rogue CTL files after the initial CTL file has been distributed.

A dedicated software tool, CTL Client, can create and manipulate CTL files. After they have been signed, they are published on a TFTP server for retrieval by the IP Phones.

The first CTL download (when there is not yet any CTL installed on the phone) must be considered insecure because it cannot be verified (any Cisco token signature is valid) and should therefore be performed over a secure network connection. The same applies when phones are reset to factory defaults and need to reload a new CTL file.

As represented in Figure 9-1, a typical CTL file would contain certificates for the following components (one or more of each).

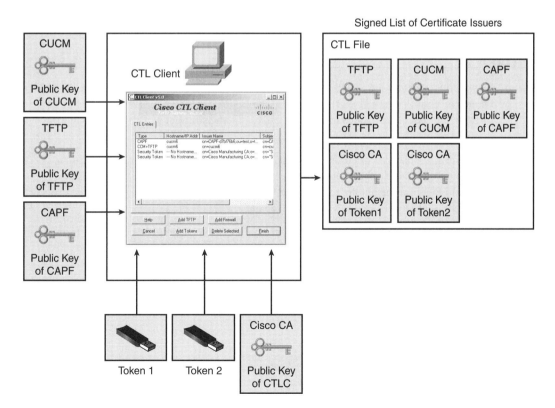

Figure 9-1 *CTL File Generation with CTL Client Software*

- Call-Manager (CUCM)

- CAPF

- TFTP

- Admin Token 1 and 2

You can find more information on the CTL Client in the CUCM Security guide: http://www.cisco.com/en/US/docs/voice_ip_comm/cucm/security/8_0_2/secugd/secuauth.html.

Certificates Distribution

This section focuses on the process used to enroll IP Phones into a local PKI, meaning that they will each have an LSC installed as result. As a reminder, all IP Phones already have a MIC installed from the factory, which might be sufficient for your needs.

Getting certificates installed (either self-signed or enrolled) on the various other UC components (CUCM, TFTP, and so on) is straightforward but specific to the software version in use; consult the product documentation for that step.

CAPF

As previously mentioned, CAPF is responsible for signing and distributing LSC to IP Phones. Let's look deeper into that process. The CAPF can be a CA, using its self-signed certificate to issue certificates to the phones. That is the simplest and default configuration for LSC.

The same CAPF is used when the phone certificate must be upgraded (renewal close to the expiration date, change in attributes, and so on). CAPF is also used to retrieve an installed LSC from the phone, for example for viewing or troubleshooting. You can also delete LSC so that the default MIC is used again.

After installation, CAPF can retrieve the information about the registered phones from the CUCM database and display an authentication string unique for each phone.

> **Note**   The previous steps to install CAPF require user interaction; to find CAPF documentation and detailed instructions, go to http://www.cisco.com/en/US/docs/voice_ip_comm/cucmbe/security/8_0_2/secugd/secucapf.html.

CAPF is the central location for all certificate-related operations and configuration, including the key size to use on the phones.

Phone Enrollment

Before working at the phone level, you must ensure that the backend infrastructure is ready. The following conditions must be met:

■ CAPF certificate must be installed on the Call Manager server.

■ CTL file must be created and contain the CAPF certificate and be published on a TFTP server.

Several authentication mechanisms are available for authenticating and enrolling phones on a CAPF server: authentication string, existing LSC, existing MIC or null string (no authentication). An authentication string requires manual user input on the phone, whereas others can be used in fully automated processes.

After triggering (manually or automatically) the phone to initiate a connection (secured through TLS) to the CAPF server, authentication can take place according to the server configuration, and the phone certificate will be installed, upgraded, or deleted through the secure channel.

Applications

After PKI is deployed to the various UC components, several applications or services can make use of it. The next section reviews some of the most common ones.

Call Authentication and Encryption

Because you have strong identity material in place (that is, digital certificates), you can now create secure communication channels between the phones and the various CUCM servers. One main application is call authentication.

In that process, as shown in Figure 9-2, both phone and server go through a challenge-response exchange, where the respective private keys are used to sign the responses, and public keys are used to validate them.

Indeed, the phone has the CTL file that contains the server certificate (and therefore its public key). In the opposite direction, the phone sends its certificate to the server.

After authentication is successful, both entities have the option (configurable) to proceed to a session key exchange mechanism to create a secure communication channel for call signaling. To maintain consistency, it is not possible to use signaling encryption without prior authentication.

When encrypted signaling is used, you can go one step further and use media authentication and encryption, which can actually secure the voice or video streams. Secure Real Time Protocol (SRTP) is used for that purpose. The CUCM server is responsible for creating session keys for media security, and those keys are transmitted to the endpoints over the signaling channel; this is why secure signaling is mandatory. Figure 9-3 illustrates secure streams between endpoints.

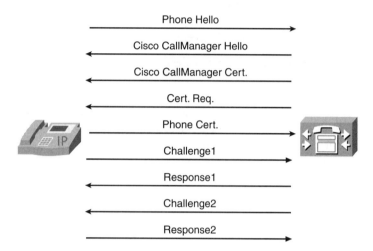

Figure 9-2   *Mutual Authentication Between Phone and CUCM Server*

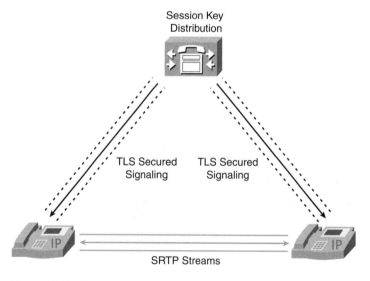

Figure 9-3   *Secure Streams Between Endpoints*

Software and Configuration Security

Because the phones are controlled entirely remotely, including the download of software images and configuration files, you need to guarantee the security of operations.

Firmware images files (typically named image.bin.sgn) are signed using a Cisco CA certificate, which is also installed on the phone (as explained in the MIC section) and can therefore be used to validate that the image has not been modified.

For the phone configuration file, you need to use both encryption so that only the target phone can read it, and authentication so that it cannot be modified in transit.

The full set of crypto functions come into play, as depicted in Figure 9-4.

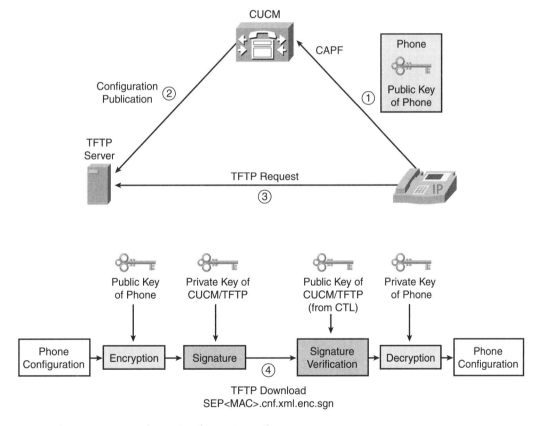

Figure 9-4   *Securing Phone Configuration Files*

On the server side:

■ The public key of the target phone (either MIC or LSC, available via CAPF) is used by CUCM to encrypt the configuration.

■ The private key of the TFTP server is used to sign the configuration.

On the phone side:

■   The TFTP server public key (available in CTL file) is used to verify the signature.

■   The phone private key (available locally by definition) is used to decrypt the configuration.

802.1x and Network Admission Control

In the previous application, the PKI was used to secure the various communication flows
between UC components (phones, CUCM servers, and TFTP servers). You can further
extend the security, earlier in the process, by increasing the control over the phones trying
to connect to the network. Indeed, as part of the global Network Admission Control
(NAC) solutions, Cisco IP Phones have an embedded 802.1x supplicant, giving them the
capability to authenticate toward the infrastructure (that is, the switch they are plugged
into) using EAP-based protocols. Figure 9-5 illustrates 802.1x authentication of IP Phones.

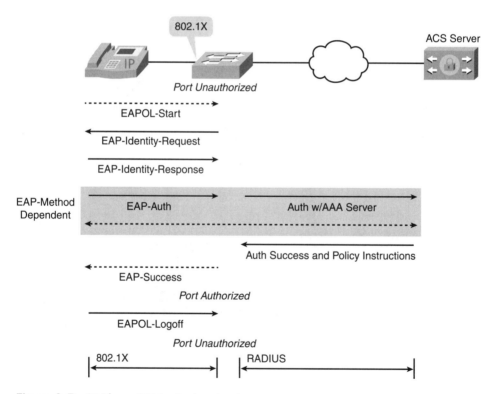

Figure 9-5   *IP Phone 802.1x Authentication*

In the early days, IP Phones were detected on a switchport using specific Cisco
Discovery Protocol (CDP) packets, bypassing NAC for those phones. Obviously that was

not secure because those packets could easily be forged and spoofed by a malicious user wanting to gain access to the network. Then came the first phone-embedded supplicant, which supports the following authentication mechanisms:

■ EAP-MD5, which relies on a password to perform challenge-based authentication.

■ EAP-TLS or EAP-FAST, which use the certificates installed on the phone, either MIC or LSC, via TLS authentication protocols.

Note   It is beyond the scope of this book to review the complete NAC-related infrastructure configuration; refer to *Cisco Network Admission Control, Volumes I and II* for additional details about NAC architectures.

For PKI-related configuration issues, most changes must be applied to the backend authentication server (namely Cisco ACS RADIUS server). For EAP-MD5 (password) authentication, each phone must have a corresponding user entry in an ACS database, with a username based on the phone model and MAC address and the associated password configured. That same password must then be manually entered on each phone.

For EAP-TLS or EAP-FAST, if only authentication is required, there is no need to configure the individual phones on ACS: Adding the issuer CA (Cisco Manufacturing and Root CAs, local CA, or self-signed CAPF certificate) to the ACS trust list is enough to verify the credentials of the phones.

Note   CN authorization must be used in ACS 4.2 and below.

However, if authorization is required, phones must be entered in an ACS database, with the certificate CN field as username.

Note   CN field content is different in MIC and LSC certificates: MIC CN=CP-<MODEL>-SEPxxxxxx whereas LSC CN=SEPxxxxxx.

Because there is no out-of-the-box integration between CUCM and ACS, you can use CSV files to perform a bulk import of all registered phones into ACS. This is required only if you need to use authorization on ACS. In ACS version 4.x, bulk import is done via CLI, whereas it is a web-based operation in ACS 5.x. Refer to the corresponding ACS User Guide, available on Cisco.com.

Furthermore, the 802.1x phone supplicant can be enabled remotely through the phone configuration on CUCM, making such deployment much easier. There is no mutual TLS authentication: The phone is authenticated toward the ACS, but the ACS server is not authenticated toward the phones.

This is applicable for both wired and wireless IP Phones; however, wireless models are enrolled using a different process: Via the embedded HTTP GUI, a Certificate Signing Request (CSR) must be generated and transmitted to the CA, which then return a certificate to the phone. The wireless phone also needs to be loaded with the CA certificate or the ACS certificate to perform a mutual authentication. This is similar to the process used to enroll Cisco IOS devices and enables the wireless phone to securely authenticate and encrypt the radio communication.

ASA TLS Phone Proxy

Voice communications usually rely on a dual connection:

- One control channel transmits various states and parameters of the call.

- At least one media channel (often two) is responsible for carrying the actual voice data.

Although the control session uses well-known TCP or UDP ports, based on the protocol in use (SIP, SCCP, H.323, and so on) the data sessions typically use dynamic port numbers, often negotiated between the endpoints through the control channel.

Firewall devices have been made smart enough to inspect the control session and detect the dynamic ports that must be open to enable the secondary channels to flow through.

Earlier in this chapter, you saw how to use some security mechanisms to encrypt the sessions (both control and data), making blind all devices on the network path, including the firewalls. The only workaround is to open a wide range of ports to ensure that the media streams will not be blocked. Obviously that can pose a security risk, which is not acceptable in a large number of situations.

To avoid such weaknesses while still using encryption for UC traffic, the Cisco ASA 5500 security appliance has been enhanced with the TLS proxy licensed feature. As shown in Figure 9-6, the ASA Firewall will now act as a termination point for TLS sessions protecting the control channels of UC calls.

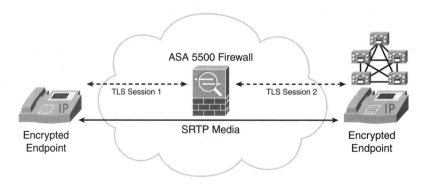

Figure 9-6 *ASA TLS Proxy*

The firewall can then decrypt signaling packets, inspect the content to identify dynamic ports that must be opened for the SRTP media streams, and then encrypt again the signaling into another TLS session toward the other UC device (typically the Call Manager).

How do you build the trust relationship between the three components?

Phone—ASA TLS Proxy

The phone can trust any certificate present in the CTL file; therefore, the ASA certificate (self-signed or from another CA) must be added into the CTL. The ASA has the CAPF CA (or other applicable CA) certificate installed and can therefore verify the authenticity of the certificate presented by the phone.

ASA TLS Proxy—CUCM Server

The ASA must have the CUCM certificate installed as trusted. For the CUCM server to authenticate the ASA TLS Proxy, it is a little more complex. The ASA can generate on-the-fly a dynamic certificate containing the identity of the phone (named Local Dynamic Certificate, or LDC), signed with the ASA certificate, and present it on behalf of the phone. The CUCM server has the ASA certificate in its trusted list and can accept those dynamic certificates because they have a signature that can be verified as valid.

> **Note**   The ASA certificates used in each step can be different; the ASA would then have the following:
>
> - An "outside" certificate, used to communicate with the phones, and present in the CTL file.
>
> - An "inside" certificate or signer certificate, used to sign LDCs and communicate with CUCM server. That certificate is installed in the CUCM trusted list.

Summary

This chapter showed how you can apply PKI to Unified Communications infrastructures.

Although some specific terminology and concepts are used (MIC, LSC, CTL, and CAPF) the basic crypto principles are applicable. The behavior should therefore be perfectly understandable after the language is acquired.

You reviewed the most common applications: from secure calls toward the ASA TLS Proxy feature that enables new extranet possibilities. You learned how Cisco IP Phones can participate in your deployed NAC solutions through the embedded 802.1x supplicant.

Chapter 10

Understanding Cisco Virtual Office

This chapter covers the integration of certificates in the Cisco virtual office solution. This solution represents an integration of certificates across multiple technologies. This chapter covers the following topics:

- Cisco Virtual Office (CVO) Overview

- PKI Integration

- 802.1x Integration

This chapter assumes that you are is familiar with the CVO solution set. This chapter's objective is to highlight certificates as they relate to CVO. If you want to learn about all the elements of CVO, go to this page about the solution and solution references: http://www.cisco.com/en/US/partner/solutions/collateral/ns340/ns517/ns430/ns855/deployment_guide_c22-493157.html.

Workplaces are becoming more diverse and distributed. This trend gives greater flexibility to a work force and enables corporations to become nimble. Remote teleworkers, who spends most of their time away from the office, can benefit from having a setup at home that is congruent in functionality to being in the office. To provide this level of flexibility in a scalable fashion, security must be in place. Certificates are a cornerstone component of security for the Cisco Virtual Office solution. Certificates are used to authenticate home routers and end users.

The Cisco Virtual Office (CVO) provides an end-user workstation and desktop IP phone access to corporate resources. End users can have a router at their home or remote site that can provide wired or wireless access to their workstation and phone, as shown in Figure 10-1.

The components involved in CVO are a router at the end-user location, PKI server, router that frontends the initial management connection, data plane VPN headend, configuration engine, Cisco Security Manager (CSM) and Cisco access control server (ACS) providing AAA.

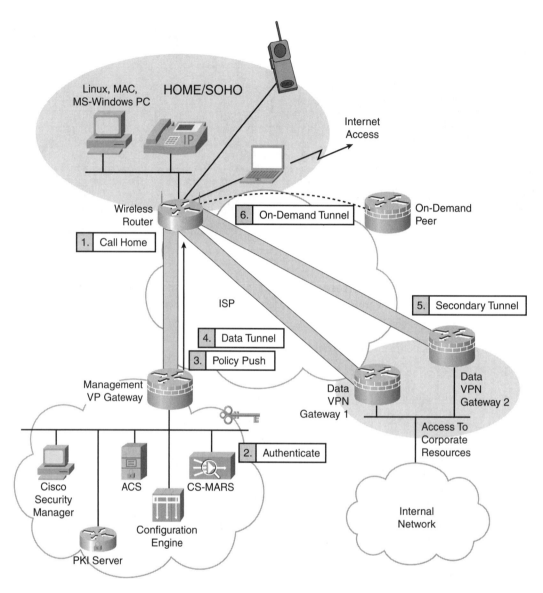

Figure 10-1 *Complete Picture for the CVO Solution*

To provide the flexibility to allow users to connect from anywhere, identity takes on an important role. Certificates are tied to the user, the user's router, and potentially the user's workstation for 802.1x. Each of these technologies has been discussed independently in separate chapters of this book. This chapter describes the application of each of these technologies. Appropriate technical references are made to the relevant chapters as necessary.

Some of the advantages CVO provides from a provisioning standpoint include the following:

■ Devices deployed only need to be seeded with a small identical set of initial configuration commands or bootstrap configuration.

■ No specialized pre-installation staging or configuration is required.

■ An end device automatically "calls homes" to the Configuration Engine (CE) and downloads its working configuration.

For a CVO to be created at a SOHO location, a series of steps occur. Before any of the technical steps occur, a user must request the service and then that request must be approved. Depending on a corporations' individual practices, this might be handled entirely online and result in a router being shipped to the user.

The next set of steps begins with a router sitting off a home Internet connection. The router has a default configuration. The user has only an Ethernet connection to a port on the back end of the 871.

When a user has a router in hand, the user needs to plug the router into the service provider's device to obtain DHCP configured information. Additionally the user needs to plug in the workstation into a LAN port on the router.

The following steps result in the router obtaining full connectivity and access to the remote network:

1. The user connects to the 800 series router using the web-based interface.

2. The user initiates Secure Device Provisioning (SDP) through the GUI.

3. The router calls home and will be challenged.

4. The user provides credentials for a response to the challenge.

5. If the challenge succeeds, the router gets a bootstrap configuration downloaded (via a template created using CSM). The bootstrap configuration will have basic data to initiate a management tunnel to a management VPN headend. This includes a certificate to connect to a management VPN gateway.

6. The router attempts to reach the configuration engine as instructed by its bootstrap config. This interesting traffic initiates a management tunnel back to the headend and authenticates with the management router using its certificate obtained in the previous step.

7. The router gets its new, full configuration from the configuration engine.

8. The configuration has new PKI trustpoint information, and the router requests a certificate from the internal sub-CA. This certificate is for authenticating the router for the data-plain VPN.

9. Now the router brings up the data-plain VPN. This data-plain VPN uses DMVPN for a standard CVO deployment.

CVO PKI Highlights

CVO has several components that use certificates simply for router setup. Optionally, certificates can be used for end device authentication and phone authentication. The areas that use PKI for router setup are for setting up the management tunnel and the DMVPN tunnel. Chapter 6, "Integration in Large-Scale, Site-to-Site VPN Solutions," describes the details of how to set up a PKI for this type of VPN deployment. To summarize, this hierarchy should use a hierarchical PKI.

The routers have trustpoints as part of their CVO templates. Chapter 5, "Generic PKI Designs," and Chapter 6 describe the trustpoint configuration elements. Example 10-1 shows a trustpoint configuration for a DMVPN headend.

Example 10-1 *Configuring Enrollment for Hub s-dmvpn-headend*

```
crypto pki trustpoint ra
 enrollment url http://192.168.159.243:12345 ! pointing to ra-subca server
 revocation-check none
 rsakeypair hub-keys
 auto-enroll 70 regenerate
```

Also included in Chapters 5 and 6 are details in how to set up a hierarchical PKI. Example 10-2 illustrates some sample configurations.

Example 10-2 *Sample Root CA and Sub-CA Configuration*

```
Example ROOT CA configuration
3845-root-ca# show run
...

crypto pki server root-ca
 database archive pkcs12 password 7 104D000A061843595F
 grant auto rollover ca-cert
 lifetime crl 12
 lifetime certificate 0 1095
 lifetime ca-certificate 1825
 cdp-url http://171.70.65.136/stenneti/root-ca.crl
 auto-rollover 185
 database url ftp://172.26.129.252
 database url crl ftp://172.26.129.252
!
crypto pki trustpoint root-ca
 revocation-check crl
 rsakeypair root-ca
!
```

```
Example Subordinate CA configuration
!
crypto pki server ra-subca
 database level complete
 database archive pkcs12 password 7 13061E010803557878
 grant auto rollover ca-cert
 grant auto
 lifetime crl 12
 lifetime certificate 1095
 cdp-url http://171.70.65.136/stenneti/ra-subca.crl
 mode sub-cs
 auto-rollover
 database url crl ftp://172.26.129.252
 database url p12 ftp://172.26.129.252
!
crypto pki trustpoint ra-subca
 enrollment url http://10.254.0.10:80
 revocation-check crl none
 rsakeypair ra-subca
 regenerate
```

The trustpoint configuration for the management tunnel trustpoint and the DMVPN trustpoint (for data) is created by the CSM template in Step 5, and the data plain configuration is distributed by the configuration engine.

What is not shown as a step is the use of network authorization based on certificates. Chapter 3, "PKI Processes and Procedures," describes network authorization based on certificates. An approach to enforce access uses AAA integration. A certificate can provide authentication; when combined with an AAA server, the AAA server provides authorization for the end host.

Fields in the certificate (such as subject and serial number) can be passed back to a RADIUS server or TACACS server. The server checks the credentials provided to it by the authorizing router to determine if the device is authorized for network access.

The advantage to using AAA as a solution is that it enables for authorization in addition to authentication. The moment an administrator decides a certificate is no longer authorized, the administrator can make the change in the AAA server, and it is immediately effective.

Example 10-3 shows the configuration required to point back to the ACS server on the headend router.

Example 10-3   *Sample Configuration for Integrating Certificates with ACS for Network Authorization*

```
aaa authentication login no-auth none
aaa authorization exec dmvpn-pki group radius
aaa authorization network dmvpn-pki group radius
!
crypto pki trustpoint ra
 enrollment url http://192.168.159.243:12345
 serial-number
 ip-address 192.168.159.242
 revocation-check crl
 rsakeypair hub-keys
 auto-enroll 70 regenerate
 authorization list dmvpn-pki
 authorization username subjectname unstructuredname
! above line will not appear in show run since it is a default !


authorization username subjectname unstructuredname
```

Note   Chapter 3 of this book contains screen captures of how ACS should be configured.

The other element that can be optionally configured for end-host authentication is 802.1x for a workstation and phone. These solutions can optionally use certificates, which are the topics of Chapter 8, "Using 802.1x Certificates in Identity-Based Networking," and Chapter 9, "PKI in Unified Communications." Example 10-4 illustrates a sample router configuration for CVO that uses 802.1x authentication.

Example 10-4   *Sample Configuration for Host Routers Using 802.1x for Workstation Authentication*

```
aaa new-model
aaa group server radius dot1x
server-private <ip address> auth-port 1812 acct-port 1813 key 0 <key>
aaa authentication dot1x default group dot1x
! Enable dot1x feature globally
dot1x system-auth-control
!
interface FastEthernet2
switchport access vlan 10
! Enable authenticator functionality
dot1x pae authenticator
! Enable dot1x on this interface
dot1x port-control auto
```

```
! Enable periodic re-authentication
dot1x reauthentication
! Re-authentication timeout.
dot1x timeout reauth-period 120
```

Summary

Cisco Virtual Office provides a workplace a high degree of flexibility and savings. Enabling a corporation to distribute a workforce allows for resiliency in operations (if a disaster recovery occurs) and full functionality for remote workers and remote offices. It also provides for savings from a facilities standpoint.

To gain these advantages, the solution needs to provide availability from anywhere. This is where the need for strong identity comes into play. Strong identity measures bring near facility-level security, down to the port level. A central part of identity is the use of certificates and PKI in this solution.

Several parts of the CVO solution suite use certificates and PKI. The following solutions rely on certificates:

■ Remote access for management tunnel, IPsec identity specifically

■ Data plane tunnel identity

■ Network authorization integrated with ACS and certificates

■ 802.1x using EAP-TLS for workstations and IP phones

These components are cornerstones to identity the CVO solution and are driven by certificates.

Chapter 11

Deploying VPNs with PKI Using Cisco Security Manager

This chapter covers the following topics:

- Deploying PKI as a Service Using CSM

- Cisco ASA IPsec VPN Remote Access Using CSM

- DMVPN Using CSM

- GETVPN Using CSM

Chapter 6, "Integration in Large-Scale Site-to-Site VPN Solutions," discusses that it takes a number of steps to deploy VPN technologies using the Cisco command-line interface, which includes configuring enrollment options, ISAKMP policy, IPsec profile, and VPN technology-specific configurations. This multistep process becomes more tedious when configuring on multiple devices. Moreover, configuring over command-line interface does not support any kind of validation of the configurations. Therefore, using a management tool to deploy these technologies would make installation and management of large number of devices easier and more efficient. This chapter illustrates the deployment of these technologies using Cisco Security Manager (CSM), which is a management tool that provides an ideal solution for large or complex deployments. The following are benefits of a CSM solution:

- Ability to configure, tune, and manage Cisco Firewalls, VPNs, intrusion prevention system (IPS) sensors, and integrated security services across multiple platforms

- Can work with Cisco Secure Access Control Server (ACS) to provide role-based access control

- Flexible device management options, including policy-based management and various methods of deploying configuration changes

The VPN deployments illustrated in Chapter 6 and Chapter 7, "Integration in Remote Access VPN Solutions," mainly illustrate the use of the Cisco command-line interface. This chapter illustrates the same deployments using CSM.

Cisco ASA IPsec VPN Remote Access

The Cisco IPsec VPN remote access solution also leverages IKE protocol for key negotiation between the clients and the gateways. As we have described in earlier chapters, two methods are available in which both the client and the gateway authenticate with each other before deriving the keys: using preshared keys or digital certificates. With remote access you can have a preshared key for every user, but that does not scale when a large number of users exists. Therefore, the remote user authenticates with s a group-based preshared key and x-auth to do per-user authentication. The disadvantage of using group-based authentication is it opens a security hole when a user leaves the group but still has the group-based keys. Therefore, to enhance better authentication, the remote users can use digital certificates and x-auth for per-user authentication. Before discussing how to use PKI as a service for remote access solutions, you need to review Easy VPN.

Easy VPN Overview

The Easy VPN Server feature enables Cisco IOS routers, Cisco Adaptive Security Appliances (ASA), and Cisco PIX Security Appliances to act as headend devices in site-to-site or remote-access VPNs. The feature pushes security policies defined at the central site to the remote device so that it has up-to-date policies in place before a connection is established. It can also terminate VPN tunnels initiated by remote workers running the Cisco VPN Client software on PCs. This flexibility enables mobile and remote workers to access critical data and applications on their corporate intranet.

Deploying IPsec VPN Remote Access on the ASA Using CSM

This section describes the deployment of a remote access solution using ASA as the VPN gateway for remote clients. Figure 11-1 illustrates the topology used in this deployment example.

Following are some of the design considerations for the topology in Figure 11-1:

- The sub-CAs should be reachable by WAN (Internet). This enables the remote clients to obtain their certificates.

- The sub-CAs and ASAs might be reachable via an internal network or through the Internet. This design assumes they would reach through the Internet.

- The ASAs are used as VPN gateways and are configured in active/standby mode.

- CSM reaches the ASA firewalls using the internal network.

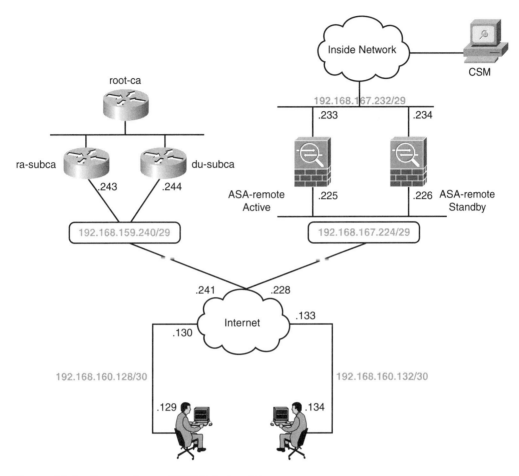

Figure 11-1 *Remote Access VPN Solution Diagram*

Adding the Device into the CSM Domain

With CSM 4.0 installed, you can use it to deploy VPN with PKI as a service. To begin, add the device into the CSM domain, as described in the upcoming steps, as shown in Figure 11-2.

Figure 11-3 shows the initial screen.

Step 1.   Add the device's general properties, as shown in Figure 11-4.

Step 2.   Add the device's credentials, as shown in Figure 11-5.

Now the device is ready to be added to the CSM domain. Click the **Test Connectivity** button to see if the connectivity is successfully established between the CSM and the device.

Initial Deployment

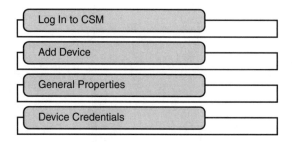

Figure 11-2 *Steps for Adding Device into CSM Domain*

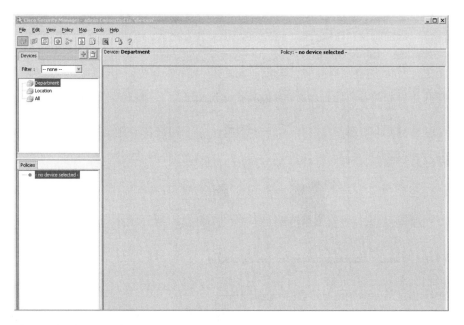

Figure 11-3 *Initial Screen*

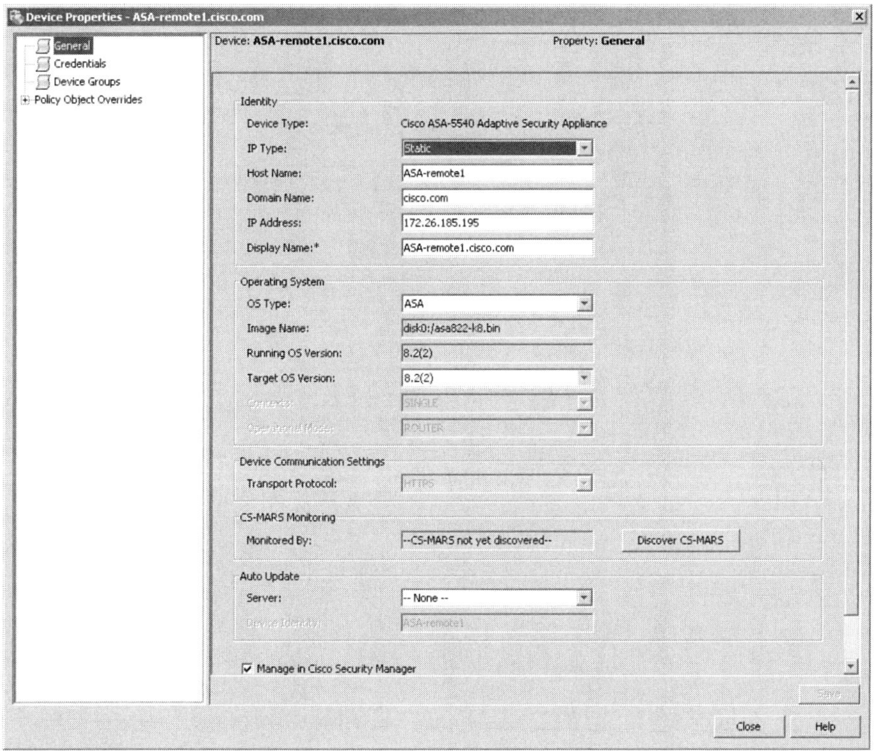

Figure 11-4 *Adding Device General Properties*

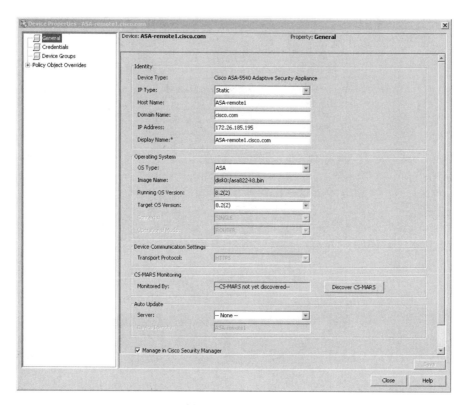

Figure 11-5 *Adding Device Credentials*

Configure Enrollment Options

With the device added to the CSM domain, now configure the enrollment options, as illustrated in Figure 11-6 and described in the following steps:

Step 1. Configure the sub-CA information (**ra-subca**), as shown in Figure 11-7. The fingerprint information must be supplied for enrollment.

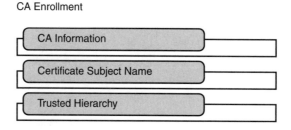

Figure 11-6 *Enrollment Option Steps*

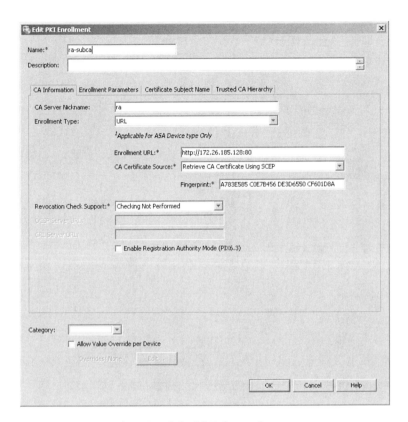

Figure 11-7   *Configuring Sub-CA Information*

Step 2.   Configure the subject name parameters for the ASA, as shown in Figure 11-8.

Step 3.   Configure the trusted hierarchy, as illustrated in Figure 11-9.

As shown in the Figure 11-9, ASA needs to obtain the root CA certificate only for the purpose of authenticating ra-subca. ASA needs to know that the CA server to which it is enrolling is truly authenticated by the root CA.

Step 4.   Obtain the root CA certificate, as illustrated in Figure 11-10.

Now the certificate chaining is complete. At this point, ASA will have not only its certificate obtained by ra-subca, but also the root CA certificate for chain verification.

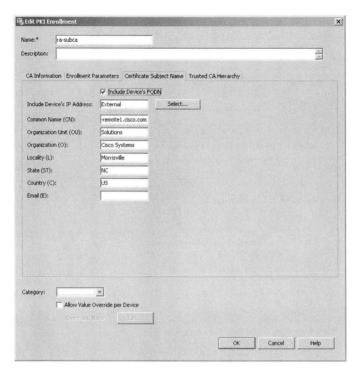

Figure 11-8 *Configuring Subject Name Parameters for ASA*

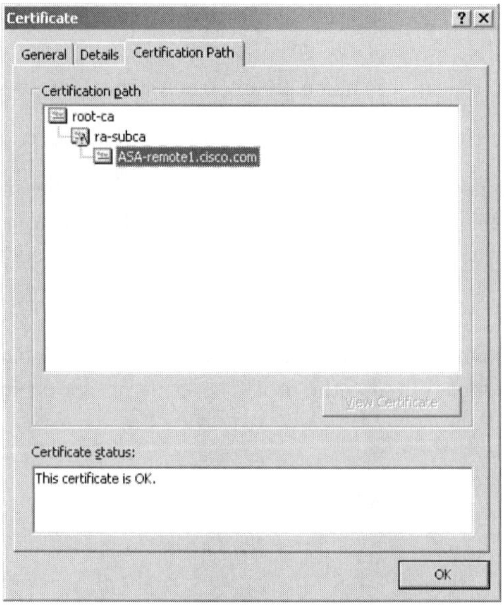

Figure 11-9 *Trusted Hierarchy*

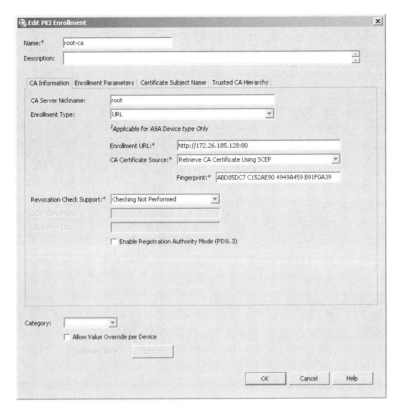

Figure 11-10   *Obtaining Root CA Certificate*

Configure the Certificate Map

The next important step is to configure the certificate map, which is used to map the incoming requests to the right tunnel group. In this example, the incoming requests are mapped to a tunnel group "testgroup." This certificate map enables certificates issued by ra-subca. Figure 11-11 shows how to configure the certificate policy.

Figure 11-12 illustrates the completed configuration of the certificate map.

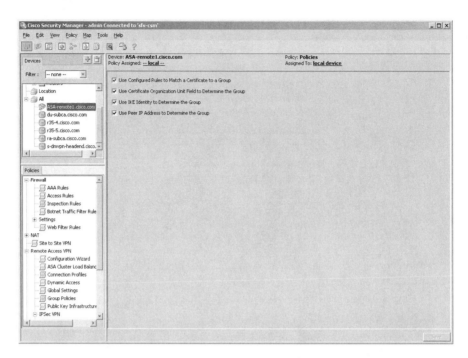

Figure 11-11 *Configuring Certificate Policy*

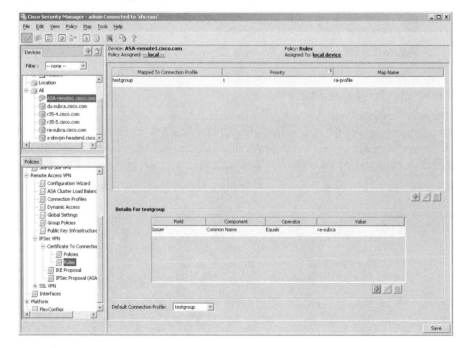

Figure 11-12 *Certificate Map*

Configure Remote Access VPN

Configure remote access configuration using CSM through the following steps, as illustrated in Figure 11-13.

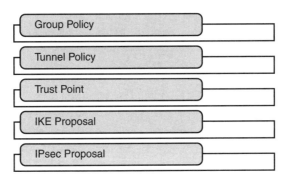

Remote Access Configuration

Figure 11-13 *Remote Access VPN Configuration Steps*

Step 1.   Configure a group policy, as illustrated in Figure 11-14.

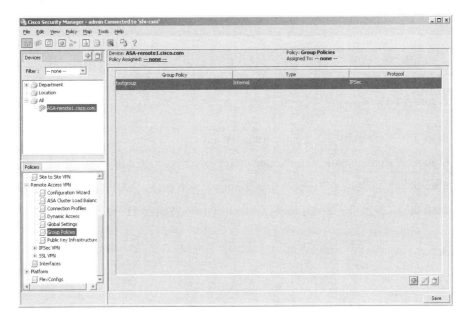

Figure 11-14 *Creating a Group Policy*

Step 2.   Configure the group's properties, as illustrated in Figure 11-15.

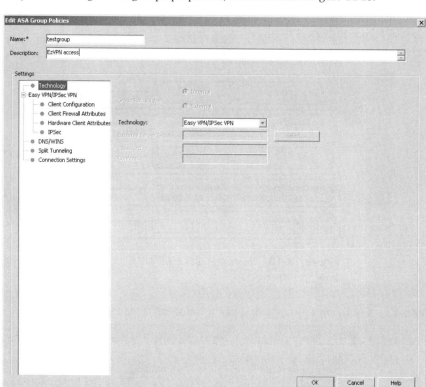

Figure 11-15   *Group Properties*

Step 3.   Configure tunnel group name, as illustrated in Figure 11-16.

Step 4.   Configure the tunnel group properties, as illustrated in Figure 11-17.

Step 5.   Configure IKE proposal, as illustrated in Figure 11-18.

Step 6.   Create the IPSec proposal, as illustrated in Figure 11-19.

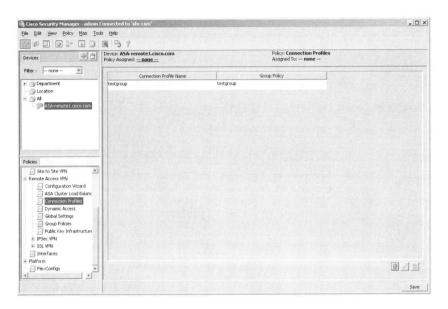

Figure 11-16 *Configuring Tunnel Group Name*

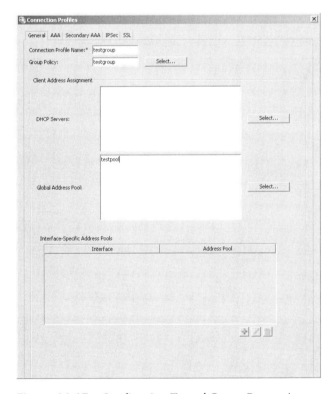

Figure 11-17 *Configuring Tunnel Group Properties*

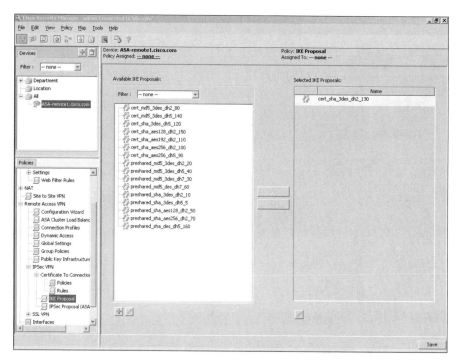

Figure 11-18 *IKE Proposal*

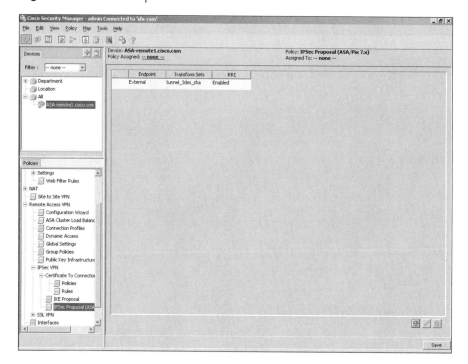

Figure 11-19 *IPsec Proposal*

Step 7.   Start the Configuration Wizard, as illustrated in Figure 11-20.

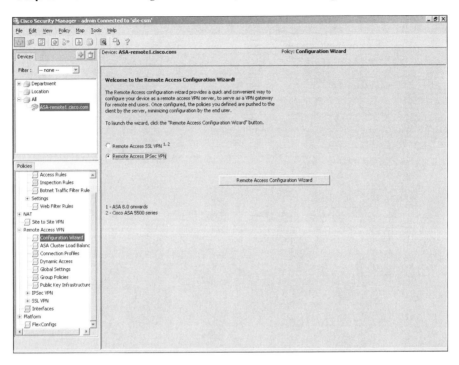

Figure 11-20   *Remote Access Configuration Wizard*

Step 8.   Configure the connection profile, as illustrated in Figure 11-21.

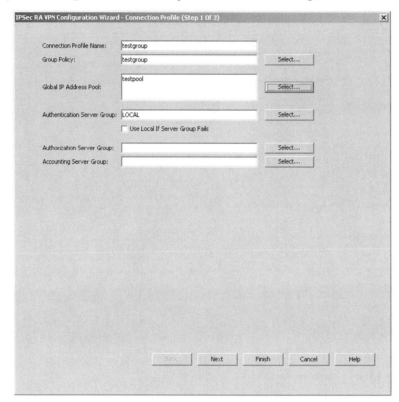

Figure 11-21   *Configuration Wizard, Connection Profile*

Step 9.   Configure the IPsec settings, as illustrated in Figure 11-22.

Step 10.   Configure the defaults, as illustrated in Figure 11-23. Click **Finish** to exit the Configuration Wizard.

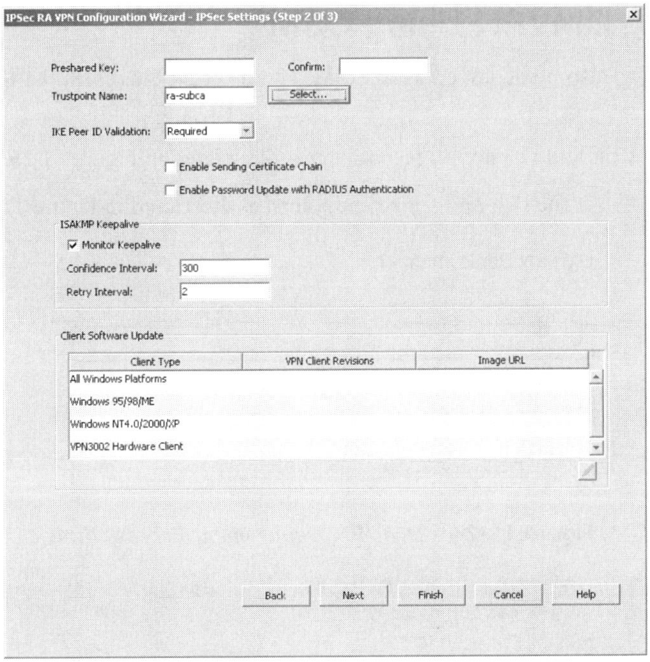

Figure 11-22 *Configuring Remote Access, IPsec Settings*

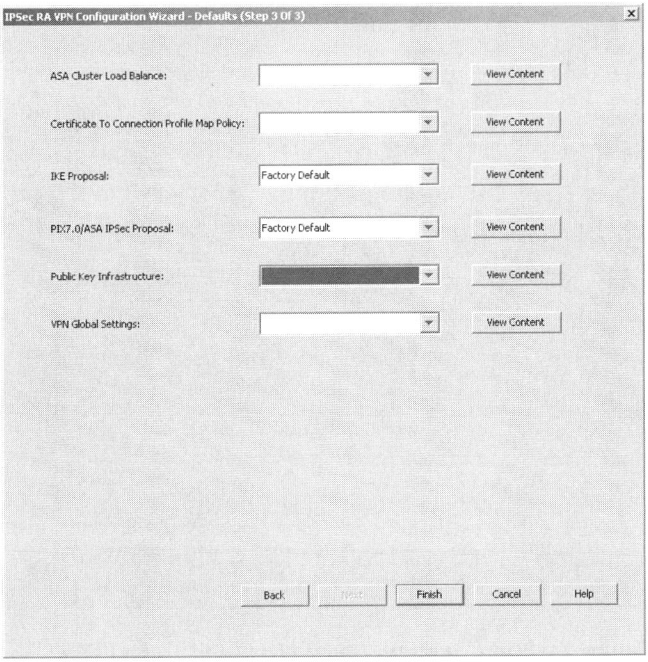

Figure 11-23 *Configuring Remote Access Defaults*

Deploying DMVPN Using CSM

DMVPM can also be deployed using CSM. Figure 11-24 illustrates the flow of this operation.

Step 1.   Configure name and technology, as illustrated in Figure 11-25.

Step 2.   Select the hub-and-spoke endpoints, as illustrated in Figure 11-26.

DMVPN Deployment - I

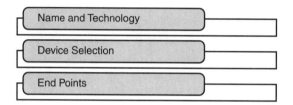

Figure 11-24   *DMVPN Deployment Process Flow*

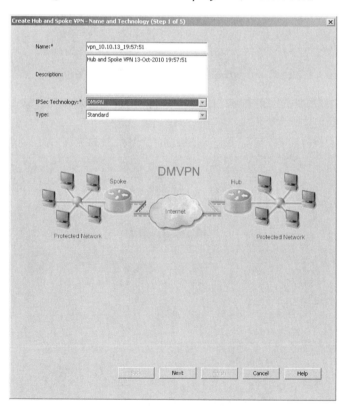

Figure 11-25   *Configuration of Name and Technology*

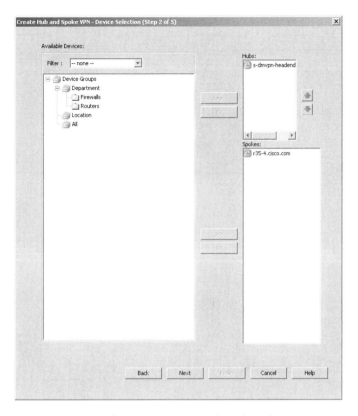

Figure 11-26 *Selecting Devices: Hub and Spoke*

Step 3.   Select the WAN interfaces and local interfaces, as illustrated in Figure 11-27.

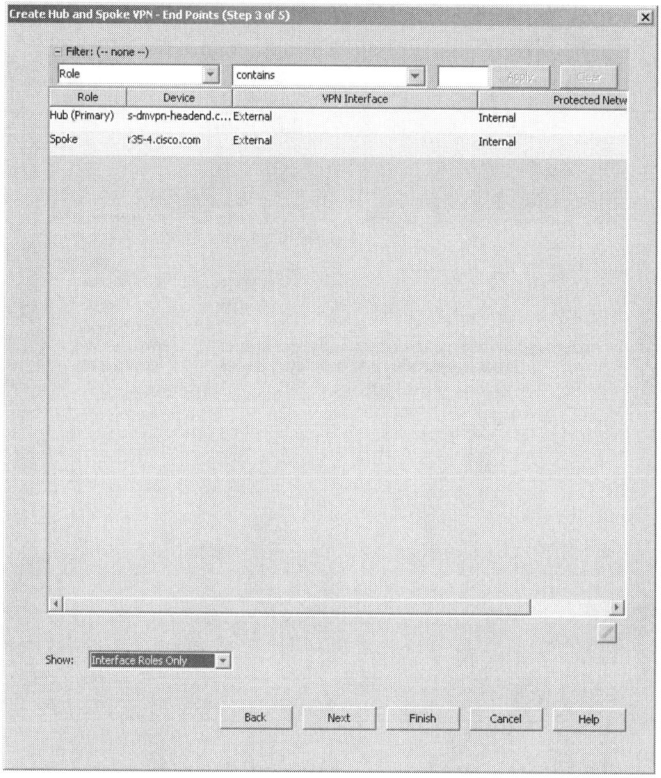

Figure 11-27   *Selecting Endpoints*

VPN Policy Configuration

You have now set up the first half of your deployment. The following steps and Figure 11-28 illustrate the second set of steps: VPN policy configuration.

DMVPN Deployment - VPN

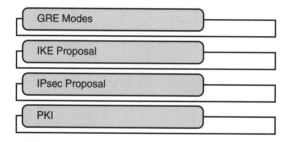

Figure 11-28   *DMVPN Deployment: VPN Policy*

Step 1.   Configure the GRE tunnel, as illustrated in Figure 11-29.

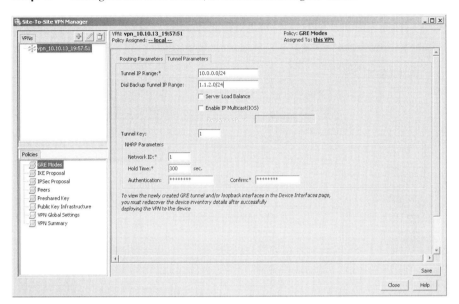

Figure 11-29   *GRE Tunnel Configuration*

Step 2.   Configure the routing associated with the DMVPN tunnel, as illustrated in Figure 11-30.

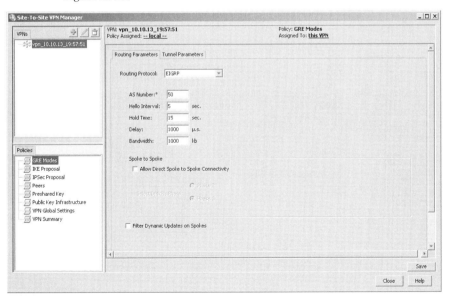

Figure 11-30   *DMVPN Routing Configuration*

Step 3.   Configure the IKE proposal, as illustrated in Figure 11-31.

Step 4.   Configure IPsec proposal, as illustrated in Figure 11-32.

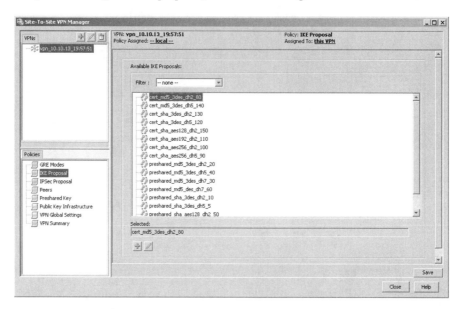

Figure 11-31   *IKE Policy Configuration*

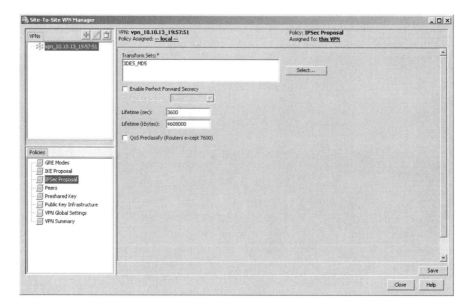

Figure 11-32   *IPsec Policy Configuration*

Step 5.   Configure the PKI trustpoint configuration. (Refer to Chapter 7 for a definition of trustpoint configuration.) Select trustpoints for DMVPN deployment,
as illustrated in Figure 11-33.

Step 6.   Review the deployment summary, as illustrated in Figure 11-34.

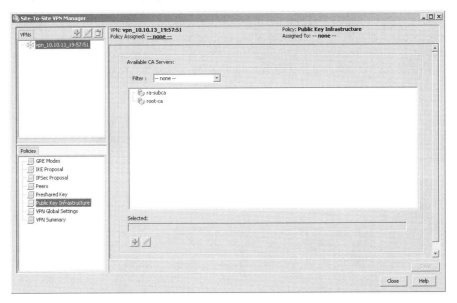

Figure 11-33   *Trustpoint Configuration*

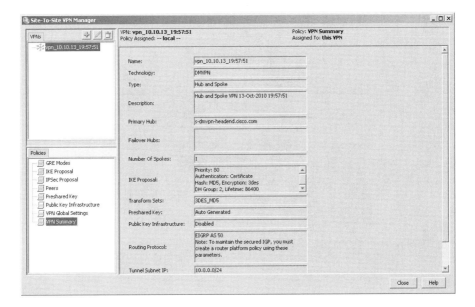

Figure 11-34   *Deployment Summary*

Step 7.   Finally, select **Submit** to deploy the configuration at both the head and spoke.

GETVPN Deployment Using CSM

GETVPN is an any-to-any technology, which means that no hub-and-spoke communication occurs; rather, GETVPN is mainly spoke-to-spoke communication. The two major components of GETVPN technology are key server and group member. A key server securely distributes keys to various group members. Group members need to register with a key server before initiating communication with other group members.

> **Note**   For more information on the GETVPN design, refer to http://www.cisco.com/en/US/prod/collateral/vpndevc/ps6525/ps9370/ps7180/GETVPN_DIG_version_1_0_External.pdf.

To deploy GETVPN using CSM, follow these steps:

Step 1.   Configure name and technology, as illustrated in Figure 11-35.

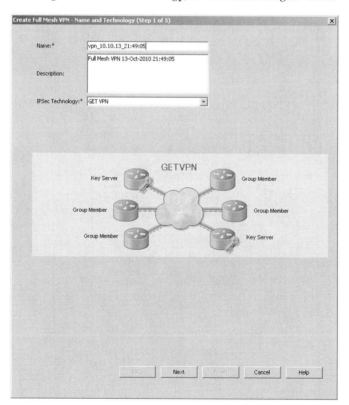

Figure 11-35   *Configuration of Name and Technology*

Step 2.   Select GETVPN, as illustrated in Figure 11-36.

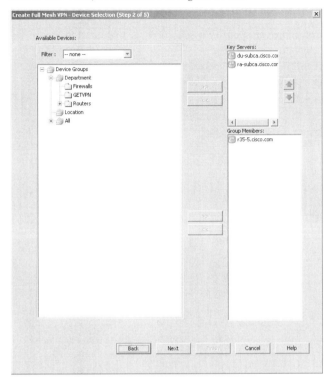

Figure 11-36   *Selecting the VPN Technology*

After selecting the technology, configure the policy. Figure 11-37 and the following steps describe the process flow for deploying a GETVPN configuration.

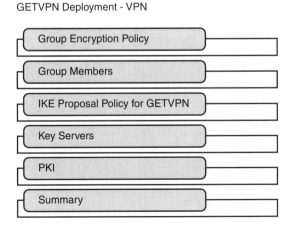

Figure 11-37   *Deploying GETVPN Process Flow*

Step 1.   The Group member policy consists of two parts: group settings and security associations. Configure the Group settings, as illustrated in Figure 11-38.

Step 2.   Configure the security association, as illustrated in Figure 11-39.

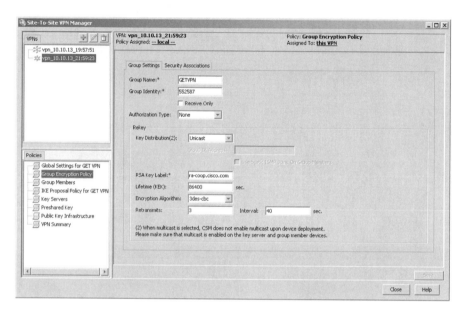

Figure 11-38   *Group Settings*

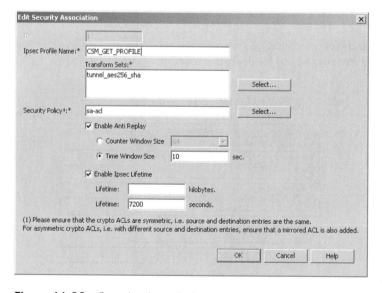

Figure 11-39   *Security Association*

Step 3.   The group member policy appears, as shown in Figure 11-40. The group member configuration consists of defining the external WAN interface and the key servers deployed.

Step 4.   Configure the IKE proposal, as illustrated in Figure 11-41.

The IKE policy uses digital certificates with 3DES for encryption and md5 for authentication.

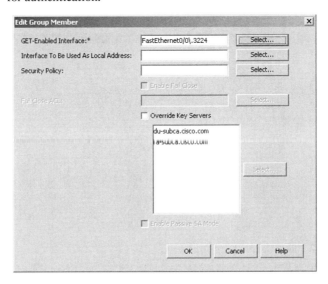

Figure 11-40   *Group Member Policy*

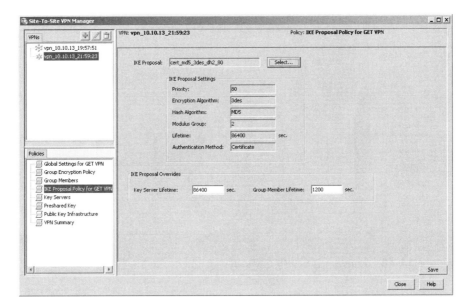

Figure 11-41   *IKE Policy Definition*

Step 5. Configure the Key server policy, as shown in Figure 11-42.

Step 6. Select the trustpoint configuration, as shown in Figure 11-43.

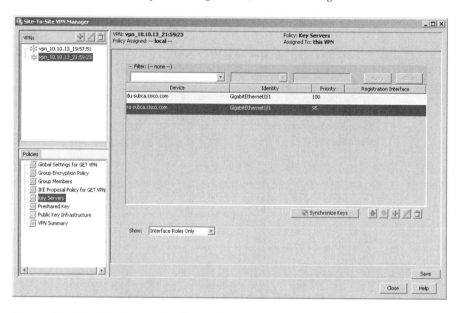

Figure 11-42 *Key Server Configuration*

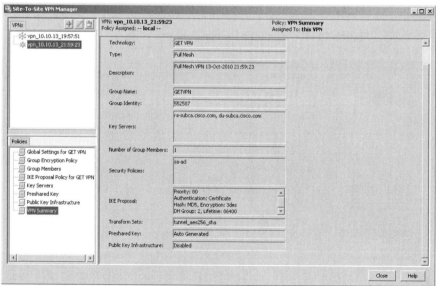

Figure 11-43 *Trustpoint Configuration*

When the preceding configuration is completed, the VPN summary shows all the pieces together, as illustrated in Figure 11-44.

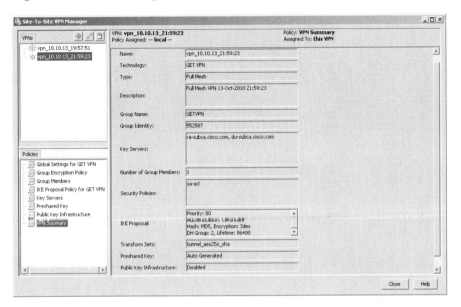

Figure 11-44   *GETVPN Summary*

Summary

This chapter looked at how to deploy VPN technologies using PKI as service with CSM as the management tool. A number of benefits exist for using CSM rather than using a command-line interface, such as validation of configs and the ability to deploy on a large number of devices.

Index

Numerics

A

B

C

X

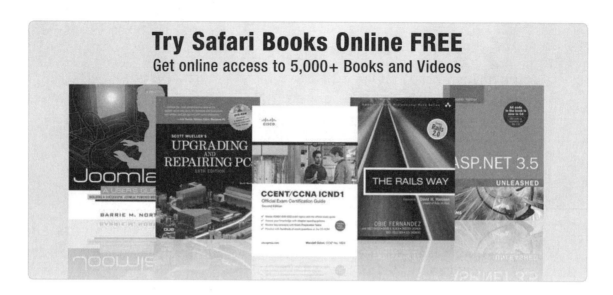

CISCO

ciscopress.com: Your Cisco Certification and Networking Learning Resource

Subscribe to the monthly Cisco Press newsletter to be the first to learn about new releases and special promotions.

Visit **ciscopress.com/newsletters.**

While you are visiting, check out the offerings available at your finger tips.

–Free Podcasts from experts:
  • OnNetworking
  • OnCertification
  • OnSecurity

Podcasts

View them at **ciscopress.com/podcasts**.

–Read the latest author **articles** and **sample chapters** at ciscopress.com/articles.

–Bookmark the Certification Reference Guide available through our partner site at **informit.com/certguide.**

Connect with Cisco Press authors and editors via Facebook and Twitter, visit **informit.com/socialconnect.**

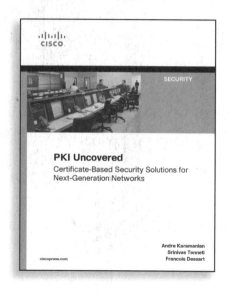

FREE Online Edition

Your purchase of **PKI Uncovered: Certificate-Based Security Solutions for Next-Generation Networks** includes access to a free online edition for 45 days through the Safari Books Online subscription service. Nearly every Cisco Press book is available online through Safari Books Online, along with more than 5,000 other technical books and videos from publishers such as Addison-Wesley Professional, Exam Cram, IBM Press, O'Reilly, Prentice Hall, Que, and Sams.

SAFARI BOOKS ONLINE allows you to search for a specific answer, cut and paste code, download chapters, and stay current with emerging technologies.

Activate your FREE Online Edition at
www.informit.com/safarifree

> **STEP 1:** Enter the coupon code: SOWYWWA.

> **STEP 2:** New Safari users, complete the brief registration form. Safari subscribers, just log in.

If you have difficulty registering on Safari or accessing the online edition, please e-mail customer-service@safaribooksonline.com